Quranic Questions Allah Asks Creation

Compiled by
Gregory Heary

The Arabic Quran is the most popular and widely memorized book of all time, believed by Muslims to be the literal speech of Allah, the Creator of the Universe. Within the Quran questions are posed by Allah to mankind and jinnkind not for lack of knowledge by Allah but for the creatures tested with such questions to think deeply, reflect and respond so a testimonial record can be made for or against them. Basically these are the most important questions to ask in order to teach as well as expose sincerity and knowledge levels. Some of these questions are even obligatory for the Prophet Muhammad and those who follow in his footsteps to ask each other and the rest of humans and jinn whom they encounter, other questions are restricted in who they address. All these questions from the Creator have correct answers which the reader will be able to discover and benefit from.

<u>Quranic Questions</u>

Quran 2:22-24

ٱلَّذِى جَعَلَ لَكُمُ ٱلْأَرْضَ فِرَٰشًا وَٱلسَّمَآءَ بِنَآءً وَأَنزَلَ مِنَ ٱلسَّمَآءِ مَآءً فَأَخْرَجَ بِهِۦ مِنَ ٱلثَّمَرَٰتِ رِزْقًا لَّكُمْ فَلَا تَجْعَلُوا۟ لِلَّهِ أَندَادًا وَأَنتُمْ تَعْلَمُونَ (٢٢) وَإِن كُنتُمْ فِى رَيْبٍ مِّمَّا نَزَّلْنَا عَلَىٰ عَبْدِنَا فَأْتُوا۟ بِسُورَةٍ مِّن مِّثْلِهِۦ وَٱدْعُوا۟ شُهَدَآءَكُم مِّن دُونِ ٱللَّهِ إِن كُنتُمْ صَٰدِقِينَ (٢٣) فَإِن لَّمْ تَفْعَلُوا۟ وَلَن تَفْعَلُوا۟ فَٱتَّقُوا۟ ٱلنَّارَ ٱلَّتِى وَقُودُهَا ٱلنَّاسُ وَٱلْحِجَارَةُ أُعِدَّتْ لِلْكَٰفِرِينَ (٢٤)

Who has made the earth a resting place for you, and the sky as a canopy, and sent down water (rain) from the sky and brought forth therewith fruits as a provision for you? Then do not set up rivals unto Allâh (in worship) while you know (that He Alone has the right to be worshipped). (22) And if you (Arab pagans, Jews, and Christians) are in doubt concerning that which We have sent down (i.e. the Qur'ân) to Our slave (Muhammad), then produce a Sûrah (chapter) of the like *thereof and call your witnesses (supporters and helpers) besides Allâh, if you are truthful. (23) But if you do it not, and you can never do it, then fear the Fire (Hell) whose fuel is men and stones, prepared for the disbelievers. (24)*

Quran 2:28-29

كَيْفَ تَكْفُرُونَ بِٱللَّهِ وَكُنتُمْ أَمْوَٰتًا فَأَحْيَـٰكُمْ ثُمَّ يُمِيتُكُمْ ثُمَّ يُحْيِيكُمْ ثُمَّ إِلَيْهِ تُرْجَعُونَ (٢٨) هُوَ ٱلَّذِى خَلَقَ لَكُم مَّا فِى ٱلْأَرْضِ جَمِيعًا ثُمَّ ٱسْتَوَىٰٓ إِلَى ٱلسَّمَآءِ فَسَوَّىٰهُنَّ سَبْعَ سَمَٰوَٰتٍ وَهُوَ بِكُلِّ شَىْءٍ عَلِيمٌ (٢٩)

How can you disbelieve in Allâh? Seeing that you were dead and He gave you life. Then He will give you death, then again will bring you to life (on the Day of Resurrection) and then unto Him you will return. (28) He it is Who created for you all that is on earth. Then He rose over (Istawâ) towards the heaven and made them seven heavens and He is the All-Knower of everything. (29)

Quran 2:30-33

وَإِذْ قَالَ رَبُّكَ لِلْمَلَـٰٓئِكَةِ إِنِّى جَاعِلٌ فِى ٱلْأَرْضِ خَلِيفَةًۖ قَالُوٓا۟
أَتَجْعَلُ فِيهَا مَن يُفْسِدُ فِيهَا وَيَسْفِكُ ٱلدِّمَآءَ وَنَحْنُ نُسَبِّحُ
بِحَمْدِكَ وَنُقَدِّسُ لَكَۖ قَالَ إِنِّىٓ أَعْلَمُ مَا لَا تَعْلَمُونَ (٣٠) وَعَلَّمَ
ءَادَمَ ٱلْأَسْمَآءَ كُلَّهَا ثُمَّ عَرَضَهُمْ عَلَى ٱلْمَلَـٰٓئِكَةِ فَقَالَ أَنۢبِـُٔونِى
بِأَسْمَآءِ هَـٰٓؤُلَآءِ إِن كُنتُمْ صَـٰدِقِينَ (٣١) قَالُوا۟ سُبْحَـٰنَكَ لَا
عِلْمَ لَنَآ إِلَّا مَا عَلَّمْتَنَآۖ إِنَّكَ أَنتَ ٱلْعَلِيمُ ٱلْحَكِيمُ (٣٢) قَالَ
يَـٰٓـَٔادَمُ أَنۢبِئْهُم بِأَسْمَآئِهِمْۖ فَلَمَّآ أَنۢبَأَهُم بِأَسْمَآئِهِمْ قَالَ أَلَمْ أَقُل لَّكُمْ
إِنِّىٓ أَعْلَمُ غَيْبَ ٱلسَّمَـٰوَٰتِ وَٱلْأَرْضِ وَأَعْلَمُ مَا تُبْدُونَ وَمَا
كُنتُمْ تَكْتُمُونَ (٣٣)

And (remember) when your Lord said to the
angels: "Verily, I am going to place
(mankind) generations after generations on
earth." They said: "Will You place therein
those who will make mischief therein and
shed blood, - while we glorify You with
praises and thanks and sanctify You." He
(Allâh) said: "I know that which you do not
know." (30) And He taught Adam all the
names (of everything), then He showed them
to the angels and said, "Tell Me the names
of these if you are truthful." (31) They
(angels) said: "Glory be to You, we have no
knowledge except what you have taught us.

Verily, it is You, the All-Knower, the All-Wise." (32) He said: "O Adam! Inform them of their names," and when he had informed them of their names, He (Allah) said: "Did I not tell you that I know the Ghaib (unseen) in the heavens and the earth, and I know what you reveal and what you have been concealing?" (33)

Quran 2:75-77

۞ أَفَتَطْمَعُونَ أَن يُؤْمِنُواْ لَكُمْ وَقَدْ كَانَ فَرِيقٌ مِّنْهُمْ يَسْمَعُونَ كَلَمَ ٱللَّهِ ثُمَّ يُحَرِّفُونَهُ ۚ مِنْ بَعْدِ مَا عَقَلُوهُ وَهُمْ يَعْلَمُونَ (٧٥) وَإِذَا لَقُواْ ٱلَّذِينَ ءَامَنُواْ قَالُواْ ءَامَنَّا وَإِذَا خَلَا بَعْضُهُمْ إِلَىٰ بَعْضٍ قَالُواْ أَتُحَدِّثُونَهُم بِمَا فَتَحَ ٱللَّهُ عَلَيْكُمْ لِيُحَاجُّوكُم بِهِ عِندَ رَبِّكُمْ أَفَلَا تَعْقِلُونَ (٧٦) أَوَلَا يَعْلَمُونَ أَنَّ ٱللَّهَ يَعْلَمُ مَا يُسِرُّونَ وَمَا يُعْلِنُونَ (٧٧)

Do you (faithful believers) covet that they will believe in your religion inspite of the fact that a party of them (Jewish rabbis) used to hear the Word of Allâh [the Taurât (Torah)], then they used to change it knowingly after they understood it? (75) And when they (Jews)

meet those who believe (Muslims), they say,
"We believe", but when they meet one
another in private, they say, "Shall you
(Jews) tell them (Muslims) what Allâh has
revealed to you [Jews, about the description
and the qualities of Prophet Muhammad,
that which are written in the Taurât
(Torah)], that they (Muslims) may argue
with you (Jews) about it before your Lord?"
**Have you (Jews) then no understanding?
(76) Know they (Jews) not that Allâh
knows what they conceal and what
they reveal? (77)**

Quran 2:80-82

وَقَالُواْ لَن تَمَسَّنَا ٱلنَّارُ إِلَّا أَيَّامًا مَّعۡدُودَةًۚ قُلۡ أَتَّخَذۡتُمۡ عِندَ ٱللَّهِ
عَهۡدًا فَلَن يُخۡلِفَ ٱللَّهُ عَهۡدَهُۥ ۖ أَمۡ تَقُولُونَ عَلَى ٱللَّهِ مَا لَا
تَعۡلَمُونَ (٨٠) بَلَىٰ مَن كَسَبَ سَيِّئَةً وَأَحَٰطَتۡ بِهِۦ خَطِيٓئَتُهُۥ
فَأُوْلَٰٓئِكَ أَصۡحَٰبُ ٱلنَّارِ ۖ هُمۡ فِيهَا خَٰلِدُونَ (٨١) وَٱلَّذِينَ
ءَامَنُواْ وَعَمِلُواْ ٱلصَّٰلِحَٰتِ أُوْلَٰٓئِكَ أَصۡحَٰبُ ٱلۡجَنَّةِۖ هُمۡ فِيهَا
خَٰلِدُونَ (٨٢)

And they (Jews) say, "The Fire (i.e. Hell-fire
on the Day of Resurrection) shall not touch

us but for a few numbered days." Say:
*"Have you taken a covenant from Allâh,
so that Allâh will not break His
Covenant? Or is it that you say of Allâh
what you know not?"* (80) Yes!
*Whosoever earns evil and his sin has
surrounded him, they are dwellers of the
Fire (i.e. Hell); they will dwell therein
forever.* (81) *And those who believe (in the
Oneness of Allâh - Islâmic Monotheism)
and do righteous good deeds, they are
dwellers of Paradise, they will dwell therein
forever.* (82)

Quran 2:85-87

ثُمَّ أَنتُمْ هَٰٓؤُلَآءِ تَقْتُلُونَ أَنفُسَكُمْ وَتُخْرِجُونَ فَرِيقًا مِّنكُم مِّن
دِيَٰرِهِمْ تَظَٰهَرُونَ عَلَيْهِم بِٱلْإِثْمِ وَٱلْعُدْوَٰنِ وَإِن يَأْتُوكُمْ
أُسَٰرَىٰ تُفَٰدُوهُمْ وَهُوَ مُحَرَّمٌ عَلَيْكُمْ إِخْرَاجُهُمْ أَفَتُؤْمِنُونَ
بِبَعْضِ ٱلْكِتَٰبِ وَتَكْفُرُونَ بِبَعْضٍ فَمَا جَزَآءُ مَن يَفْعَلُ ذَٰلِكَ
مِنكُمْ إِلَّا خِزْيٌ فِى ٱلْحَيَوٰةِ ٱلدُّنْيَا وَيَوْمَ ٱلْقِيَٰمَةِ يُرَدُّونَ إِلَىٰٓ
أَشَدِّ ٱلْعَذَابِ وَمَا ٱللَّهُ بِغَٰفِلٍ عَمَّا تَعْمَلُونَ (٨٥) أُوْلَٰٓئِكَ ٱلَّذِينَ
ٱشْتَرَوُاْ ٱلْحَيَوٰةَ ٱلدُّنْيَا بِٱلْأَخِرَةِ فَلَا يُخَفَّفُ عَنْهُمُ ٱلْعَذَابُ وَلَا
هُمْ يُنصَرُونَ (٨٦) وَلَقَدْ ءَاتَيْنَا مُوسَى ٱلْكِتَٰبَ وَقَفَّيْنَا مِنۢ
بَعْدِهِ بِٱلرُّسُلِ وَءَاتَيْنَا عِيسَى ٱبْنَ مَرْيَمَ ٱلْبَيِّنَٰتِ وَأَيَّدْنَٰهُ

بِرُوحِ ٱلْقُدُسِ ۗ أَفَكُلَّمَا جَاءَكُمْ رَسُولٌ بِمَا لَا تَهْوَىٰ أَنفُسُكُمُ ٱسْتَكْبَرْتُمْ فَفَرِيقًا كَذَّبْتُمْ وَفَرِيقًا تَقْتُلُونَ (٨٧)

After this, it is you who kill one another and drive out a party of you from their homes, assist (their enemies) against them, in sin and transgression. And if they come to you as captives, you ransom them, although their expulsion was forbidden to you. **Then do you believe in a part of the Scripture and reject the rest?** Then what is the recompense of those who do so among you, except disgrace in the life of this world, and on the Day of Resurrection they shall be consigned to the most grievous torment. And Allâh is not unaware of what you do. (85) Those are they who have bought the life of this world at the price of the Hereafter. Their torment shall not be lightened nor shall they be helped. (86) And indeed, We gave Mûsa (Moses) the Book and followed him up with a succession of Messengers. And We gave 'Îsâ (Jesus), the son of Maryam (Mary), clear signs and supported

him with Rûh-ul-Qudus [Jibrael (Gabriel)].
Is it that whenever there came to you a Messenger with what you yourselves desired not, you grew arrogant? *Some you disbelieved and some you killed. (87)*

Quran 2:91

وَإِذَا قِيلَ لَهُمْ ءَامِنُواْ بِمَآ أَنزَلَ ٱللَّهُ قَالُواْ نُؤْمِنُ بِمَآ أُنزِلَ عَلَيْنَا وَيَكْفُرُونَ بِمَا وَرَآءَهُ ۥ وَهُوَ ٱلْحَقُّ مُصَدِّقًا لِّمَا مَعَهُمْ قُلْ فَلِمَ تَقْتُلُونَ أَنْبِيَآءَ ٱللَّهِ مِن قَبْلُ إِن كُنتُم مُّؤْمِنِينَ (٩١)

And when it is said to them (the Jews), "Believe in what Allâh has sent down," they say, "We believe in what was sent down to us." And they disbelieve in that which came after it, while it is the truth confirming what is with them. Say (O Muhammad to them): **"Why then have you killed the Prophets of Allâh aforetime, if you indeed have been believers?"** *(91)*

Quran 2:99-100

وَلَقَدْ أَنزَلْنَا إِلَيْكَ ءَايَتٍ بَيِّنَتٍ وَمَا يَكْفُرُ بِهَا إِلَّا ٱلْفَسِقُونَ
(٩٩) أَوَكُلَّمَا عَهَدُواْ عَهْدًا نَّبَذَهُ فَرِيقٌ مِّنْهُم بَلْ أَكْثَرُهُمْ
لَا يُؤْمِنُونَ (١٠٠)

*And indeed We have sent down to you
manifest Ayât (these Verses of the Qur'ân
which inform in detail about the news of the
Jews and their secret intentions, etc.), and
none disbelieve in them but Fâsiqûn (those
who rebel against Allâh's Command).*
(99) **Is it not (the case) that every time
they make a covenant, some party
among them throw it aside?** *Nay! (the
truth) is most of them believe not.* (100)

Quran 2:130-133

وَمَن يَرْغَبُ عَن مِّلَّةِ إِبْرَٰهِۦمَ إِلَّا مَن سَفِهَ نَفْسَهُ وَلَقَدِ
ٱصْطَفَيْنَٰهُ فِى ٱلدُّنْيَا وَإِنَّهُ فِى ٱلْأَخِرَةِ لَمِنَ ٱلصَّٰلِحِينَ
(١٣٠) إِذْ قَالَ لَهُ رَبُّهُ أَسْلِمْ قَالَ أَسْلَمْتُ لِرَبِّ ٱلْعَٰلَمِينَ
(١٣١) وَوَصَّىٰ بِهَا إِبْرَٰهِۦمُ بَنِيهِ وَيَعْقُوبُ يَٰبَنِىَّ إِنَّ ٱللَّهَ
ٱصْطَفَىٰ لَكُمُ ٱلدِّينَ فَلَا تَمُوتُنَّ إِلَّا وَأَنتُم مُّسْلِمُونَ (١٣٢) أَمْ
كُنتُمْ شُهَدَآءَ إِذْ حَضَرَ يَعْقُوبَ ٱلْمَوْتُ إِذْ قَالَ لِبَنِيهِ مَا تَعْبُدُونَ
مِنْ بَعْدِى قَالُواْ نَعْبُدُ إِلَٰهَكَ وَإِلَٰهَ ءَابَآئِكَ إِبْرَٰهِۦمَ وَإِسْمَٰعِيلَ
وَإِسْحَٰقَ إِلَٰهًا وَٰحِدًا وَنَحْنُ لَهُ مُسْلِمُونَ (١٣٣)

And who turns away from the religion of Ibrâhim (Abraham) (i.e. Islâmic Monotheism) except him who befools himself? Truly, We chose him in this world and verily, in the Hereafter he will be among the righteous. (130) When his Lord said to him, "Submit (i.e. be a Muslim)!" He said, "I have submitted myself (as a Muslim) to the Lord of the 'Alamîn (mankind, jinn and all that exists)." (131) And this (submission to Allâh, Islâm) was enjoined by Ibrâhim (Abraham) upon his sons and by Ya'qûb (Jacob), (saying), "O my sons! Allâh has chosen for you the (true) religion, then die not except in the Faith of Islâm (as Muslims - Islâmic Monotheism)." (132) *Or were you witnesses when death approached Ya'qûb (Jacob)? When he said unto his sons, "What will you worship after me?"* They said, "We shall worship your Ilâh (God - Allâh), the Ilâh (God) of your fathers, Ibrâhim (Abraham), Ismâ'il

(Ishmael), Ishâq (Isaac), One Ilâh (God), and to Him we submit (in Islâm)." (133)

Quran 2:138-140

صِبْغَةَ ٱللَّهِ وَمَنْ أَحْسَنُ مِنَ ٱللَّهِ صِبْغَةً وَنَحْنُ لَهُ عَٰبِدُونَ (١٣٨) قُلْ أَتُحَآجُّونَنَا فِى ٱللَّهِ وَهُوَ رَبُّنَا وَرَبُّكُمْ وَلَنَآ أَعْمَٰلُنَا وَلَكُمْ أَعْمَٰلُكُمْ وَنَحْنُ لَهُ مُخْلِصُونَ (١٣٩) أَمْ تَقُولُونَ إِنَّ إِبْرَٰهِۦمَ وَإِسْمَٰعِيلَ وَإِسْحَٰقَ وَيَعْقُوبَ وَٱلْأَسْبَاطَ كَانُوا۟ هُودًا أَوْ نَصَٰرَىٰ قُلْ ءَأَنتُمْ أَعْلَمُ أَمِ ٱللَّهُ وَمَنْ أَظْلَمُ مِمَّن كَتَمَ شَهَٰدَةً عِندَهُۥ مِنَ ٱللَّهِ وَمَا ٱللَّهُ بِغَٰفِلٍ عَمَّا تَعْمَلُونَ (١٤٠)

[Our Sibghah (religion) is] the Sibghah (Religion) of Allâh (Islâm) and which Sibghah (religion) can be better than Allâh's? And we are His worshippers. (138) Say (O Muhammad to the Jews and Christians), "*Dispute you with us about Allâh while He is our Lord and your Lord?* And we are to be rewarded for our deeds and you for your deeds. And we are sincere to Him [in worship and obedience (i.e. we worship Him Alone and none else, and we obey His Orders).]" (139) *Or say*

you that Ibrâhim (Abraham), Ismâ'il (Ishmael), Ishâque (Isaac), Ya'qûb (Jacob) and Al-Asbât [the offspring twelve sons of Ya'qûb (Jacob)] were Jews or Christians? Say, "Do you know better or does Allâh ? And who is more unjust than he who conceals the testimony [i.e. to believe in Prophet Muhammad when he comes, as is written in their Books.] he has from Allâh? And Allâh is not unaware of what you do." (140)

Quran 2:210

هَلْ يَنظُرُونَ إِلَّا أَن يَأْتِيَهُمُ ٱللَّهُ فِى ظُلَلٍ مِّنَ ٱلْغَمَامِ وَٱلْمَلَـٰٓئِكَةُ وَقُضِىَ ٱلْأَمْرُ ۚ وَإِلَى ٱللَّهِ تُرْجَعُ ٱلْأُمُورُ (٢١٠)

Do they then wait for anything other than that Allâh should come to them in the shadows of the clouds and the angels? (Then) the case would be already judged. And to Allâh return all matters (for decision). (210)

Quran 2:214

أَمْ حَسِبْتُمْ أَن تَدْخُلُوا ٱلْجَنَّةَ وَلَمَّا يَأْتِكُم مَّثَلُ ٱلَّذِينَ خَلَوْا مِن قَبْلِكُم مَّسَّتْهُمُ ٱلْبَأْسَاءُ وَٱلضَّرَّاءُ وَزُلْزِلُوا حَتَّىٰ يَقُولَ ٱلرَّسُولُ وَٱلَّذِينَ ءَامَنُوا مَعَهُ ۥ مَتَىٰ نَصْرُ ٱللَّهِ أَلَا إِنَّ نَصْرَ ٱللَّهِ قَرِيبٌ (٢١٤)

Or think you that you will enter Paradise without such (trials) as came to those who passed away before you? They were afflicted with severe poverty and ailments and were so shaken that even the Messenger and those who believed along with him said, "When (will come) the Help of Allâh?" Yes! Certainly, the Help of Allâh is near! (214)

Quran 2:243-246

۞ أَلَمْ تَرَ إِلَى ٱلَّذِينَ خَرَجُوا مِن دِيَٰرِهِمْ وَهُمْ أُلُوفٌ حَذَرَ ٱلْمَوْتِ فَقَالَ لَهُمُ ٱللَّهُ مُوتُوا ثُمَّ أَحْيَٰهُمْ إِنَّ ٱللَّهَ لَذُو فَضْلٍ عَلَى ٱلنَّاسِ وَلَٰكِنَّ أَكْثَرَ ٱلنَّاسِ لَا يَشْكُرُونَ (٢٤٣) وَقَٰتِلُوا فِى سَبِيلِ ٱللَّهِ وَٱعْلَمُوا أَنَّ ٱللَّهَ سَمِيعٌ عَلِيمٌ (٢٤٤) مَّن ذَا ٱلَّذِى يُقْرِضُ ٱللَّهَ قَرْضًا حَسَنًا فَيُضَٰعِفَهُ ۥ لَهُ ۥ أَضْعَافًا كَثِيرَةً وَٱللَّهُ يَقْبِضُ وَيَبْصُۜطُ وَإِلَيْهِ تُرْجَعُونَ (٢٤٥) أَلَمْ تَرَ إِلَى ٱلْمَلَإِ مِنۢ بَنِى إِسْرَٰءِيلَ مِنۢ بَعْدِ مُوسَىٰ إِذْ قَالُوا لِنَبِىٍّ لَّهُمُ ٱبْعَثْ لَنَا مَلِكًا نُّقَٰتِلْ فِى سَبِيلِ ٱللَّهِ قَالَ هَلْ عَسَيْتُمْ إِن كُتِبَ عَلَيْكُمُ ٱلْقِتَالُ أَلَّا تُقَٰتِلُوا قَالُوا وَمَا لَنَا أَلَّا نُقَٰتِلَ فِى

سَبِيلِ ٱللَّهِ وَقَدْ أُخْرِجْنَا مِن دِيَـٰرِنَا وَأَبْنَآئِنَاۖ فَلَمَّا كُتِبَ عَلَيْهِمُ ٱلْقِتَالُ تَوَلَّوْاْ إِلَّا قَلِيلاً مِّنْهُمْۗ وَٱللَّهُ عَلِيمُۢ بِٱلظَّـٰلِمِينَ (٢٤٦)

Did you (O Muhammad) not think of those who went forth from their homes in thousands, fearing death? Allâh said to them, "Die". And then He restored them to life. Truly, Allâh is full of Bounty to mankind, but most men thank not. (243) *And fight in the Way of Allâh and know that Allâh is All-Hearer, All-Knower.* (244) **Who is he that will lend to Allâh a goodly loan so that He may multiply it to him many times?** *And it is Allâh that decreases or increases (your provisions), and unto Him you shall return.* (245) **Have you not thought about the group of the Children of Israel after (the time of) Musâ (Moses)?** *When they said to a Prophet of theirs, "Appoint for us a king and we will fight in Allâh's Way." He said, "Would you then refrain from fighting, if fighting was prescribed for you?" They said, "Why should we not fight in Allâh's Way*

*while we have been driven out of our homes
and our children (families have been taken
as captives)?" But when fighting was
ordered for them, they turned away, all
except a few of them. And Allâh is All-
Aware of the Zâlimûn (polytheists and
wrong-doers). (246)*

Quran 2:255

ٱللَّهُ لَا إِلَٰهَ إِلَّا هُوَ ٱلْحَىُّ ٱلْقَيُّومُ لَا تَأْخُذُهُ سِنَةٌ وَلَا نَوْمٌ لَّهُ
مَا فِى ٱلسَّمَٰوَٰتِ وَمَا فِى ٱلْأَرْضِ مَن ذَا ٱلَّذِى يَشْفَعُ عِندَهُ
إِلَّا بِإِذْنِهِ يَعْلَمُ مَا بَيْنَ أَيْدِيهِمْ وَمَا خَلْفَهُمْ وَلَا يُحِيطُونَ
بِشَىْءٍ مِّنْ عِلْمِهِ إِلَّا بِمَا شَآءَ وَسِعَ كُرْسِيُّهُ ٱلسَّمَٰوَٰتِ
وَٱلْأَرْضَ وَلَا يَـُٔودُهُ حِفْظُهُمَا وَهُوَ ٱلْعَلِىُّ ٱلْعَظِيمُ (٢٥٥)

*Allâh! Lâ ilâha illa Huwa (none has the
right to be worshipped but He), the Ever
Living, the One Who sustains and protects
all that exists. Neither slumber, nor sleep
overtake Him. To Him belongs whatever is
in the heavens and whatever is on earth.*
**Who is he that can intercede with Him
except with His Permission?** *He knows
what happens to them (His creatures) in this*

world, and what will happen to them in the
Hereafter. And they will never compass
anything of His Knowledge except that
which He wills. His Kursî extends over the
heavens and the earth, and He feels no
fatigue in guarding and preserving them.
And He is the Most High, the Most Great.
(255)

Quran 2:258-260

أَلَمْ تَرَ إِلَى ٱلَّذِى حَاجَّ إِبْرَاهِمَ فِى رَبِّهِ أَنْ ءَاتَىٰهُ ٱللَّهُ ٱلْمُلْكَ
إِذْ قَالَ إِبْرَاهِمُ رَبِّىَ ٱلَّذِى يُحْيِ وَيُمِيتُ قَالَ أَنَا أُحْيِ
وَأُمِيتُ قَالَ إِبْرَاهِمُ فَإِنَّ ٱللَّهَ يَأْتِى بِٱلشَّمْسِ مِنَ ٱلْمَشْرِقِ فَأْتِ
بِهَا مِنَ ٱلْمَغْرِبِ فَبُهِتَ ٱلَّذِى كَفَرَ وَٱللَّهُ لَا يَهْدِى ٱلْقَوْمَ
ٱلظَّٰلِمِينَ (٢٥٨) أَوْ كَٱلَّذِى مَرَّ عَلَىٰ قَرْيَةٍ وَهِىَ خَاوِيَةٌ عَلَىٰ
عُرُوشِهَا قَالَ أَنَّىٰ يُحْيِ هَٰذِهِ ٱللَّهُ بَعْدَ مَوْتِهَا فَأَمَاتَهُ ٱللَّهُ مِائَةَ
عَامٍ ثُمَّ بَعَثَهُ قَالَ كَمْ لَبِثْتَ قَالَ لَبِثْتُ يَوْمًا أَوْ بَعْضَ يَوْمٍ
قَالَ بَل لَّبِثْتَ مِائَةَ عَامٍ فَٱنظُرْ إِلَىٰ طَعَامِكَ وَشَرَابِكَ لَمْ يَتَسَنَّهْ
وَٱنظُرْ إِلَىٰ حِمَارِكَ وَلِنَجْعَلَكَ ءَايَةً لِّلنَّاسِ وَٱنظُرْ إِلَى ٱلْعِظَامِ
كَيْفَ نُنشِزُهَا ثُمَّ نَكْسُوهَا لَحْمًا فَلَمَّا تَبَيَّنَ لَهُ قَالَ أَعْلَمُ أَنَّ
ٱللَّهَ عَلَىٰ كُلِّ شَىْءٍ قَدِيرٌ (٢٥٩) وَإِذْ قَالَ إِبْرَاهِمُ رَبِّ
أَرِنِى كَيْفَ تُحْيِ ٱلْمَوْتَىٰ قَالَ أَوَلَمْ تُؤْمِن قَالَ بَلَىٰ وَلَٰكِن
لِّيَطْمَئِنَّ قَلْبِى قَالَ فَخُذْ أَرْبَعَةً مِّنَ ٱلطَّيْرِ فَصُرْهُنَّ إِلَيْكَ ثُمَّ

أَجْعَلْ عَلَىٰ كُلِّ جَبَلٍ مِّنْهُنَّ جُزْءًا ثُمَّ ٱدْعُهُنَّ يَأْتِينَكَ سَعْيًا وَٱعْلَمْ أَنَّ ٱللَّهَ عَزِيزٌ حَكِيمٌ (٢٦٠)

Have you not looked at him who disputed with Ibrâhim (Abraham) about his Lord (Allâh), because Allâh had given him the kingdom? When Ibrâhim (Abraham) said (to him): "My Lord (Allâh) is He Who gives life and causes death." He said, "I give life and cause death." Ibrâhim (Abraham) said, "Verily! Allâh causes the sun to rise from the east; then cause it you to rise from the west." So the disbeliever was utterly defeated. And Allâh guides not the people, who are Zâlimûn (wrong-doers). (258) **Or like the one who passed by a town and it had tumbled over its roofs?** He said: "Oh! How will Allâh ever bring it to life after its death?" So Allâh caused him to die for a hundred years, then raised him up (again). He said: **"How long did you remain (dead)?"** He (the man) said: "(Perhaps) I remained (dead) a day or part of a day". He said: "Nay, you have remained (dead) for a hundred years, look at your food and your drink, they show no change; and look at your donkey! And thus We have made of you a sign for the people. Look at the bones, how We bring them together and clothe them with flesh". When this was clearly shown to him, he said, "I know (now) that Allâh is Able to do all things." (259) And (remember) when Ibrâhim (Abraham) said, "My Lord! Show me how You give life to the dead." He (Allâh) said: **"Do you not believe?"** He [Ibrâhim (Abraham)] said: "Yes (I believe), but to be stronger in Faith." He said: "Take four birds, then cause them to incline towards you (then slaughter them, cut them into pieces), and then put a portion of them on every hill, and call them, they will come to you in haste. And know that Allâh is All-Mighty, All-Wise." (260)

Quran 2:265-266

وَمَثَلُ ٱلَّذِينَ يُنفِقُونَ أَمْوَٰلَهُمُ ٱبْتِغَآءَ مَرْضَاتِ ٱللَّهِ وَتَثْبِيتًا مِّنْ أَنفُسِهِمْ كَمَثَلِ جَنَّةٍ بِرَبْوَةٍ أَصَابَهَا وَابِلٌ فَآتَتْ أُكُلَهَا ضِعْفَيْنِ

فَإِن لَّمْ يُصِبْهَا وَابِلٌ فَطَلٌّ ۗ وَٱللَّهُ بِمَا تَعْمَلُونَ بَصِيرٌ
(٢٦٥) أَيَوَدُّ أَحَدُكُمْ أَن تَكُونَ لَهُ ۥ جَنَّةٌ مِّن نَّخِيلٍ وَأَعْنَابٍ
تَجْرِى مِن تَحْتِهَا ٱلْأَنْهَـٰرُ لَهُ ۥ فِيهَا مِن كُلِّ ٱلثَّمَرَٰتِ
وَأَصَابَهُ ٱلْكِبَرُ وَلَهُ ۥ ذُرِّيَّةٌ ضُعَفَآءُ فَأَصَابَهَآ إِعْصَارٌ فِيهِ نَارٌ
فَٱحْتَرَقَتْ ۗ كَذَٰلِكَ يُبَيِّنُ ٱللَّهُ لَكُمُ ٱلْـَٔايَـٰتِ لَعَلَّكُمْ تَتَفَكَّرُونَ
(٢٦٦)

And the likeness of those who spend their wealth seeking Allâh's Pleasure while they in their ownselves are sure and certain that Allâh will reward them (for their spending in His Cause), is the likeness of a garden on a height; heavy rain falls on it and it doubles its yield of harvest. And if it does not receive heavy rain, light rain suffices it. And Allâh is All-Seer of (knows well) what you do. **(265)** **Would any of you wish to have a garden with date-palms and vines, with rivers flowing underneath, and all kinds of fruits for him therein, while he is striken with old age, and his children are weak (not able to look after themselves), then it is struck with a fiery whirlwind, so that it is burnt?**

Thus does Allâh make clear His Ayât
(proofs, evidences, verses) to you that you
may give thought. (266)

Quran 3:20

فَإِنْ حَاجُّوكَ فَقُلْ أَسْلَمْتُ وَجْهِيَ لِلَّهِ وَمَنِ ٱتَّبَعَنِّ وَقُل لِّلَّذِينَ
أُوتُواْ ٱلْكِتَـٰبَ وَٱلْأُمِّيِّـۧنَ ءَأَسْلَمْتُمْ فَإِنْ أَسْلَمُواْ فَقَدِ ٱهْتَدَواْ وَّإِن
تَوَلَّوْاْ فَإِنَّمَا عَلَيْكَ ٱلْبَلَـٰغُ وَٱللَّهُ بَصِيرُۢ بِٱلْعِبَادِ (٢٠)

So if they dispute with you (Muhammad)
say: "I have submitted myself to Allâh (in
Islâm), and (so have) those who follow me."
And say to those who were given the
Scripture (Jews and Christians) and to those
*who are illiterates (Arab pagans): "**Do you***
(also) submit yourselves (to Allâh in
***Islâm)?"** If they do, they are rightly guided;*
but if they turn away, your duty is only to
convey the Message; and Allâh is All-Seer of
(His) slaves(20)

Quran 3:23-25

أَلَمْ تَرَ إِلَى ٱلَّذِينَ أُوتُواْ نَصِيبًا مِّنَ ٱلْكِتَـٰبِ يُدْعَوْنَ إِلَىٰ
كِتَـٰبِ ٱللَّهِ لِيَحْكُمَ بَيْنَهُمْ ثُمَّ يَتَوَلَّىٰ فَرِيقٌ مِّنْهُمْ وَهُم

مُعْرِضُونَ (٢٣) ذَٰلِكَ بِأَنَّهُمْ قَالُوا لَن تَمَسَّنَا ٱلنَّارُ إِلَّا أَيَّامًا مَّعْدُودَٰتٍ وَغَرَّهُمْ فِى دِينِهِم مَّا كَانُوا يَفْتَرُونَ (٢٤) فَكَيْفَ إِذَا جَمَعْنَٰهُمْ لِيَوْمٍ لَّا رَيْبَ فِيهِ وَوُفِّيَتْ كُلُّ نَفْسٍ مَّا كَسَبَتْ وَهُمْ لَا يُظْلَمُونَ (٢٥)

Have you not seen those who have been given a portion of the Scripture? They are being invited to the Book of Allâh to settle their dispute, then a party of them turn away, and they are averse. (23) This is because they say: "The Fire shall not touch us but for a number of days." And that which they used to invent regarding their religion has deceived them. (24) **How (will it be) when We gather them together on the Day about which there is no doubt (i.e. the Day of Resurrection) and each person will be paid in full what he has earned?** *And they will not be dealt with unjustly. (25)*

Quran 3:65-71

يَٰأَهْلَ ٱلْكِتَٰبِ لِمَ تُحَآجُّونَ فِىٓ إِبْرَٰهِيمَ وَمَآ أُنزِلَتِ ٱلتَّوْرَٰةُ وَٱلْإِنجِيلُ إِلَّا مِنۢ بَعْدِهِۦٓ أَفَلَا تَعْقِلُونَ (٦٥) هَٰٓأَنتُمْ هَٰٓؤُلَآءِ

حَاجَجْتُمْ فِيمَا لَكُم بِهِ عِلْمٌ فَلِمَ تُحَاجُّونَ فِيمَا لَيْسَ لَكُم بِهِ
عِلْمٌ وَٱللَّهُ يَعْلَمُ وَأَنتُمْ لَا تَعْلَمُونَ (٦٦) مَا كَانَ إِبْرَٰهِيمُ يَهُودِيًّا
وَلَا نَصْرَانِيًّا وَلَٰكِن كَانَ حَنِيفًا مُّسْلِمًا وَمَا كَانَ مِنَ
ٱلْمُشْرِكِينَ (٦٧) إِنَّ أَوْلَى ٱلنَّاسِ بِإِبْرَٰهِيمَ لَلَّذِينَ ٱتَّبَعُوهُ
وَهَٰذَا ٱلنَّبِىُّ وَٱلَّذِينَ ءَامَنُوا وَٱللَّهُ وَلِىُّ ٱلْمُؤْمِنِينَ (٦٨) وَدَّت
طَّآئِفَةٌ مِّنْ أَهْلِ ٱلْكِتَٰبِ لَوْ يُضِلُّونَكُمْ وَمَا يُضِلُّونَ إِلَّا أَنفُسَهُمْ
وَمَا يَشْعُرُونَ (٦٩) يَٰأَهْلَ ٱلْكِتَٰبِ لِمَ تَكْفُرُونَ بِـَٔايَٰتِ ٱللَّهِ
وَأَنتُمْ تَشْهَدُونَ (٧٠) يَٰأَهْلَ ٱلْكِتَٰبِ لِمَ تَلْبِسُونَ ٱلْحَقَّ بِٱلْبَٰطِلِ
وَتَكْتُمُونَ ٱلْحَقَّ وَأَنتُمْ تَعْلَمُونَ (٧١)

O people of the Scripture (Jews and Christians)! Why do you dispute about Ibrâhim (Abraham), while the Taurât (Torah) and the Injeel were not revealed till after him? Have you then no sense? (65) Verily, you are those who have disputed about that of which you have knowledge. *Why do you then dispute concerning that of which you have no knowledge?* It is Allâh Who knows, and you know not. (66) Ibrâhim (Abraham) was neither a Jew nor a Christian, but he was a true Muslim Hanifa (Islâmic Monotheism - to worship none but Allâh Alone) and he was not of Al-

Mushrikûn[polytheists] (67) Verily, among mankind who have the best claim to Ibrâhim (Abraham) are those who followed him, and this Prophet (Muhammad) and those who have believed (Muslims). And Allâh is the Walî (Protector and Helper) of the believers. (68) A party of the people of the Scripture (Jews and Christians) wish to lead you astray. But they shall not lead astray anyone except themselves, and they perceive not. (69) O people of the Scripture! (Jews and Christians): **"Why do you disbelieve in the Ayât of Allâh, [the Verses about Prophet Muhammad present in the Taurât (Torah) and the Injeel] while you (yourselves) bear witness (to their truth)?"** *(70) O people of the Scripture (Jews and Christians):* **"Why do you mix truth with falsehood and conceal the truth while you know?"** *(71)*

Quran 3:79-83

مَا كَانَ لِبَشَرٍ أَن يُؤْتِيَهُ ٱللَّهُ ٱلْكِتَـٰبَ وَٱلْحُكْمَ وَٱلنُّبُوَّةَ ثُمَّ يَقُولَ
لِلنَّاسِ كُونُواْ عِبَادًا لِّى مِن دُونِ ٱللَّهِ وَلَـٰكِن كُونُواْ رَبَّـٰنِيِّنَ
بِمَا كُنتُمْ تُعَلِّمُونَ ٱلْكِتَـٰبَ وَبِمَا كُنتُمْ تَدْرُسُونَ (٧٩) وَلَا
يَأْمُرَكُمْ أَن تَتَّخِذُواْ ٱلْمَلَـٰٓئِكَةَ وَٱلنَّبِيِّنَ أَرْبَابًا أَيَأْمُرُكُم بِٱلْكُفْرِ
بَعْدَ إِذْ أَنتُم مُّسْلِمُونَ (٨٠) وَإِذْ أَخَذَ ٱللَّهُ مِيثَـٰقَ ٱلنَّبِيِّنَ لَمَآ
ءَاتَيْتُكُم مِّن كِتَـٰبٍ وَحِكْمَةٍ ثُمَّ جَآءَكُمْ رَسُولٌ مُّصَدِّقٌ لِّمَا
مَعَكُمْ لَتُؤْمِنُنَّ بِهِۦ وَلَتَنصُرُنَّهُۥ ۚ قَالَ ءَأَقْرَرْتُمْ وَأَخَذْتُمْ عَلَىٰ
ذَٰلِكُمْ إِصْرِى ۖ قَالُوٓاْ أَقْرَرْنَا ۚ قَالَ فَٱشْهَدُواْ وَأَنَا۠ مَعَكُم مِّنَ
ٱلشَّـٰهِدِينَ (٨١) فَمَن تَوَلَّىٰ بَعْدَ ذَٰلِكَ فَأُوْلَـٰٓئِكَ هُمُ ٱلْفَـٰسِقُونَ
(٨٢) أَفَغَيْرَ دِينِ ٱللَّهِ يَبْغُونَ وَلَهُۥٓ أَسْلَمَ مَن فِى ٱلسَّمَـٰوَٰتِ
وَٱلْأَرْضِ طَوْعًا وَكَرْهًا وَإِلَيْهِ يُرْجَعُونَ (٨٣)

It is not (possible) for any human being to whom Allâh has given the Book and Al-Hukm (the knowledge and understanding of the laws of religion) and Prophethood to say to the people: "Be my worshippers rather than Allâh's." On the contrary (he would say): "Be you Rabbaniyyun (learned men of religion who practise what they know and also preach others), because you are teaching the Book, and you are studying it." (79) Nor would he order you to take angels and Prophets for lords (gods). **Would he order** *you to disbelieve after you have submitted to Allâh's Will?* (80) *And (remember) when Allâh took the Covenant of the Prophets, saying: "Take whatever I gave you from the Book and Hikmah (understanding of the Laws of Allâh), and afterwards there will come to you a Messenger (Muhammad) confirming what is with you; you must, then, believe in him and help him." Allâh said:* **"Do you agree (to it) and will you take up My Covenant (which I conclude with you)?"** *They said: "We agree." He said: "Then bear witness; and I am with you among the witnesses (for this)."* (81) *Then whoever turns away after this, they are the Fâsiqûn (rebellious: those who turn away from Allâh's Obedience).* (82**) Do they seek other than the religion of Allâh (the true Islâmic Monotheism worshipping none but Allâh Alone), while to Him submitted all creatures in the heavens**

and the earth, willingly or unwillingly?
And to Him shall they all be returned. (83)

Quran 3:85-86

وَمَن يَبْتَغِ غَيْرَ ٱلْإِسْلَٰمِ دِينًا فَلَن يُقْبَلَ مِنْهُ وَهُوَ فِى ٱلْأَخِرَةِ
مِنَ ٱلْخَٰسِرِينَ (٨٥) كَيْفَ يَهْدِى ٱللَّهُ قَوْمًا كَفَرُواْ بَعْدَ
إِيمَٰنِهِمْ وَشَهِدُوٓاْ أَنَّ ٱلرَّسُولَ حَقٌّ وَجَآءَهُمُ ٱلْبَيِّنَٰتُ وَٱللَّهُ لَا
يَهْدِى ٱلْقَوْمَ ٱلظَّٰلِمِينَ (٨٦)

And whoever seeks a religion other than
Islâm, it will never be accepted of him, and
in the Hereafter he will be one of the losers.
(85) **How shall Allâh guide a people**
who disbelieved after their belief and
after they bore witness that the
Messenger (Muhammad) is true and
after clear proofs had come unto them?
And Allâh guides not the people who are
Zâlimûn (polytheists and wrong-doers).
(86)

Quran 3:98-101

قُلْ يَٰٓأَهْلَ ٱلْكِتَٰبِ لِمَ تَكْفُرُونَ بِـَٔايَٰتِ ٱللَّهِ وَٱللَّهُ شَهِيدٌ عَلَىٰ مَا
تَعْمَلُونَ (٩٨) قُلْ يَٰٓأَهْلَ ٱلْكِتَٰبِ لِمَ تَصُدُّونَ عَن سَبِيلِ ٱللَّهِ

مَنْ ءَامَنَ تَبْغُونَهَا عِوَجًا وَأَنتُمْ شُهَدَآءُ وَمَا ٱللَّهُ بِغَٰفِلٍ عَمَّا
تَعْمَلُونَ (٩٩) يَٰٓأَيُّهَا ٱلَّذِينَ ءَامَنُوٓاْ إِن تُطِيعُواْ فَرِيقًا مِّنَ
ٱلَّذِينَ أُوتُواْ ٱلْكِتَٰبَ يَرُدُّوكُم بَعْدَ إِيمَٰنِكُمْ كَٰفِرِينَ
(١٠٠) وَكَيْفَ تَكْفُرُونَ وَأَنتُمْ تُتْلَىٰ عَلَيْكُمْ ءَايَٰتُ ٱللَّهِ وَفِيكُمْ
رَسُولُهُ ۗ وَمَن يَعْتَصِم بِٱللَّهِ فَقَدْ هُدِىَ إِلَىٰ صِرَٰطٍ مُّسْتَقِيمٍ
(١٠١)

Say: "**O people of the Scripture (Jews and Christians)! Why do you reject the Ayât of Allâh (proofs, evidences, verses, lessons, signs, revelations, etc.) while Allâh is Witness to what you do?"**
(98) Say: "O people of the Scripture (Jews and Christians)! **Why do you stop those who have believed, from the Path of Allâh, seeking to make it seem crooked, while you (yourselves) are witnesses [to Muhammad as a Messenger of Allâh and Islâm (Allâh's Religion, i.e. to worship none but Him Alone)]?** And Allâh is not unaware of what you do."
(99) O you who believe! If you obey a group of those who were given the Scripture (Jews and Christians), they would (indeed) render

you disbelievers after you have believed!
(100) **And how would you disbelieve,**
while unto you are recited the Verses of
Allâh, and among you is His Messenger
(Muhammad)? *And whoever holds firmly*
to Allâh, (i.e. follows Islâm — Allâh's
Religion, and obeys all that Allâh has
ordered, practically), then he is indeed
guided to a Right Path. (101)

Quran 3:106

يَوْمَ تَبْيَضُّ وُجُوهٌ وَتَسْوَدُّ وُجُوهٌ فَأَمَّا ٱلَّذِينَ ٱسْوَدَّتْ وُجُوهُهُمْ
أَكَفَرْتُم بَعْدَ إِيمَـٰنِكُمْ فَذُوقُواْ ٱلْعَذَابَ بِمَا كُنتُمْ تَكْفُرُونَ (١٠٦)

On the Day (i.e. the Day of Resurrection)
when some faces will become white and some
faces will become black; as for those whose
faces will become black (to them will be
said): **"Did you reject Faith after**
accepting it? *Then taste the torment (in*
Hell) for rejecting Faith." (106)

Quran 3:142-144

أَمْ حَسِبْتُمْ أَن تَدْخُلُواْ ٱلْجَنَّةَ وَلَمَّا يَعْلَمِ ٱللَّهُ ٱلَّذِينَ جَـٰهَدُواْ مِنكُمْ
وَيَعْلَمَ ٱلصَّـٰبِرِينَ (١٤٢) وَلَقَدْ كُنتُمْ تَمَنَّوْنَ ٱلْمَوْتَ مِن قَبْلِ
أَن تَلْقَوْهُ فَقَدْ رَأَيْتُمُوهُ وَأَنتُمْ تَنظُرُونَ (١٤٣) وَمَا مُحَمَّدٌ إِلَّا
رَسُولٌ قَدْ خَلَتْ مِن قَبْلِهِ ٱلرُّسُلُ أَفَإِيْن مَّاتَ أَوْ قُتِلَ ٱنقَلَبْتُمْ
عَلَىٰٓ أَعْقَـٰبِكُمْ وَمَن يَنقَلِبْ عَلَىٰ عَقِبَيْهِ فَلَن يَضُرَّ ٱللَّهَ شَيْـًٔا
وَسَيَجْزِى ٱللَّهُ ٱلشَّـٰكِرِينَ (١٤٤)

Do you think that you will enter
Paradise before Allâh tests those of you
who fought (in His Cause) and (also)
tests those who are As-Sâbirun (the
patient)? (142) You did indeed wish for
death (Ash¬Shahâdah - martyrdom) before
you met it. Now you have seen it openly
with your own eyes. (143) **Muhammad is**
no more than a Messenger, and indeed
(many) Messengers have passed away
before him. If he dies or is killed, will
you then turn back on your heels (as
disbelievers)? *And he who turns back on*
his heels, not the least harm will he do to
Allâh, and Allâh will give reward to those
who are grateful. (144)

Quran 3:183

ٱلَّذِينَ قَالُوٓاْ إِنَّ ٱللَّهَ عَهِدَ إِلَيْنَآ أَلَّا نُؤْمِنَ لِرَسُولٍ حَتَّىٰ يَأْتِيَنَا بِقُرْبَانٍ تَأْكُلُهُ ٱلنَّارُ قُلْ قَدْ جَآءَكُمْ رُسُلٌ مِّن قَبْلِى بِٱلْبَيِّنَٰتِ وَبِٱلَّذِى قُلْتُمْ فَلِمَ قَتَلْتُمُوهُمْ إِن كُنتُمْ صَٰدِقِينَ (١٨٣)

Those (Jews) who said: "Verily, Allâh has
taken our promise not to believe in any
Messenger unless he brings to us an offering
which the fire (from heaven) shall devour."
Say: "Verily, there came to you
Messengers before me, with clear signs
and even with what you speak of; why
then did you kill them, if you are
truthful?" *(183)*

Quran 4:41

فَكَيْفَ إِذَا جِئْنَا مِن كُلِّ أُمَّةٍ بِشَهِيدٍ وَجِئْنَا بِكَ عَلَىٰ هَٰٓؤُلَآءِ شَهِيدًا (٤١)

How (will it be) then, when We bring
from each nation a witness and We
bring you (O Muhammad) as a witness
against these people? (41)

Quran 4:44

أَلَمْ تَرَ إِلَى ٱلَّذِينَ أُوتُواْ نَصِيبًا مِّنَ ٱلْكِتَـٰبِ يَشْتَرُونَ ٱلضَّلَـٰلَةَ وَيُرِيدُونَ أَن تَضِلُّواْ ٱلسَّبِيلَ (٤٤)

Have you not seen those who were given a portion of the book (the Jews), purchasing the wrong path, and wish that you should go astray from the Right Path?(44)

Quran 4:49-54

أَلَمْ تَرَ إِلَى ٱلَّذِينَ يُزَكُّونَ أَنفُسَهُمْ بَلِ ٱللَّهُ يُزَكِّى مَن يَشَاءُ وَلَا يُظْلَمُونَ فَتِيلاً (٤٩) ٱنظُرْ كَيْفَ يَفْتَرُونَ عَلَى ٱللَّهِ ٱلْكَذِبَ وَكَفَىٰ بِهِ إِثْمًا مُّبِينًا (٥٠) أَلَمْ تَرَ إِلَى ٱلَّذِينَ أُوتُواْ نَصِيبًا مِّنَ ٱلْكِتَـٰبِ يُؤْمِنُونَ بِٱلْجِبْتِ وَٱلطَّـٰغُوتِ وَيَقُولُونَ لِلَّذِينَ كَفَرُواْ هَـٰٓؤُلَاءِ أَهْدَىٰ مِنَ ٱلَّذِينَ ءَامَنُواْ سَبِيلاً (٥١) أُوْلَـٰٓئِكَ ٱلَّذِينَ لَعَنَهُمُ ٱللَّهُ وَمَن يَلْعَنِ ٱللَّهُ فَلَن تَجِدَ لَهُ نَصِيرًا (٥٢) أَمْ لَهُمْ نَصِيبٌ مِّنَ ٱلْمُلْكِ فَإِذًا لَّا يُؤْتُونَ ٱلنَّاسَ نَقِيرًا (٥٣) أَمْ يَحْسُدُونَ ٱلنَّاسَ عَلَىٰ مَآ ءَاتَىٰهُمُ ٱللَّهُ مِن فَضْلِهِ فَقَدْ ءَاتَيْنَآ ءَالَ إِبْرَٰهِيمَ ٱلْكِتَـٰبَ وَٱلْحِكْمَةَ وَءَاتَيْنَـٰهُم مُّلْكًا عَظِيمًا (٥٤)

Have you not seen those (Jews and Christians) who claim sanctity for themselves? Nay, but Allâh sanctifies whom He wills, and they will not be dealt with injustice even equal to the extent of a scalish thread in the long slit of a date-stone. (49) Look, how they invent a lie against Allâh, and enough is that as a manifest sin. (50) **Have you not seen those who were given a portion of the Scripture?** They believe in Jibt and Tâghût and say to the disbelievers that they are better guided as regards the way than the believers (Muslims). (51) They are those whom Allâh has cursed, and he whom Allâh curses, you will not find for him (any) helper, (52) **Or have they a share in the dominion?** Then in that case they would not give mankind even a speck on the back of a date-stone. (53) **Or do they envy men (Muhammad and his followers) for what Allâh has given them of His Bounty?** Then We had already given the family of Ibrâhim (Abraham) the Book and Al-Hikmah (As¬Sunnah - Divine Revelation to those Prophets not written in the form of a book), and conferred upon them a great kingdom (54)

Quran 4:82

أَفَلَا يَتَدَبَّرُونَ ٱلْقُرْءَانَ وَلَوْ كَانَ مِنْ عِندِ غَيْرِ ٱللَّهِ لَوَجَدُواْ فِيهِ ٱخْتِلَٰفًا كَثِيرًا (٨٢)

Do they not then consider the Qur'ân carefully? Had it been from other than Allâh, they would surely have found therein many contradictions. (82)

Quran 4:86-88

ٱللَّهُ لَآ إِلَٰهَ إِلَّا هُوَ لَيَجْمَعَنَّكُمْ إِلَىٰ يَوْمِ ٱلْقِيَٰمَةِ لَا رَيْبَ فِيهِ وَمَنْ أَصْدَقُ مِنَ ٱللَّهِ حَدِيثًا ﴿٨٧﴾ فَمَا لَكُمْ فِى ٱلْمُنَٰفِقِينَ فِئَتَيْنِ وَٱللَّهُ أَرْكَسَهُم بِمَا كَسَبُوٓاْ أَتُرِيدُونَ أَن تَهْدُواْ مَنْ أَضَلَّ ٱللَّهُ وَمَن يُضْلِلِ ٱللَّهُ فَلَن تَجِدَ لَهُۥ سَبِيلًا (٨٨)

Allâh! Lâ ilâha illa Huwa (none has the right to be worshipped but He). Surely, He will gather you together on the Day of Resurrection about which there is no doubt. **And who is truer in statement than Allâh?** *(87)* **Then what is the matter with you that you are divided into two parties about the hypocrites?** *Allâh has cast them back (to disbelief) because of what* *they have earned.* **Do you want to guide him whom Allâh has made to go astray?** *And he whom Allâh has made to go astray, you will never find for him any way (of guidance). (88)*

Quran 4:109

هَـٰٓأَنتُمْ هَـٰٓؤُلَاءِ جَـٰدَلْتُمْ عَنْهُمْ فِى ٱلْحَيَوٰةِ ٱلدُّنْيَا فَمَن يُجَـٰدِلُ ٱللَّهَ عَنْهُمْ يَوْمَ ٱلْقِيَـٰمَةِ أَم مَّن يَكُونُ عَلَيْهِمْ وَكِيلاً (١٠٩)

Lo! **You are those who have argued for them in the life of this world, but who will argue for them on the Day of Resurrection against Allâh, or who will then be their defender?** *(109)*

Quran 4:122

وَٱلَّذِينَ ءَامَنُواْ وَعَمِلُواْ ٱلصَّـٰلِحَـٰتِ سَنُدْخِلُهُمْ جَنَّـٰتٍ تَجْرِى مِن تَحْتِهَا ٱلْأَنْهَـٰرُ خَـٰلِدِينَ فِيهَا أَبَداً وَعْدَ ٱللَّهِ حَقّاً وَمَنْ أَصْدَقُ مِنَ ٱللَّهِ قِيلاً (١٢٢)

But those who believe (in the Oneness of Allâh - Islâmic Monotheism) and do deeds of righteousness, We shall admit them to the Gardens under which rivers flow (i.e. in

Paradise) to dwell therein forever. **Allâh's Promise is the Truth, and whose words can be truer than those of Allâh?** *(Of course, none). (122)*

Quran 4:125

وَمَنْ أَحْسَنُ دِينًا مِّمَّنْ أَسْلَمَ وَجْهَهُ لِلَّهِ وَهُوَ مُحْسِنٌ وَٱتَّبَعَ مِلَّةَ إِبْرَٰهِيمَ حَنِيفًا وَٱتَّخَذَ ٱللَّهُ إِبْرَٰهِيمَ خَلِيلًا (١٢٥)

And who can be better in religion than one who submits his face (himself) to Allâh (i.e. follows Allâh's religion of Islâmic Monotheism); and he is a Muhsin (a good-doer), and follows the religion of Ibrâhim (Abraham) Hanifa (Islâmic Monotheism - to worship none but Allâh Alone)? *And Allâh did take Ibrâhim (Abraham) as a Khalil (an intimate friend)! (125)*

Quran 4:139

ٱلَّذِينَ يَتَّخِذُونَ ٱلْكَٰفِرِينَ أَوْلِيَآءَ مِن دُونِ ٱلْمُؤْمِنِينَ أَيَبْتَغُونَ عِندَهُمُ ٱلْعِزَّةَ فَإِنَّ ٱلْعِزَّةَ لِلَّهِ جَمِيعًا (١٣٩)

Those who take disbelievers for Auliyâ'
(protectors or helpers or friends) instead
of believers, do they seek honour, power
and glory with them? *Verily, then to*
Allâh belongs all honour, power and glory.
(139)

Quran 4:144

يَٰٓأَيُّهَا ٱلَّذِينَ ءَامَنُوا۟ لَا تَتَّخِذُوا۟ ٱلْكَٰفِرِينَ أَوْلِيَآءَ مِن دُونِ
ٱلْمُؤْمِنِينَ أَتُرِيدُونَ أَن تَجْعَلُوا۟ لِلَّهِ عَلَيْكُمْ سُلْطَٰنًا مُّبِينًا
(١٤٤)

O you who believe! Take not for Auliyâ'
(protectors or helpers or friends) disbelievers
instead of believers. **Do you wish to offer**
Allâh a manifest proof against
yourselves? *(144)*

Quran 5:17-18

لَّقَدْ كَفَرَ ٱلَّذِينَ قَالُوٓا۟ إِنَّ ٱللَّهَ هُوَ ٱلْمَسِيحُ ٱبْنُ مَرْيَمَ قُلْ فَمَن
يَمْلِكُ مِنَ ٱللَّهِ شَيْـًٔا إِنْ أَرَادَ أَن يُهْلِكَ ٱلْمَسِيحَ ٱبْنَ مَرْيَمَ
وَأُمَّهُ وَمَن فِى ٱلْأَرْضِ جَمِيعًا وَلِلَّهِ مُلْكُ ٱلسَّمَٰوَٰتِ
وَٱلْأَرْضِ وَمَا بَيْنَهُمَا يَخْلُقُ مَا يَشَآءُ وَٱللَّهُ عَلَىٰ كُلِّ شَىْءٍ
قَدِيرٌ (١٧) وَقَالَتِ ٱلْيَهُودُ وَٱلنَّصَٰرَىٰ نَحْنُ أَبْنَٰٓؤُا۟ ٱللَّهِ
وَأَحِبَّٰٓؤُهُ قُلْ فَلِمَ يُعَذِّبُكُم بِذُنُوبِكُم بَلْ أَنتُم بَشَرٌ مِّمَّنْ خَلَقَ

يَغْفِرُ لِمَن يَشَاءُ وَيُعَذِّبُ مَن يَشَاءُ وَلِلَّهِ مُلْكُ ٱلسَّمَـٰوَٰتِ
وَٱلْأَرْضِ وَمَا بَيْنَهُمَا ۚ وَإِلَيْهِ ٱلْمَصِيرُ (١٨)

*Surely, in disbelief are they who say that
Allâh is the Messiah, son of Maryam
(Mary). Say (O Muhammad): "**Who then
has the least power against Allâh, if He
were to destroy the Messiah, son of
Maryam (Mary), his mother, and all
those who are on the earth together?**"
And to Allâh belongs the dominion of the
heavens and the earth, and all that is
between them. He creates what He wills.
And Allâh is Able to do all things. (17) And
(both) the Jews and the Christians say: "We
are the children of Allâh and His loved
ones." Say: "**Why then does He punish
you for your sins?**" Nay, you are but
human beings, of those He has created, He
forgives whom He wills and He punishes
whom He wills. And to Allâh belongs the
dominion of the heavens and the earth and
all that is between them, and to Him is the
return (of all). (18)*

Quran 5:59

قُلْ يَـٰٓأَهْلَ ٱلْكِتَـٰبِ هَلْ تَنقِمُونَ مِنَّآ إِلَّآ أَنْ ءَامَنَّا بِٱللَّهِ وَمَآ أُنزِلَ إِلَيْنَا وَمَآ أُنزِلَ مِن قَبْلُ وَأَنَّ أَكْثَرَكُمْ فَـٰسِقُونَ (٥٩)

Say: "O people of the Scripture (Jews and Christians)! **Do you criticize us for no other reason than that we believe in Allâh, and in (the revelation) which has been sent down to us and in that which has been sent down before (us), and that most of you are Fâsiqûn [rebellious and disobedient (to Allâh)]?"** *(59)*

Quran 5:72-76

لَقَدْ كَفَرَ ٱلَّذِينَ قَالُوٓاْ إِنَّ ٱللَّهَ هُوَ ٱلْمَسِيحُ ٱبْنُ مَرْيَمَ وَقَالَ ٱلْمَسِيحُ يَـٰبَنِىٓ إِسْرَٰٓءِيلَ ٱعْبُدُواْ ٱللَّهَ رَبِّى وَرَبَّكُمْ إِنَّهُۥ مَن يُشْرِكْ بِٱللَّهِ فَقَدْ حَرَّمَ ٱللَّهُ عَلَيْهِ ٱلْجَنَّةَ وَمَأْوَىٰهُ ٱلنَّارُ وَمَا لِلظَّـٰلِمِينَ مِنْ أَنصَارٍ (٧٢) لَقَدْ كَفَرَ ٱلَّذِينَ قَالُوٓاْ إِنَّ ٱللَّهَ ثَالِثُ ثَلَـٰثَةٍ وَمَا مِنْ إِلَـٰهٍ إِلَّآ إِلَـٰهٌ وَٰحِدٌ وَإِن لَّمْ يَنتَهُواْ عَمَّا يَقُولُونَ لَيَمَسَّنَّ ٱلَّذِينَ كَفَرُواْ مِنْهُمْ عَذَابٌ أَلِيمٌ (٧٣) أَفَلَا يَتُوبُونَ إِلَى ٱللَّهِ وَيَسْتَغْفِرُونَهُۥ وَٱللَّهُ غَفُورٌ رَّحِيمٌ (٧٤) مَّا ٱلْمَسِيحُ ٱبْنُ مَرْيَمَ إِلَّا رَسُولٌ قَدْ خَلَتْ مِن قَبْلِهِ ٱلرُّسُلُ وَأُمُّهُۥ صِدِّيقَةٌ كَانَا يَأْكُلَانِ ٱلطَّعَامَ ٱنظُرْ كَيْفَ نُبَيِّنُ لَهُمُ ٱلْأَيَـٰتِ

ثُمَّ ٱنظُرْ أَنَّىٰ يُؤْفَكُونَ (٧٥) قُلْ أَتَعْبُدُونَ مِن دُونِ ٱللَّهِ مَا لَا
يَمْلِكُ لَكُمْ ضَرًّا وَلَا نَفْعًا وَٱللَّهُ هُوَ ٱلسَّمِيعُ ٱلْعَلِيمُ (٧٦)

Surely, they have disbelieved who say:
"Allâh is the Messiah Īsā (Jesus), son of
Maryam (Mary)." But the Messiah
Īsā(Jesus) said: "O Children of Israel!
Worship Allâh, my Lord and your Lord."
Verily, whosoever sets up partners (in
worship) with Allâh, then Allâh has
forbidden Paradise to him, and the Fire will
be his abode. And for the Zâlimûn
(polytheists and wrong-doers) there are no
helpers (72) Surely, disbelievers are those
who said: "Allâh is the third of the three (in
a Trinity)." But there is no Ilâh (god) (none
who has the right to be worshipped) but One
Ilâh (God -Allâh). And if they cease not from
what they say, verily, a painful torment will
befall on the disbelievers among them
(73) ***Will they not turn with repentance***
to Allâh and ask His Forgiveness? *For*
Allâh is Oft-Forgiving, Most Merciful.
(74) The Messiah ['Īsā (Jesus)], son of

Maryam (Mary), was no more than a Messenger; many were the Messengers that passed away before him. His mother [Maryam (Mary)] was a Siddiqah [i.e. she believed in the words of Allâh and His Books]. They both used to eat food (as any other human being, while Allâh does not eat). Look how We make the Ayât (proofs, evidences, verses, lessons, signs, revelations, etc.) clear to them, yet look how they are deluded away (from the truth) (75) Say (O Muhammad to mankind): "**How do you worship besides Allâh something which has no power either to harm or to benefit you?** But it is Allâh Who is the All¬Hearer, All¬Knower." (76)

Quran 5:116-119

وَإِذْ قَالَ ٱللَّهُ يَـٰعِيسَى ٱبْنَ مَرْيَمَ ءَأَنتَ قُلْتَ لِلنَّاسِ ٱتَّخِذُونِى وَأُمِّىَ إِلَـٰهَيْنِ مِن دُونِ ٱللَّهِ قَالَ سُبْحَـٰنَكَ مَا يَكُونُ لِىٓ أَنْ أَقُولَ مَا لَيْسَ لِى بِحَقٍّ إِن كُنتُ قُلْتُهُۥ فَقَدْ عَلِمْتَهُۥ تَعْلَمُ مَا فِى نَفْسِى وَلَآ أَعْلَمُ مَا فِى نَفْسِكَ إِنَّكَ أَنتَ عَلَّـٰمُ ٱلْغُيُوبِ (١١٦) مَا قُلْتُ لَهُمْ إِلَّا مَآ أَمَرْتَنِى بِهِۦٓ أَنِ ٱعْبُدُواْ ٱللَّهَ رَبِّى وَرَبَّكُمْ وَكُنتُ عَلَيْهِمْ شَهِيدًا مَّا دُمْتُ فِيهِمْ فَلَمَّا تَوَفَّيْتَنِى كُنتَ

أنتَ ٱلرَّقِيبَ عَلَيْهِمْ وَأَنتَ عَلَىٰ كُلِّ شَىْءٍ شَهِيدٌ (١١٧) إِن تُعَذِّبْهُمْ فَإِنَّهُمْ عِبَادُكَ وَإِن تَغْفِرْ لَهُمْ فَإِنَّكَ أَنتَ ٱلْعَزِيزُ ٱلْحَكِيمُ (١١٨) قَالَ ٱللَّهُ هَٰذَا يَوْمُ يَنفَعُ ٱلصَّٰدِقِينَ صِدْقُهُمْ لَهُمْ جَنَّٰتٌ تَجْرِى مِن تَحْتِهَا ٱلْأَنْهَٰرُ خَٰلِدِينَ فِيهَا أَبَدًا رَّضِىَ ٱللَّهُ عَنْهُمْ وَرَضُوا عَنْهُ ذَٰلِكَ ٱلْفَوْزُ ٱلْعَظِيمُ (١١٩)

And (remember) when Allâh will say (on the Day of Resurrection): **"O 'Īsā (Jesus), son of Maryam (Mary)! Did you say unto men: 'Worship me and my mother as two gods besides Allâh?'"** *He will say: "Glory be to You! It was not for me to say what I had no right (to say). Had I said such a thing, You would surely have known it. You know what is in my inner-self though I do not know what is in Yours, truly, You, only You, are the All-Knower of all that is hidden (and unseen). (116) "Never did I say to them aught except what You (Allâh) did command me to say: 'Worship Allâh, my Lord and your Lord.' And I was a witness over them while I dwelt amongst them, but when You took me up, You were the Watcher over them, and You are a Witness*

to all things. (117) "If You punish them,
they are Your slaves, and if You forgive
them, verily You, only You are the
All¬Mighty, the All¬Wise.' (118) Allâh
will say: "This is a Day on which the
truthful will profit from their truth: theirs
are Gardens under which rivers flow (in
Paradise) - they shall abide therein forever.
Allâh is pleased with them and they with
Him. That is the great success (Paradise).
(119)

Quran 6:12-14

قُل لِّمَن مَّا فِى ٱلسَّمَٰوَٰتِ وَٱلْأَرْضِ ۖ قُل لِّلَّهِ ۚ كَتَبَ عَلَىٰ نَفْسِهِ
ٱلرَّحْمَةَ ۚ لَيَجْمَعَنَّكُمْ إِلَىٰ يَوْمِ ٱلْقِيَٰمَةِ لَا رَيْبَ فِيهِ ۚ ٱلَّذِينَ خَسِرُوٓاْ
أَنفُسَهُمْ فَهُمْ لَا يُؤْمِنُونَ (١٢) ۞ وَلَهُۥ مَا سَكَنَ فِى ٱلَّيْلِ
وَٱلنَّهَارِ ۚ وَهُوَ ٱلسَّمِيعُ ٱلْعَلِيمُ (١٣) قُلْ أَغَيْرَ ٱللَّهِ أَتَّخِذُ وَلِيًّا
فَاطِرِ ٱلسَّمَٰوَٰتِ وَٱلْأَرْضِ وَهُوَ يُطْعِمُ وَلَا يُطْعَمُ ۗ قُلْ إِنِّىٓ
أُمِرْتُ أَنْ أَكُونَ أَوَّلَ مَنْ أَسْلَمَ ۖ وَلَا تَكُونَنَّ مِنَ ٱلْمُشْرِكِينَ
(١٤)

Say: "To whom belongs all that is in the
heavens and the earth?" Say: "To Allâh.
He has prescribed Mercy for Himself. Indeed

He will gather you together on the Day of Resurrection, about which there is no doubt. Those who have lost themselves will not believe [in Allâh as being the only Ilâh (God), and Muhammad as being one of His Messengers, and in Resurrection]. (12) And to Him belongs whatsoever exists in the night and the day, and He is the All¬Hearing, the All¬Knowing." (13) Say (O Muhammad): "**Shall I take as a Walî (helper, protector, Lord or God) any other than Allâh, the Creator of the heavens and the earth?** And it is He Who feeds but is not fed." Say: "Verily, I am commanded to be the first of those who submit themselves to Allâh (as Muslims)." And be not you (O Muhammad) of the Mushrikûn (polytheists, pagans, idolaters and disbelievers in the Oneness of Allâh). (14)

Quran 6:19-22

قُلْ أَىُّ شَىْءٍ أَكْبَرُ شَهَٰدَةًۖ قُلِ ٱللَّهُۖ شَهِيدُۢ بَيْنِى وَبَيْنَكُمْۚ وَأُوحِىَ إِلَىَّ هَٰذَا ٱلْقُرْءَانُ لِأُنذِرَكُم بِهِۦ وَمَنۢ بَلَغَۚ أَئِنَّكُمْ لَتَشْهَدُونَ أَنَّ

مَعَ ٱللَّهِ ءَالِهَةً أُخْرَىٰ قُل لَّا أَشْهَدُ قُلْ إِنَّمَا هُوَ إِلَٰهٌ وَٰحِدٌ
وَإِنَّنِى بَرِىٓءٌ مِّمَّا تُشْرِكُونَ (١٩) ٱلَّذِينَ ءَاتَيْنَٰهُمُ ٱلْكِتَٰبَ
يَعْرِفُونَهُۥ كَمَا يَعْرِفُونَ أَبْنَآءَهُمُ ٱلَّذِينَ خَسِرُوٓاْ أَنفُسَهُمْ فَهُمْ لَا
يُؤْمِنُونَ (٢٠) وَمَنْ أَظْلَمُ مِمَّنِ ٱفْتَرَىٰ عَلَى ٱللَّهِ كَذِبًا أَوْ
كَذَّبَ بِـَٔايَٰتِهِۦٓ إِنَّهُۥ لَا يُفْلِحُ ٱلظَّٰلِمُونَ (٢١) وَيَوْمَ نَحْشُرُهُمْ
جَمِيعًا ثُمَّ نَقُولُ لِلَّذِينَ أَشْرَكُوٓاْ أَيْنَ شُرَكَآؤُكُمُ ٱلَّذِينَ كُنتُمْ
تَزْعُمُونَ (٢٢)

*Say(O Muhammad): "**What thing is the most great in witness?**" Say: "Allâh (the Most Great!) is Witness between me and you; this Qur'ân has been revealed to me that I may therewith warn you and whomsoever it may reach. **Can you verily bear witness that besides Allâh there are other alihâh (gods)?**" Say "I bear no (such) witness!" Say: "But in truth He (Allâh) is the only one Ilâh (God). And truly I am innocent of what you join in worship with Him." (19) Those to whom We have given the Scripture (Jews and Christians) recognize him (i.e. Muhammad as a Messenger of Allâh, and they also know that there is no Ilah (God) but Allâh and Islâm is*

Allâh's religion), as they recognize their own sons. Those who have lost (destroyed) themselves will not believe. (20) **And who does more wrong and aggression than he who invents a lie against Allâh or rejects His Ayât (proofs, evidences, verses, lessons, or revelations)?** *Verily, the Zâlimûn (polytheists and wrong-doers,) shall never be successful. (21) And on the Day when We shall gather them all together, We shall say to those who joined partners (in worship with Us):* **"Where are your partners (false deities) whom you used to assert (as partners in worship with Allâh)?"** *(22)*

Quran 6:40-41

قُلْ أَرَءَيْتَكُمْ إِنْ أَتَنكُمْ عَذَابُ ٱللَّهِ أَوْ أَتَتْكُمُ ٱلسَّاعَةُ أَغَيْرَ ٱللَّهِ تَدْعُونَ إِن كُنتُمْ صَٰدِقِينَ (٤٠) بَلْ إِيَّاهُ تَدْعُونَ فَيَكْشِفُ مَا تَدْعُونَ إِلَيْهِ إِن شَآءَ وَتَنسَوْنَ مَا تُشْرِكُونَ (٤١)

Say: **"Tell me if Allâh's Torment comes upon you, or the Hour comes upon you, would you then call upon any one other**

*than Allâh? (Reply) if you are truthful!"
(40) Nay! To Him Alone you would call,
and, if He wills, He would remove that
(distress) for which you call upon Him, and
you would forget at that time whatever
partners you joined (with Him in worship)!
(41)*

Quran 6:46-47

قُلْ أَرَءَيْتُمْ إِنْ أَخَذَ ٱللَّهُ سَمْعَكُمْ وَأَبْصَـٰرَكُمْ وَخَتَمَ عَلَىٰ قُلُوبِكُم
مَّنْ إِلَـٰهٌ غَيْرُ ٱللَّهِ يَأْتِيكُم بِهِ ٱنظُرْ كَيْفَ نُصَرِّفُ ٱلْأَيَـٰتِ ثُمَّ
هُمْ يَصْدِفُونَ (٤٦) قُلْ أَرَءَيْتَكُمْ إِنْ أَتَنكُمْ عَذَابُ ٱللَّهِ بَغْتَةً أَوْ
جَهْرَةً هَلْ يُهْلَكُ إِلَّا ٱلْقَوْمُ ٱلظَّـٰلِمُونَ (٤٧)

*Say (to the disbelievers): "**Tell me, if Allâh
took away your hearing and your sight,
and sealed up your hearts, who is there -
an ilâh (a god) other than Allâh who
could restore them to you?"** See how
variously We explain the Ayât (proofs,
evidences, verses, lessons, signs, revelations,
etc.), yet they turn aside. (46) Say: "**Tell
me, if the punishment of Allâh comes to
you suddenly (during the night), or***

openly (during the day), will any be destroyed except the Zâlimûn (polytheists and wrong-doing people)?" (47)

Quran 6:50

قُل لَّآ أَقُولُ لَكُمۡ عِندِى خَزَآئِنُ ٱللَّهِ وَلَآ أَعۡلَمُ ٱلۡغَيۡبَ وَلَآ أَقُولُ لَكُمۡ إِنِّى مَلَكٌۖ إِنۡ أَتَّبِعُ إِلَّا مَا يُوحَىٰٓ إِلَىَّۚ قُلۡ هَلۡ يَسۡتَوِى ٱلۡأَعۡمَىٰ وَٱلۡبَصِيرُۚ أَفَلَا تَتَفَكَّرُونَ (٥٠)

Say (O Muhammad): "I don't tell you that with me are the treasures of Allâh, nor (that) I know the unseen; nor I tell you that I am an angel. I but follow what is revealed to me." Say: **"Are the blind and the one who sees equal? will you not then take thought?"** (50)

Quran 6:53

وَكَذَٰلِكَ فَتَنَّا بَعۡضَهُم بِبَعۡضٍ لِّيَقُولُوٓاْ أَهَٰٓؤُلَآءِ مَنَّ ٱللَّهُ عَلَيۡهِم مِّنۢ بَيۡنِنَآۗ أَلَيۡسَ ٱللَّهُ بِأَعۡلَمَ بِٱلشَّـٰكِرِينَ (٥٣)

Thus We have tried some of them with others, that they might say: "Is it these (poor believers) that Allâh has favoured from amongst us?" **Does not Allâh know best those who are grateful?** *(53)*

Quran 6:63-64

قُلْ مَن يُنَجِّيكُم مِّن ظُلُمَـٰتِ ٱلۡبَرِّ وَٱلۡبَحۡرِ تَدۡعُونَهُۥ تَضَرُّعًا وَخُفۡيَةً لَّئِنۡ أَنجَىٰنَا مِنۡ هَـٰذِهِۦ لَنَكُونَنَّ مِنَ ٱلشَّـٰكِرِينَ (٦٣) قُلِ ٱللَّهُ يُنَجِّيكُم مِّنۡهَا وَمِن كُلِّ كَرۡبٍ ثُمَّ أَنتُمۡ تُشۡرِكُونَ (٦٤)

Say: 'Who rescues you from the darkness of the land and the sea (dangers like storms), when you call upon Him in humility and in secret (saying): "If He (Allâh) only saves us from this (danger), we shall truly be grateful."?' *(63) Say: "Allâh rescues you from this and from all (other) distresses, and yet you worship others besides Allâh." (64)*

Quran 6:71

قُلۡ أَنَدۡعُواْ مِن دُونِ ٱللَّهِ مَا لَا يَنفَعُنَا وَلَا يَضُرُّنَا وَنُرَدُّ عَلَىٰٓ أَعۡقَابِنَا بَعۡدَ إِذۡ هَدَىٰنَا ٱللَّهُ كَٱلَّذِى ٱسۡتَهۡوَتۡهُ ٱلشَّيَـٰطِينُ فِى ٱلۡأَرۡضِ حَيۡرَانَ لَهُۥٓ أَصۡحَـٰبٌ يَدۡعُونَهُۥٓ إِلَى ٱلۡهُدَى ٱئۡتِنَا قُلۡ إِنَّ هُدَى ٱللَّهِ هُوَ ٱلۡهُدَىٰ وَأُمِرۡنَا لِنُسۡلِمَ لِرَبِّ ٱلۡعَـٰلَمِينَ (٧١)

*Say (O Muhammad): "**Shall we invoke others besides Allâh (false deities), that can do us neither good nor harm, and shall we turn back on our heels after Allâh has guided us (to true Monotheism)?** - like one whom the Shayâtin (devils) have made to go astray, in the land in confusion, his companions calling him to guidance (saying): 'Come to us.' " Say: "Verily, Allâh's Guidance is the only guidance, and we have been commanded to submit (ourselves) to the Lord of the 'Alamîn (mankind, jinn and all that exists); (71)*

Quran 6:95

﴿ إِنَّ ٱللَّهَ فَالِقُ ٱلْحَبِّ وَٱلنَّوَىٰ يُخْرِجُ ٱلْحَىَّ مِنَ ٱلْمَيِّتِ وَمُخْرِجُ ٱلْمَيِّتِ مِنَ ٱلْحَيِّ ذَٰلِكُمُ ٱللَّهُ فَأَنَّىٰ تُؤْفَكُونَ (٩٥)

*Verily! It is Allâh Who causes the seed-grain and the fruit-stone (like date-stone) to split and sprout. He brings forth the living from the dead, and it is He Who brings forth the dead from the living. **Such is Allâh,*** *then how are you deluded away from the truth? (95)*

Quran 6:109

وَأَقْسَمُواْ بِٱللَّهِ جَهْدَ أَيْمَٰنِهِمْ لَئِن جَاءَتْهُمْ ءَايَةٌ لَّيُؤْمِنُنَّ بِهَا ۚ قُلْ إِنَّمَا ٱلْأَيَٰتُ عِندَ ٱللَّهِ ۖ وَمَا يُشْعِرُكُمْ أَنَّهَا إِذَا جَاءَتْ لَا يُؤْمِنُونَ (١٠٩)

And they swear their strongest oaths by Allâh, that if there came to them a sign, they would surely believe therein. Say: **"Signs are but with Allâh and what will make you (Muslims) perceive that (even) if it (the sign) came, they will not believe?"** *(109)*

Quran 6:114

أَفَغَيْرَ ٱللَّهِ أَبْتَغِى حَكَمًا وَهُوَ ٱلَّذِى أَنزَلَ إِلَيْكُمُ ٱلْكِتَٰبَ مُفَصَّلًا ۚ وَٱلَّذِينَ ءَاتَيْنَٰهُمُ ٱلْكِتَٰبَ يَعْلَمُونَ أَنَّهُ ۥ مُنَزَّلٌ مِّن رَّبِّكَ بِٱلْحَقِّ ۖ فَلَا تَكُونَنَّ مِنَ ٱلْمُمْتَرِينَ (١١٤)

[Say (O Muhammad)] "Shall I seek a judge other than Allâh while it is He Who has sent down unto you the Book (the Qur'ân), explained in detail?" Those

unto whom We gave the Scripture [the Taurât (Torah) and the Injeel] know that it is revealed from your Lord in truth. So be not you of those who doubt. (114)

Quran 6:119

وَمَا لَكُمْ أَلَّا تَأْكُلُواْ مِمَّا ذُكِرَ ٱسْمُ ٱللَّهِ عَلَيْهِ وَقَدْ فَصَّلَ لَكُم مَّا حَرَّمَ عَلَيْكُمْ إِلَّا مَا ٱضْطُرِرْتُمْ إِلَيْهِ وَإِنَّ كَثِيرًا لَّيُضِلُّونَ بِأَهْوَآئِهِم بِغَيْرِ عِلْمٍ إِنَّ رَبَّكَ هُوَ أَعْلَمُ بِٱلْمُعْتَدِينَ (١١٩)

And why should you not eat of that (meat) on which Allâh's Name has been pronounced (at the time of slaughtering the animal), while He has explained to you in detail what is forbidden to you, except under compulsion of necessity? And surely many do lead (mankind) astray by their own desires through lack of knowledge. Certainly your Lord knows best the transgressors (119)

Quran 6:122

أَوَمَن كَانَ مَيْتًا فَأَحْيَيْنَـٰهُ وَجَعَلْنَا لَهُ نُورًا يَمْشِى بِهِۦ فِى ٱلنَّاسِ كَمَن مَّثَلُهُۥ فِى ٱلظُّلُمَـٰتِ لَيْسَ بِخَارِجٍ مِّنْهَاۚ كَذَٰلِكَ زُيِّنَ لِلْكَـٰفِرِينَ مَا كَانُوا۟ يَعْمَلُونَ (١٢٢)

Is he who was dead (without Faith by ignorance and disbelief) and We gave him life (by knowledge and Faith) and set for him a light (of Belief) whereby he can walk amongst men— like him who is in the darkness (of disbelief, polytheism and hypocrisy) from which he can never come out? Thus it is made fair¬seeming to the disbelievers that which they used to do. (122)

Quran 6:130

يَـٰمَعْشَرَ ٱلْجِنِّ وَٱلْإِنسِ أَلَمْ يَأْتِكُمْ رُسُلٌ مِّنكُمْ يَقُصُّونَ عَلَيْكُمْ ءَايَـٰتِى وَيُنذِرُونَكُمْ لِقَآءَ يَوْمِكُمْ هَـٰذَاۚ قَالُوا۟ شَهِدْنَا عَلَىٰ أَنفُسِنَاۖ وَغَرَّتْهُمُ ٱلْحَيَوٰةُ ٱلدُّنْيَا وَشَهِدُوا۟ عَلَىٰ أَنفُسِهِمْ أَنَّهُمْ كَانُوا۟ كَـٰفِرِينَ (١٣٠)

*O you assembly of jinn and mankind! "**Did not there come to you Messengers from amongst you, reciting unto you My Verses and warning you of the meeting***

of this Day of yours?" They will say: "We
bear witness against ourselves." It was the
life of this world that deceived them. And
they will bear witness against themselves
that they were disbelievers (130)

Quran 6:143-144

ثَمَٰنِيَةَ أَزْوَٰجٍ مِّنَ ٱلضَّأْنِ ٱثْنَيْنِ وَمِنَ ٱلْمَعْزِ ٱثْنَيْنِ قُلْ
ءَآلذَّكَرَيْنِ حَرَّمَ أَمِ ٱلْأُنثَيَيْنِ أَمَّا ٱشْتَمَلَتْ عَلَيْهِ أَرْحَامُ
ٱلْأُنثَيَيْنِ نَبِّـُٔونِى بِعِلْمٍ إِن كُنتُمْ صَٰدِقِينَ (١٤٣) وَمِنَ ٱلْإِبِلِ
ٱثْنَيْنِ وَمِنَ ٱلْبَقَرِ ٱثْنَيْنِ قُلْ ءَآلذَّكَرَيْنِ حَرَّمَ أَمِ ٱلْأُنثَيَيْنِ أَمَّا
ٱشْتَمَلَتْ عَلَيْهِ أَرْحَامُ ٱلْأُنثَيَيْنِ أَمْ كُنتُمْ شُهَدَآءَ إِذْ وَصَّىٰكُمُ
ٱللَّهُ بِهَٰذَا فَمَنْ أَظْلَمُ مِمَّنِ ٱفْتَرَىٰ عَلَى ٱللَّهِ كَذِبًا لِّيُضِلَّ
ٱلنَّاسَ بِغَيْرِ عِلْمٍ إِنَّ ٱللَّهَ لَا يَهْدِى ٱلْقَوْمَ ٱلظَّٰلِمِينَ (١٤٤)

*Eight pairs; of the sheep two (male and
female), and of the goats two (male and
female). Say: "**Has He forbidden the two
males or the two females, or (the young)
which the wombs of the two females
enclose?** Inform me with knowledge if you
are truthful." (143) And of the camels two
(male and female), and of oxen two (male
and female). Say: "**Has He forbidden the***

*two males or the two females or (the
young) which the wombs of the two
females enclose? Or were you present
when Allâh ordered you such a thing?*
*Then who does more wrong than one who
invents a lie against Allâh, to lead mankind
astray without knowledge. Certainly Allâh
guides not the people who are Zâlimûn
(polytheists and wrong-doers)." (144)*

Quran 6:148

سَيَقُولُ ٱلَّذِينَ أَشْرَكُواْ لَوْ شَاءَ ٱللَّهُ مَآ أَشْرَكْنَا وَلَآ ءَابَآؤُنَا
وَلَا حَرَّمْنَا مِن شَيْءٍ كَذَٰلِكَ كَذَّبَ ٱلَّذِينَ مِن قَبْلِهِمْ حَتَّىٰ
ذَاقُواْ بَأْسَنَا قُلْ هَلْ عِندَكُم مِّنْ عِلْمٍ فَتُخْرِجُوهُ لَنَآ إِن
تَتَّبِعُونَ إِلَّا ٱلظَّنَّ وَإِنْ أَنتُمْ إِلَّا تَخْرُصُونَ (١٤٨)

*Those who took partners (in worship) with
Allâh will say: "If Allâh had willed, we
would not have taken partners (in worship)
with Him, nor would our fathers, and we
would not have forbidden anything (against
His Will)." Likewise belied those who were
before them, (they argued falsely with
Allâh's Messengers), till they tasted Our*

*Wrath. Say: "**Have you any knowledge (proof) that you can produce before us?** Verily, you follow nothing but guess and you do nothing but lie." (148)*

Quran 6:157-158

أَوْ تَقُولُوٓا۟ لَوْ أَنَّآ أُنزِلَ عَلَيْنَا ٱلْكِتَـٰبُ لَكُنَّآ أَهْدَىٰ مِنْهُمْ ۚ فَقَدْ جَآءَكُم بَيِّنَةٌ مِّن رَّبِّكُمْ وَهُدًى وَرَحْمَةٌ ۚ فَمَنْ أَظْلَمُ مِمَّن كَذَّبَ بِـَٔايَـٰتِ ٱللَّهِ وَصَدَفَ عَنْهَا ۗ سَنَجْزِى ٱلَّذِينَ يَصْدِفُونَ عَنْ ءَايَـٰتِنَا سُوٓءَ ٱلْعَذَابِ بِمَا كَانُوا۟ يَصْدِفُونَ (١٥٧) هَلْ يَنظُرُونَ إِلَّآ أَن تَأْتِيَهُمُ ٱلْمَلَـٰٓئِكَةُ أَوْ يَأْتِىَ رَبُّكَ أَوْ يَأْتِىَ بَعْضُ ءَايَـٰتِ رَبِّكَ ۗ يَوْمَ يَأْتِى بَعْضُ ءَايَـٰتِ رَبِّكَ لَا يَنفَعُ نَفْسًا إِيمَـٰنُهَا لَمْ تَكُنْ ءَامَنَتْ مِن قَبْلُ أَوْ كَسَبَتْ فِى إِيمَـٰنِهَا خَيْرًا ۗ قُلِ ٱنتَظِرُوٓا۟ إِنَّا مُنتَظِرُونَ (١٥٨)

*Or lest you (pagan Arabs) should say: "If only the Book had been sent down to us, we would surely have been better guided than they (Jews and Christians)." So now has come unto you a clear proof (the Qur'ân) from your Lord, and a guidance and a mercy. **Who then does more wrong than one who rejects the Ayât (proofs, evidences, verses, lessons, signs,***

*revelations, etc.) of Allâh and turns
away therefrom?* We shall requite those
who turn away from Our Ayât with an evil
torment, because of their turning away
(from them). (157) **Do they then wait for
anything other than that the angels
should come to them, or that your Lord
(Allah) should come, or that some of the
Signs of your Lord should come?** The day
that some of the Signs of your Lord do come,
no good will it do to a person to believe then,
if he believed not before, nor earned good (by
performing deeds of righteousness) through
his Faith. Say: "Wait you! we (too) are
waiting." (158)*

Quran 6:164

قُلۡ أَغَيۡرَ ٱللَّهِ أَبۡغِى رَبًّا وَهُوَ رَبُّ كُلِّ شَىۡءٍۚ وَلَا تَكۡسِبُ كُلُّ
نَفۡسٍ إِلَّا عَلَيۡهَاۚ وَلَا تَزِرُ وَازِرَةٌ وِزۡرَ أُخۡرَىٰۚ ثُمَّ إِلَىٰ رَبِّكُم
مَّرۡجِعُكُمۡ فَيُنَبِّئُكُم بِمَا كُنتُمۡ فِيهِ تَخۡتَلِفُونَ (١٦٤)

*Say: "**Shall I seek a lord other than
Allâh, while He is the Lord of all
things?** No person earns any (sin) except*

against himself (only), and no bearer of burdens shall bear the burden of another. Then unto your Lord is your return, so He will tell you that wherein you have been differing." (164)

Quran 7:12-18

قَالَ مَا مَنَعَكَ أَلَّا تَسْجُدَ إِذْ أَمَرْتُكَ قَالَ أَنَا۟ خَيْرٌ مِّنْهُ خَلَقْتَنِى مِن نَّارٍ وَخَلَقْتَهُۥ مِن طِينٍ (١٢) قَالَ فَٱهْبِطْ مِنْهَا فَمَا يَكُونُ لَكَ أَن تَتَكَبَّرَ فِيهَا فَٱخْرُجْ إِنَّكَ مِنَ ٱلصَّٰغِرِينَ (١٣) قَالَ أَنظِرْنِىٓ إِلَىٰ يَوْمِ يُبْعَثُونَ (١٤) قَالَ إِنَّكَ مِنَ ٱلْمُنظَرِينَ (١٥) قَالَ فَبِمَآ أَغْوَيْتَنِى لَأَقْعُدَنَّ لَهُمْ صِرَٰطَكَ ٱلْمُسْتَقِيمَ (١٦) ثُمَّ لَءَاتِيَنَّهُم مِّنۢ بَيْنِ أَيْدِيهِمْ وَمِنْ خَلْفِهِمْ وَعَنْ أَيْمَٰنِهِمْ وَعَن شَمَآئِلِهِمْ وَلَا تَجِدُ أَكْثَرَهُمْ شَٰكِرِينَ (١٧) قَالَ ٱخْرُجْ مِنْهَا مَذْءُومًا مَّدْحُورًا لَّمَن تَبِعَكَ مِنْهُمْ لَأَمْلَأَنَّ جَهَنَّمَ مِنكُمْ أَجْمَعِينَ (١٨)

(Allâh) said: "**What prevented you (O Iblîs) that you did not prostrate yourself, when I commanded you?**" Iblîs said: "I am better than him (Adam), You created me from fire, and him You created from clay." (12) (Allâh) said: "(O Iblîs) get down from this (Paradise), it is not for you to be arrogant here. Get out, for you are of those humiliated and disgraced." (13) (Iblîs) said: "Allow me respite till the Day they are raised up (i.e. the Day of Resurrection)." (14) (Allâh) said: "You are of those respited." (15) (Iblîs) said: "Because You have sent me astray, surely I will sit in wait against them (human beings) on Your Straight Path (16) Then I will come to them from before them and behind them, from their right and from their left, and You will not find most of them as thankful ones (i.e. they will not be dutiful to You)." (17) (Allâh) said (to Iblîs) "Get out from this (Paradise) disgraced and expelled. Whoever of them (mankind) will follow you, then surely I will fill Hell with you all." (18)

Quran 7:22-23

فَدَلَّىٰهُمَا بِغُرُورٍ ۚ فَلَمَّا ذَاقَا ٱلشَّجَرَةَ بَدَتْ لَهُمَا سَوْءَٰتُهُمَا وَطَفِقَا يَخْصِفَانِ عَلَيْهِمَا مِن وَرَقِ ٱلْجَنَّةِ ۖ وَنَادَىٰهُمَا رَبُّهُمَآ أَلَمْ أَنْهَكُمَا عَن تِلْكُمَا ٱلشَّجَرَةِ وَأَقُل لَّكُمَآ إِنَّ ٱلشَّيْطَٰنَ لَكُمَا عَدُوٌّ مُّبِينٌ

قَالَا رَبَّنَا ظَلَمْنَا أَنفُسَنَا وَإِن لَّمْ تَغْفِرْ لَنَا وَتَرْحَمْنَا (٢٢)
لَنَكُونَنَّ مِنَ ٱلْخَـٰسِرِينَ (٢٣)

So he misled them with deception. Then when they tasted of the tree, that which was hidden from them of their shame (private parts) became manifest to them and they began to cover themselves with the leaves of Paradise (in order to cover their shame). And their Lord called out to them (saying): **"Did I not forbid you that tree and tell you: Verily, Shaitân (Satan) is an open enemy unto you?"** *(22) They said: "Our Lord! We have wronged ourselves. If You forgive us not, and bestow not upon us Your Mercy, we shall certainly be of the losers."* *(23)*

Quran 7:32

قُلْ مَنْ حَرَّمَ زِينَةَ ٱللَّهِ ٱلَّتِىٓ أَخْرَجَ لِعِبَادِهِۦ وَٱلطَّيِّبَـٰتِ مِنَ
ٱلرِّزْقِ قُلْ هِىَ لِلَّذِينَ ءَامَنُواْ فِى ٱلْحَيَوٰةِ ٱلدُّنْيَا خَالِصَةً يَوْمَ
ٱلْقِيَـٰمَةِ كَذَٰلِكَ نُفَصِّلُ ٱلْءَايَـٰتِ لِقَوْمٍ يَعْلَمُونَ (٣٢)

Say (O Muhammad): **"Who has forbidden the adornment with clothes given by**

Allâh, which He has produced for His slaves, and At-Taiyyibât [all kinds of Halâl (lawful) things] of food?" Say: "They are, in the life of this world, for those who believe, (and) exclusively for them (believers) on the Day of Resurrection (the disbelievers will not share them)." Thus We explain the Ayât (Islâmic laws) in detail for people who have knowledge. (32)

Quran 7:37

فَمَنْ أَظْلَمُ مِمَّنِ ٱفْتَرَىٰ عَلَى ٱللَّهِ كَذِبًا أَوْ كَذَّبَ بِـَٔايَٰتِهِۦٓ أُوْلَٰٓئِكَ يَنَالُهُمْ نَصِيبُهُم مِّنَ ٱلْكِتَٰبِ حَتَّىٰٓ إِذَا جَآءَتْهُمْ رُسُلُنَا يَتَوَفَّوْنَهُمْ قَالُوٓاْ أَيْنَ مَا كُنتُمْ تَدْعُونَ مِن دُونِ ٱللَّهِ قَالُوٓاْ ضَلُّواْ عَنَّا وَشَهِدُواْ عَلَىٰٓ أَنفُسِهِمْ أَنَّهُمْ كَانُواْ كَٰفِرِينَ (٣٧)

Who is more unjust than one who invents a lie against Allâh or rejects His Ayât (proofs, evidences, verses, lessons, signs, revelations)? For such their appointed portion (good things of this worldly life and their period of stay therein) will reach them from the Book (of Decrees) until, when Our Messengers (the angel of death and his assistants) come to them to take their souls, they (the angels) will say: "Where are those whom you used to invoke and worship besides Allâh," they will reply, "They have vanished and deserted us." And they will bear witness against themselves, that they were disbelievers. (37)

Quran 7:147-148

وَٱلَّذِينَ كَذَّبُواْ بِـَٔايَـٰتِنَا وَلِقَآءِ ٱلْأَخِرَةِ حَبِطَتْ أَعْمَـٰلُهُمْ هَلْ يُجْزَوْنَ إِلَّا مَا كَانُواْ يَعْمَلُونَ (١٤٧) وَٱتَّخَذَ قَوْمُ مُوسَىٰ مِنْ بَعْدِهِ مِنْ حُلِيِّهِمْ عِجْلاً جَسَدًا لَّهُ خُوَارٌ أَلَمْ يَرَوْاْ أَنَّهُ لَا يُكَلِّمُهُمْ وَلَا يَهْدِيهِمْ سَبِيلاً ٱتَّخَذُوهُ وَكَانُواْ ظَـٰلِمِينَ (١٤٨)

Those who deny Our Ayât (proofs, evidences, verses, lessons, signs, revelations, etc.) and the Meeting in the Hereafter (Day of Resurrection,), vain are their deeds. **Are they requited with anything except what they used to do?** (147) And the people of Mûsa (Moses) made in his absence, out of their ornaments, the image of a calf (for worship). It had a sound (as if it was mooing). **Did they not see that it could** *neither speak to them nor guide them to the way?* *They took it (for worship) and they were Zâlimûn (wrong-doers). (148)*

Quran 7:163

وَسْئَلْهُمْ عَنِ ٱلْقَرْيَةِ ٱلَّتِى كَانَتْ حَاضِرَةَ ٱلْبَحْرِ إِذْ يَعْدُونَ فِى ٱلسَّبْتِ إِذْ تَأْتِيهِمْ حِيتَانُهُمْ يَوْمَ سَبْتِهِمْ شُرَّعًا وَيَوْمَ لَا يَسْبِتُونَ لَا تَأْتِيهِمْ كَذَٰلِكَ نَبْلُوهُم بِمَا كَانُواْ يَفْسُقُونَ (١٦٣)

And ask them (O Muhammad) about the town that was by the sea; when they transgressed in the matter of the Sabbath (i.e. Saturday): when their fish came to them openly on the Sabbath day, and did not come to them on the day they had no Sabbath. Thus We made a trial of them, for they used to rebel against Allâh's Command (disobey Allâh) (163)

Quran 7:169

فَخَلَفَ مِنۢ بَعْدِهِمْ خَلْفٌ وَرِثُواْ ٱلْكِتَٰبَ يَأْخُذُونَ عَرَضَ هَٰذَا ٱلْأَدْنَىٰ وَيَقُولُونَ سَيُغْفَرُ لَنَا وَإِن يَأْتِهِمْ عَرَضٌ مِّثْلُهُۥ يَأْخُذُوهُ أَلَمْ يُؤْخَذْ عَلَيْهِم مِّيثَٰقُ ٱلْكِتَٰبِ أَن لَّا يَقُولُواْ عَلَى ٱللَّهِ إِلَّا

ٱلْحَقَّ وَدَرَسُواْ مَا فِيهِۗ وَٱلدَّارُ ٱلْأَخِرَةُ خَيْرٌ لِّلَّذِينَ يَتَّقُونَۚ أَفَلَا تَعْقِلُونَ (١٦٩)

Then after them succeeded an (evil) generation, which inherited the Book, but they chose (for themselves) the goods of this low life (evil pleasures of this world) saying (as an excuse): "(Everything) will be forgiven to us." And if (again) the offer of the like (evil pleasures of this world) came their way, they would (again) seize them (would commit those sins). **Was not the covenant of the Book taken from them that they would not say about Allâh anything but the truth?** *And they have studied what is in it (the Book). And the home of the Hereafter is better for those who are Al-Muttaqûn (the pious).* **Do not you then understand?** *(169)*

Quran 7:172

وَإِذْ أَخَذَ رَبُّكَ مِنْ بَنِىٓ ءَادَمَ مِن ظُهُورِهِمْ ذُرِّيَّتَهُمْ وَأَشْهَدَهُمْ عَلَىٰٓ أَنفُسِهِمْ أَلَسْتُ بِرَبِّكُمْۖ قَالُواْ بَلَىٰۚ شَهِدْنَآۚ أَن تَقُولُواْ يَوْمَ ٱلْقِيَٰمَةِ إِنَّا كُنَّا عَنْ هَٰذَا غَٰفِلِينَ (١٧٢)

*And (remember) when your Lord brought forth from the Children of Adam, from their loins, their seed (or from Adam's loin his offspring) and made them testify as to themselves (saying): "**Am I not your Lord?**" They said: "Yes! We testify," lest you should say on the Day of Resurrection: "Verily, we have been unaware of this." (172)*

Quran 7:184-185

أَوَلَمْ يَتَفَكَّرُوا۟ مَا بِصَاحِبِهِم مِّن جِنَّةٍ إِنْ هُوَ إِلَّا نَذِيرٌ مُّبِينٌ (١٨٤) أَوَلَمْ يَنظُرُوا۟ فِى مَلَكُوتِ ٱلسَّمَٰوَٰتِ وَٱلْأَرْضِ وَمَا خَلَقَ ٱللَّهُ مِن شَىْءٍ وَأَنْ عَسَىٰ أَن يَكُونَ قَدِ ٱقْتَرَبَ أَجَلُهُمْ فَبِأَىِّ حَدِيثٍ بَعْدَهُ يُؤْمِنُونَ (١٨٥)

Do they not reflect? There is no madness in their companion (Muhammad). He is but a plain warner. (184) Do they not look in the dominion of the heavens and the earth and all things that Allâh has created, and that it may be that the end of their lives is near? In what message after this will they then believe? (185)

Quran 7:191

أَيُشْرِكُونَ مَا لَا يَخْلُقُ شَيْئًا وَهُمْ يُخْلَقُونَ (١٩١)

Do they attribute as partners to Allâh those who created nothing but they themselves are created? (191)

Quran 7:194-195

إِنَّ ٱلَّذِينَ تَدْعُونَ مِن دُونِ ٱللَّهِ عِبَادٌ أَمْثَالُكُمْ فَٱدْعُوهُمْ فَلْيَسْتَجِيبُواْ لَكُمْ إِن كُنتُمْ صَـٰدِقِينَ (١٩٤) أَلَهُمْ أَرْجُلٌ يَمْشُونَ بِهَآ أَمْ لَهُمْ أَيْدٍ يَبْطِشُونَ بِهَآ أَمْ لَهُمْ أَعْيُنٌ يُبْصِرُونَ بِهَآ أَمْ لَهُمْ ءَاذَانٌ يَسْمَعُونَ بِهَا قُلِ ٱدْعُواْ شُرَكَآءَكُمْ ثُمَّ كِيدُونِ فَلَا تُنظِرُونِ (١٩٥)

Verily, those whom you call upon besides Allâh are slaves like you. So call upon them and let them answer you if you are truthful (194) **Have they feet wherewith they walk? Or have they hands wherewith they hold? Or have they eyes wherewith they see? Or have they ears wherewith they hear?** *Say (O Muhammad): "Call your (so-called) partners (of Allâh) and then*

plot against me, and give me no respite!
(195)

Quran 8:33-34

وَمَا كَانَ ٱللَّهُ لِيُعَذِّبَهُمْ وَأَنتَ فِيهِمْ وَمَا كَانَ ٱللَّهُ مُعَذِّبَهُمْ وَهُمْ
يَسْتَغْفِرُونَ (٣٣) وَمَا لَهُمْ أَلَّا يُعَذِّبَهُمُ ٱللَّهُ وَهُمْ يَصُدُّونَ عَنِ
ٱلْمَسْجِدِ ٱلْحَرَامِ وَمَا كَانُوٓا۟ أَوْلِيَآءَهُۥٓ ۚ إِنْ أَوْلِيَآؤُهُۥٓ إِلَّا
ٱلْمُتَّقُونَ وَلَٰكِنَّ أَكْثَرَهُمْ لَا يَعْلَمُونَ (٣٤)

*And Allâh would not punish them while
you (Muhammad) are amongst them, nor
will He punish them while they seek
(Allâh's) Forgiveness (33)* **And why
should not Allâh punish them while
they hinder (men) from Al-Masjid-Al-
Harâm, and they are not its guardians?**
*None can be its guardian except Al-
Muttaqûn (the pious), but most of them
know not (34)*

Quran 9:7-8

كَيْفَ يَكُونُ لِلْمُشْرِكِينَ عَهْدٌ عِندَ ٱللَّهِ وَعِندَ رَسُولِهِۦٓ إِلَّا
ٱلَّذِينَ عَٰهَدتُّمْ عِندَ ٱلْمَسْجِدِ ٱلْحَرَامِ فَمَا ٱسْتَقَٰمُوا۟ لَكُمْ
فَٱسْتَقِيمُوا۟ لَهُمْ إِنَّ ٱللَّهَ يُحِبُّ ٱلْمُتَّقِينَ (٧) كَيْفَ وَإِن

يَظْهَرُواْ عَلَيْكُمْ لَا يَرْقُبُواْ فِيكُمْ إِلَّا وَلَا ذِمَّةً يُرْضُونَكُم بِأَفْوَاهِهِمْ وَتَأْبَىٰ قُلُوبُهُمْ وَأَكْثَرُهُمْ فَٰسِقُونَ ﴿٨﴾

How can there be a covenant with Allâh and with His Messenger for the Mushrikûn (polytheists, idolaters, pagans, disbelievers in the Oneness of Allâh) except those with whom you made a covenant near Al-Masjid-al-Harâm (at Makkah)? So long, as they are true to you, stand you true to them. Verily, Allâh loves Al-Muttaqûn (the pious) (7) *How (can there be such a covenant with them) that when you are overpowered by them, they regard not the ties, either of kinship or of covenant with you?* With (good words from) their mouths they please you, but their hearts are averse to you, and most of them are Fâsiqûn (rebellious, disobedient to Allâh). (8)

Quran 9:13-16

أَلَا تُقَٰتِلُونَ قَوْمًا نَّكَثُوٓاْ أَيْمَٰنَهُمْ وَهَمُّواْ بِإِخْرَاجِ ٱلرَّسُولِ وَهُم بَدَءُوكُمْ أَوَّلَ مَرَّةٍ أَتَخْشَوْنَهُمْ فَٱللَّهُ أَحَقُّ أَن تَخْشَوْهُ إِن كُنتُم

مُّؤْمِنِينَ (١٣) قَٰتِلُوهُمْ يُعَذِّبْهُمُ ٱللَّهُ بِأَيْدِيكُمْ وَيُخْزِهِمْ وَيَنصُرْكُمْ عَلَيْهِمْ وَيَشْفِ صُدُورَ قَوْمٍ مُّؤْمِنِينَ (١٤) وَيُذْهِبْ غَيْظَ قُلُوبِهِمْ وَيَتُوبُ ٱللَّهُ عَلَىٰ مَن يَشَآءُ وَٱللَّهُ عَلِيمٌ حَكِيمٌ (١٥) أَمْ حَسِبْتُمْ أَن تُتْرَكُواْ وَلَمَّا يَعْلَمِ ٱللَّهُ ٱلَّذِينَ جَٰهَدُواْ مِنكُمْ وَلَمْ يَتَّخِذُواْ مِن دُونِ ٱللَّهِ وَلَا رَسُولِهِ وَلَا ٱلْمُؤْمِنِينَ وَلِيجَةٌ وَٱللَّهُ خَبِيرٌ بِمَا تَعْمَلُونَ (١٦)

Will you not fight a people who have violated their oaths (pagans of Makkah) and intended to expel the Messenger, while they did attack you first? Do you fear them? Allâh has more right that you should fear Him, if you are believers. (13) Fight against them so that Allâh will punish them by your hands and disgrace them and give you victory over them and heal the breasts of a believing people, (14) And remove the anger of their (believers') hearts. Allâh accepts the repentance of whom He wills. Allâh is All-Knowing, All-Wise. (15) Do you think that you shall be left alone while Allâh has not yet tested those among you who have striven hard and fought and have

*not taken Walîjah [(Batanah - helpers,
advisors and consultants from
disbelievers, pagans) giving openly to
them their secrets] besides Allâh and
His Messenger, and the believers?* Allâh
is Well-Acquainted with what you do. (16)

Quran 9:19

﴿۞ أَجَعَلْتُمْ سِقَايَةَ ٱلْحَاجِّ وَعِمَارَةَ ٱلْمَسْجِدِ ٱلْحَرَامِ كَمَنْ ءَامَنَ
بِٱللَّهِ وَٱلْيَوْمِ ٱلْأَخِرِ وَجَٰهَدَ فِى سَبِيلِ ٱللَّهِ لَا يَسْتَوُۥنَ عِندَ ٱللَّهِ
وَٱللَّهُ لَا يَهْدِى ٱلْقَوْمَ ٱلظَّٰلِمِينَ (١٩) ﴾

**Do you consider the providing of
drinking water to the pilgrims and the
maintenance of Al-Masjid-al-Harâm (at
Makkah) as equal to the worth of those
who believe in Allâh and the Last Day,
and strive hard and fight in the Cause of
Allâh?** They are not equal before Allâh. And
Allâh guides not those people who are the
Zâlimûn (polytheists and wrong-doers).
(19)

Quran 9:38

يَـٰٓأَيُّهَا ٱلَّذِينَ ءَامَنُوا۟ مَا لَكُمْ إِذَا قِيلَ لَكُمُ ٱنفِرُوا۟ فِى سَبِيلِ ٱللَّهِ ٱثَّاقَلْتُمْ إِلَى ٱلْأَرْضِ أَرَضِيتُم بِٱلْحَيَوٰةِ ٱلدُّنْيَا مِنَ ٱلْأَخِرَةِ فَمَا مَتَـٰعُ ٱلْحَيَوٰةِ ٱلدُّنْيَا فِى ٱلْأَخِرَةِ إِلَّا قَلِيلٌ (٣٨)

O you who believe! **What is the matter with you, that when you are asked to march forth in the Cause of Allâh (i.e. Jihâd) you cling heavily to the earth? Are you pleased with the life of this world rather than the Hereafter?** *But little is the enjoyment of the life of this world as compared to the Hereafter. (38)*

Quran 9:43

عَفَا ٱللَّهُ عَنكَ لِمَ أَذِنتَ لَهُمْ حَتَّىٰ يَتَبَيَّنَ لَكَ ٱلَّذِينَ صَدَقُوا۟ وَتَعْلَمَ ٱلْكَـٰذِبِينَ (٤٣)

May Allâh forgive you (O Muhammad). **Why did you grant them leave (for remaining behind, you should have persisted as regards your order to them to proceed on Jihâd), until those who told the truth were seen by you in a clear light, and you had known the liars?** *(43)*

Quran 9:52

قُلْ هَلْ تَرَبَّصُونَ بِنَآ إِلَّآ إِحْدَى ٱلْحُسْنَيَيْنِ وَنَحْنُ نَتَرَبَّصُ بِكُمْ أَن يُصِيبَكُمُ ٱللَّهُ بِعَذَابٍ مِّنْ عِندِهِ أَوْ بِأَيْدِينَا فَتَرَبَّصُوٓاْ إِنَّا مَعَكُم مُّتَرَبِّصُونَ (٥٢)

*Say: "**Do you wait for us (anything) except one of the two best things (martyrdom or victory); while we await for you either that Allâh will afflict you with a punishment from Himself or at our hands?** So wait, we too are waiting with you." (52)*

Quran 9:70

أَلَمْ يَأْتِهِمْ نَبَأُ ٱلَّذِينَ مِن قَبْلِهِمْ قَوْمِ نُوحٍ وَعَادٍ وَثَمُودَ وَقَوْمِ إِبْرَاهِيمَ وَأَصْحَابِ مَدْيَنَ وَٱلْمُؤْتَفِكَاتِ أَتَتْهُمْ رُسُلُهُم بِٱلْبَيِّنَاتِ فَمَا كَانَ ٱللَّهُ لِيَظْلِمَهُمْ وَلَكِن كَانُوٓاْ أَنفُسَهُمْ يَظْلِمُونَ (٧٠)

Has not the story reached them of those before them? - The people of Nûh (Noah), 'Âd, and Thamûd, the people of Ibrâhîm (Abraham), the dwellers of Madyan (Midian) and the cities overthrown [i.e. the people to whom Lût (Lot) preached]; to them came their Messengers with clear proofs. So it was not Allâh Who wronged them, but they used to wrong themselves. (70)

Quran 9:104

أَلَمْ يَعْلَمُوٓاْ أَنَّ ٱللَّهَ هُوَ يَقْبَلُ ٱلتَّوْبَةَ عَنْ عِبَادِهِۦ وَيَأْخُذُ ٱلصَّدَقَٰتِ وَأَنَّ ٱللَّهَ هُوَ ٱلتَّوَّابُ ٱلرَّحِيمُ (١٠٤)

Know they not that Allâh accepts repentance from His slaves and takes the Sadaqât (alms, charity) and that Allah Alone is the One Who forgives and accepts repentance, Most Merciful? (104)

Quran 9:111

۞ إِنَّ ٱللَّهَ ٱشْتَرَىٰ مِنَ ٱلْمُؤْمِنِينَ أَنفُسَهُمْ وَأَمْوَٰلَهُم بِأَنَّ لَهُمُ ٱلْجَنَّةَ يُقَٰتِلُونَ فِى سَبِيلِ ٱللَّهِ فَيَقْتُلُونَ وَيُقْتَلُونَ وَعْدًا عَلَيْهِ حَقًّا فِى ٱلتَّوْرَىٰةِ وَٱلْإِنجِيلِ وَٱلْقُرْءَانِ وَمَنْ أَوْفَىٰ بِعَهْدِهِۦ مِنَ ٱللَّهِ فَٱسْتَبْشِرُواْ بِبَيْعِكُمُ ٱلَّذِى بَايَعْتُم بِهِۦ وَذَٰلِكَ هُوَ ٱلْفَوْزُ ٱلْعَظِيمُ (١١١)

Verily, Allâh has purchased of the believers their lives and their properties for (the price) that theirs shall be the Paradise. They fight in Allâh's Cause, so they kill (others) and are killed. It is a promise in truth which is binding on Him in the Taurât (Torah) and the Injeel and the Qur'ân. **And who is truer to his covenant than Allâh?** *Then rejoice in the bargain which you have concluded. That is the supreme success. (111)*

Quran 9:126

أَوَلَا يَرَوْنَ أَنَّهُمْ يُفْتَنُونَ فِى كُلِّ عَامٍ مَّرَّةً أَوْ مَرَّتَيْنِ ثُمَّ لَا يَتُوبُونَ وَلَا هُمْ يَذَّكَّرُونَ (١٢٦)

See they not that they are put in trial once or twice every year (with different kinds of calamities, disease, famine)? *Yet, they turn not in repentance, nor do they learn a lesson (from it). (126)*

Quran 10:2-3

أَكَانَ لِلنَّاسِ عَجَبًا أَنْ أَوْحَيْنَآ إِلَىٰ رَجُلٍ مِّنْهُمْ أَنْ أَنذِرِ ٱلنَّاسَ وَبَشِّرِ ٱلَّذِينَ ءَامَنُوٓاْ أَنَّ لَهُمْ قَدَمَ صِدْقٍ عِندَ رَبِّهِمْ قَالَ ٱلْكَٰفِرُونَ إِنَّ هَٰذَا لَسَٰحِرٌ مُّبِينٌ (٢) إِنَّ رَبَّكُمُ ٱللَّهُ ٱلَّذِى

خَلَقَ ٱلسَّمَـٰوَٰتِ وَٱلْأَرْضَ فِى سِتَّةِ أَيَّامٍ ثُمَّ ٱسْتَوَىٰ عَلَى ٱلْعَرْشِ يُدَبِّرُ ٱلْأَمْرَ مَا مِن شَفِيعٍ إِلَّا مِنۢ بَعْدِ إِذْنِهِ ذَٰلِكُمُ ٱللَّهُ رَبُّكُمْ فَٱعْبُدُوهُ أَفَلَا تَذَكَّرُونَ (٣)

Is it wonder for mankind that We have sent Our Revelation to a man from among themselves (i.e. Muhammad) (saying): "Warn mankind (of the coming torment in Hell), and give good news to those who believe (in the Oneness of Allâh and in His Muhammad) that they shall have with their Lord the rewards of their good deeds?" (But) the disbelievers say: "This is indeed an evident sorcerer (i.e. Prophet Muhammad and the Qur'ân)! (2) Surely, your Lord is Allâh Who created the heavens and the earth in six Days and then rose over (Istawâ) the Throne (really in a manner that suits His Majesty), disposing the affair of all things. No intercessor (can plead with Him) except after His Leave. That is Allâh, your Lord; so worship Him (Alone). **Then, will you not remember?** (3)

Quran 10:15-18

وَإِذَا تُتْلَىٰ عَلَيْهِمْ ءَايَاتُنَا بَيِّنَتٍ قَالَ ٱلَّذِينَ لَا يَرْجُونَ لِقَاءَنَا ٱئْتِ بِقُرْءَانٍ غَيْرِ هَذَآ أَوْ بَدِّلْهُ قُلْ مَا يَكُونُ لِىٓ أَنْ أُبَدِّلَهُ مِن تِلْقَآىِٕ نَفْسِىٓ إِنْ أَتَّبِعُ إِلَّا مَا يُوحَىٰٓ إِلَىَّ إِنِّىٓ أَخَافُ إِنْ عَصَيْتُ رَبِّى عَذَابَ يَوْمٍ عَظِيمٍ (١٥) قُل لَّوْ شَآءَ ٱللَّهُ مَا تَلَوْتُهُ عَلَيْكُمْ وَلَآ أَدْرَىٰكُم بِهِۦ فَقَدْ لَبِثْتُ فِيكُمْ عُمُرًا مِّن قَبْلِهِۦٓ أَفَلَا تَعْقِلُونَ (١٦) فَمَنْ أَظْلَمُ مِمَّنِ ٱفْتَرَىٰ عَلَى ٱللَّهِ كَذِبًا أَوْ كَذَّبَ بِـَٔايَتِهِۦٓ إِنَّهُ لَا يُفْلِحُ ٱلْمُجْرِمُونَ (١٧) وَيَعْبُدُونَ مِن دُونِ ٱللَّهِ مَا لَا يَضُرُّهُمْ وَلَا يَنفَعُهُمْ وَيَقُولُونَ هَٰٓؤُلَآءِ شُفَعَٰٓؤُنَا عِندَ ٱللَّهِ قُلْ أَتُنَبِّئُونَ ٱللَّهَ بِمَا لَا يَعْلَمُ فِى ٱلسَّمَٰوَٰتِ وَلَا فِى ٱلْأَرْضِ سُبْحَٰنَهُ وَتَعَٰلَىٰ عَمَّا يُشْرِكُونَ (١٨)

And when Our Clear Verses are recited unto them, those who hope not for their meeting with Us, say: Bring us a Qur'ân other than this, or change it." Say (O Muhammad): "It is not for me to change it on my own accord; I only follow that which is revealed unto me. Verily, I fear the torment of the Great Day (i.e. the Day of Resurrection). if I were to disobey my Lord." (15) Say (O Muhammad): "If Allâh had so willed, I should not have recited it to you

nor would He have made it known to you.
Verily, I have stayed amongst you a life time
before this. **Have you then no sense?**"
(16) **So who does more wrong than he
who forges a lie against Allâh or denies
His Ayât (proofs, evidences, verses,
lessons, signs, revelations, etc.)?** Surely,
the Mujrimûn (criminals, sinners,
disbelievers and polytheists) will never be
successful! (17) And they worship besides
Allâh things that hurt them not, nor profit
them, and they say: "These are our
intercessors with Allâh." Say: **"Do you
inform Allâh of that which He knows
not in the heavens and on the earth?"**
Glorified and Exalted is He above all that
which they associate as partners (with
Him)! (18)

Quran 10:32-37

فَذَٰلِكُمُ ٱللَّهُ رَبُّكُمُ ٱلْحَقُّ فَمَاذَا بَعْدَ ٱلْحَقِّ إِلَّا ٱلضَّلَٰلُ فَأَنَّىٰ
تُصْرَفُونَ (٣٢) كَذَٰلِكَ حَقَّتْ كَلِمَتُ رَبِّكَ عَلَى ٱلَّذِينَ فَسَقُوٓاْ
أَنَّهُمْ لَا يُؤْمِنُونَ (٣٣) قُلْ هَلْ مِن شُرَكَآئِكُم مَّن يَبْدَؤُاْ ٱلْخَلْقَ
ثُمَّ يُعِيدُهُ قُلِ ٱللَّهُ يَبْدَؤُاْ ٱلْخَلْقَ ثُمَّ يُعِيدُهُ فَأَنَّىٰ تُؤْفَكُونَ

(٣٤) قُلْ هَلْ مِن شُرَكَآئِكُم مَّن يَهْدِىٓ إِلَى ٱلْحَقِّ قُلِ ٱللَّهُ يَهْدِى لِلْحَقِّ أَفَمَن يَهْدِىٓ إِلَى ٱلْحَقِّ أَحَقُّ أَن يُتَّبَعَ أَمَّن لَّا يَهِدِّىٓ إِلَّآ أَن يُهْدَىٰ فَمَا لَكُمْ كَيْفَ تَحْكُمُونَ (٣٥) وَمَا يَتَّبِعُ أَكْثَرُهُمْ إِلَّا ظَنًّا إِنَّ ٱلظَّنَّ لَا يُغْنِى مِنَ ٱلْحَقِّ شَيْئًا إِنَّ ٱللَّهَ عَلِيمٌ بِمَا يَفْعَلُونَ (٣٦) وَمَا كَانَ هَٰذَا ٱلْقُرْءَانُ أَن يُفْتَرَىٰ مِن دُونِ ٱللَّهِ وَلَٰكِن تَصْدِيقَ ٱلَّذِى بَيْنَ يَدَيْهِ وَتَفْصِيلَ ٱلْكِتَٰبِ لَا رَيْبَ فِيهِ مِن رَّبِّ ٱلْعَٰلَمِينَ (٣٧)

Such is Allâh, your Lord in truth. **So after the truth, what else can there be, save error? How then are you turned away?** *(32) Thus is the Word of your Lord justified against those who rebel (disobey Allâh) that they will not believe (in the Oneness of Allâh and in Muhammad as the Messenger of Allâh) (33) Say:* **"Is there of your (Allâh's so-called) partners one that originates the creation and then repeats it?"** *Say: "Allâh originates the creation and then He repeats it. Then how are you deluded away (from the truth)?" (34) Say:* **"Is there of your (Allâh's so-called) partners one that guides to the truth?"** *Say: "It is Allâh Who guides to the truth. Is*

*then He, Who guides to the truth, more
worthy to be followed, or he who finds
not guidance (himself) unless he is
guided? Then, what is the matter with
you? How judge you?"* (35) *And most of
them follow nothing but conjecture.
Certainly, conjecture can be of no avail
against the truth. Surely, Allâh is All-
Aware of what they do.* (36) *And this
Qur'ân is not such as could ever be
produced by other than Allâh (Lord of the
heavens and the earth), but it is a
confirmation of (the revelation) which was
before it [i.e. the Taurât (Torah), and the
Injeel] and a full explanation of the Book (i.e.
laws decreed for mankind) - wherein there is
no doubt from the the Lord of the 'Alamîn
(mankind, jinn,and all that exists).* (37)

Quran 10:50-52

قُلْ أَرَءَيْتُمْ إِنْ أَتَلٰكُمْ عَذَابُهُ بَيَٰتًا أَوْ نَهَارًا مَّاذَا يَسْتَعْجِلُ مِنْهُ
ٱلْمُجْرِمُونَ (٥٠) أَثُمَّ إِذَا مَا وَقَعَ ءَامَنتُم بِهِ ءَآلْـَٰٔنَ وَقَدْ كُنتُم
بِهِ تَسْتَعْجِلُونَ (٥١) ثُمَّ قِيلَ لِلَّذِينَ ظَلَمُوا ذُوقُوا عَذَابَ
ٱلْخُلْدِ هَلْ تُجْزَوْنَ إِلَّا بِمَا كُنتُمْ تَكْسِبُونَ (٥٢)

Say: "Tell me, - if His torment should come to you by night or by day, - which portion thereof would the Mujrimûn (disbelievers, polytheists, sinners, criminals) hasten on?" (50) *Is it then, that when it has actually befallen, you will believe in it? What!* **Now?** *And you used (aforetime) to hasten it on!"* (51) *Then it will be said to them who wronged themselves: "Taste you the everlasting torment!* **Are you recompensed (aught) save what you used to earn?"** (52)

Quran 10:59-60

قُلْ أَرَءَيْتُم مَّآ أَنزَلَ ٱللَّهُ لَكُم مِّن رِّزْقٍ فَجَعَلْتُم مِّنْهُ حَرَامًا وَحَلَٰلاً قُلْ ءَآللَّهُ أَذِنَ لَكُمْ أَمْ عَلَى ٱللَّهِ تَفْتَرُونَ (٥٩) وَمَا ظَنُّ ٱلَّذِينَ يَفْتَرُونَ عَلَى ٱللَّهِ ٱلْكَذِبَ يَوْمَ ٱلْقِيَٰمَةِ إِنَّ ٱللَّهَ لَذُو فَضْلٍ عَلَى ٱلنَّاسِ وَلَٰكِنَّ أَكْثَرَهُمْ لَا يَشْكُرُونَ (٦٠)

Say (O Muhammad to these polytheists): "Tell me, what provision Allâh has sent down to you! And you have made of it lawful and unlawful." Say (O Muhammad): **"Has Allâh permitted you (to do so), or**

do you invent a lie against Allâh?"
(59) And what think those who invent
lie against Allâh, on the Day of
Resurrection? [i.e. Do they think that they
will be forgiven and excused! Nay, they will
have an eternal punishment in the Fire of
Hell]. Truly, Allâh is full of Bounty to
mankind, but most of them are ungrateful
(60)

Quran 10:98

فَلَوْلَا كَانَتْ قَرْيَةٌ ءَامَنَتْ فَنَفَعَهَآ إِيمَـٰنُهَآ إِلَّا قَوْمَ يُونُسَ لَمَّآ
ءَامَنُواْ كَشَفْنَا عَنْهُمْ عَذَابَ ٱلْخِزْىِ فِى ٱلْحَيَوٰةِ ٱلدُّنْيَا وَمَتَّعْنَـٰهُمْ
إِلَىٰ حِينٍ (٩٨)

Was there any town (community) that
believed (after seeing the punishment),
and its Faith (at that moment) saved it
(from the punishment)? (The answer is
none,) - except the people of Yûnus (Jonah);
when they believed, We removed from them
the torment of disgrace in the life of the
(present) world, and permitted them to
enjoy for a while. (98)

Quran 11:13-14

أَمْ يَقُولُونَ ٱفْتَرَىٰهُ قُلْ فَأْتُواْ بِعَشْرِ سُوَرٍ مِّثْلِهِ مُفْتَرَيَٰتٍ
وَٱدْعُواْ مَنِ ٱسْتَطَعْتُم مِّن دُونِ ٱللَّهِ إِن كُنتُمْ صَٰدِقِينَ
(١٣) فَإِلَّمْ يَسْتَجِيبُواْ لَكُمْ فَٱعْلَمُواْ أَنَّمَآ أُنزِلَ بِعِلْمِ ٱللَّهِ وَأَن لَّا
إِلَٰهَ إِلَّا هُوَ فَهَلْ أَنتُم مُّسْلِمُونَ (١٤)

*Or they say, "He (Prophet Muhammad)
forged it (the Qur'an)." Say: "Bring you
then ten forged Sûrahs (chapters) like unto
it, and call whomsoever you can, other than
Allâh (to your help), if you speak the truth!"
(13) If then they answer you not, know then
that it [the Revelation (this Qur'ân)] is sent
down with the Knowledge of Allâh and that
Lâ ilâha illa Huwa: (none has the right to be
worshipped but He)!* **Will you then be
Muslims (those who submit to Islâm)?**
(14)

Quran 11:24

۞ مَثَلُ ٱلْفَرِيقَيْنِ كَٱلْأَعْمَىٰ وَٱلْأَصَمِّ وَٱلْبَصِيرِ وَٱلسَّمِيعِ
هَلْ يَسْتَوِيَانِ مَثَلاً أَفَلَا تَذَكَّرُونَ (٢٤)

The likeness of the two parties is as the blind and the deaf and the seer and the hearer. **Are they equal when compared? Will you not then take heed?** *(24)*

Quran 12:109

وَمَآ أَرْسَلْنَا مِن قَبْلِكَ إِلَّا رِجَالًا نُّوحِىٓ إِلَيْهِم مِّنْ أَهْلِ ٱلْقُرَىٰٓ أَفَلَمْ يَسِيرُواْ فِى ٱلْأَرْضِ فَيَنظُرُواْ كَيْفَ كَانَ عَٰقِبَةُ ٱلَّذِينَ مِن قَبْلِهِمْ وَلَدَارُ ٱلْأَخِرَةِ خَيْرٌ لِّلَّذِينَ ٱتَّقَوْاْ أَفَلَا تَعْقِلُونَ (١٠٩)

And We sent not before you (as Messengers) any but men, whom We revealed from among the people of townships. **Have they not travelled in the land and seen what was the end of those who were before them?** *And verily, the home of the Hereafter is the best for those who fear Allâh and obey Him (by abstaining from sins and evil deeds, and by performing righteous good deeds).* **Do you not then understand?** *(109)*

Quran 13:16-17

قُلْ مَن رَّبُّ ٱلسَّمَٰوَٰتِ وَٱلْأَرْضِ قُلِ ٱللَّهُ قُلْ أَفَٱتَّخَذْتُم مِّن دُونِهِۦٓ أَوْلِيَآءَ لَا يَمْلِكُونَ لِأَنفُسِهِمْ نَفْعًا وَلَا ضَرًّا قُلْ هَلْ

يَسْتَوِى ٱلْأَعْمَىٰ وَٱلْبَصِيرُ أَمْ هَلْ تَسْتَوِى ٱلظُّلُمَـٰتُ وَٱلنُّورُ أَمْ جَعَلُواْ لِلَّهِ شُرَكَآءَ خَلَقُواْ كَخَلْقِهِۦ فَتَشَـٰبَهَ ٱلْخَلْقُ عَلَيْهِمْ قُلِ ٱللَّهُ خَـٰلِقُ كُلِّ شَىْءٍ وَهُوَ ٱلْوَٰحِدُ ٱلْقَهَّـٰرُ (١٦) أَنزَلَ مِنَ ٱلسَّمَآءِ مَآءً فَسَالَتْ أَوْدِيَةٌۢ بِقَدَرِهَا فَٱحْتَمَلَ ٱلسَّيْلُ زَبَدًا رَّابِيًا وَمِمَّا يُوقِدُونَ عَلَيْهِ فِى ٱلنَّارِ ٱبْتِغَآءَ حِلْيَةٍ أَوْ مَتَـٰعٍ زَبَدٌ مِّثْلُهُۥ كَذَٰلِكَ يَضْرِبُ ٱللَّهُ ٱلْحَقَّ وَٱلْبَـٰطِلَ فَأَمَّا ٱلزَّبَدُ فَيَذْهَبُ جُفَآءً وَأَمَّا مَا يَنفَعُ ٱلنَّاسَ فَيَمْكُثُ فِى ٱلْأَرْضِ كَذَٰلِكَ يَضْرِبُ ٱللَّهُ ٱلْأَمْثَالَ (١٧)

Say (O Muhammad): "**Who is the Lord of the heavens and the earth?**" Say: "(It is) Allâh." Say: "**Have you then taken (for worship) Auliyâ' (protectors) other than Him, such as have no power either for benefit or for harm to themselves?**" Say: "**Is the blind equal to the one who sees? Or darkness equal to light? Or do they assign to Allâh partners who created the like of His creation, so that the creation (which they made and His creation) seemed alike to them?**" Say: "**Allâh is the Creator of all things, He is the One, the Irresistible.**" (16) He sends down water (rain) from the sky, and the valleys

flow according to their measure, but the
flood bears away the foam that mounts up to
the surface, — and (also) from that (ore)
which they heat in the fire in order to make
ornaments or utensils, rises a foam like unto
it, thus does Allâh (by parables) show forth
truth and falsehood. Then, as for the foam it
passes away as scum upon the banks, while
that which is for the good of mankind
remains in the earth. Thus Allâh sets forth
parables (for the truth and falsehood, i.e.
Belief and disbelief). (17)

Quran 13:19

﴿۞ أَفَمَن يَعْلَمُ أَنَّمَآ أُنزِلَ إِلَيْكَ مِن رَّبِّكَ ٱلْحَقُّ كَمَنْ هُوَ
أَعْمَىٰٓ إِنَّمَا يَتَذَكَّرُ أُوْلُواْ ٱلْأَلْبَـٰبِ (١٩)

**Shall he then who knows that what has
been revealed unto you (O Muhammad)
from your Lord is the truth be like him
who is blind?** But it is only the men of
understanding that pay heed. (19)

Quran 13:31

وَلَوْ أَنَّ قُرْءَانًا سُيِّرَتْ بِهِ ٱلْجِبَالُ أَوْ قُطِّعَتْ بِهِ ٱلْأَرْضُ أَوْ كُلِّمَ بِهِ ٱلْمَوْتَىٰ بَل لِّلَّهِ ٱلْأَمْرُ جَمِيعًا أَفَلَمْ يَأْيْئَسِ ٱلَّذِينَ ءَامَنُوٓاْ أَن لَّوْ يَشَآءُ ٱللَّهُ لَهَدَى ٱلنَّاسَ جَمِيعًا وَلَا يَزَالُ ٱلَّذِينَ كَفَرُواْ تُصِيبُهُم بِمَا صَنَعُواْ قَارِعَةٌ أَوْ تَحُلُّ قَرِيبًا مِّن دَارِهِمْ حَتَّىٰ يَأْتِيَ وَعْدُ ٱللَّهِ إِنَّ ٱللَّهَ لَا يُخْلِفُ ٱلْمِيعَادَ (٣١)

*And if there had been a Qur'ân with which
mountains could be moved (from their
places), or the earth could be cloven asunder,
or the dead could be made to speak (it would
not have been other than this Qur'ân). But
the decision of all things is certainly with
Allâh.* **Have not then those who believed
yet known that had Allâh willed, He
could have guided all mankind?** *And a
disaster will not cease to strike those who
disbelieve because of their (evil) deeds or it
(i.e. the disaster) settle close to their homes,
until the Promise of Allâh comes to pass.
Certainly, Allâh does not fail in His
Promise. (31)*

Quran 13:33

أَفَمَنْ هُوَ قَآئِمٌ عَلَىٰ كُلِّ نَفْسٍ بِمَا كَسَبَتْ ۗ وَجَعَلُواْ لِلَّهِ شُرَكَآءَ
قُلْ سَمُّوهُمْ ۚ أَمْ تُنَبِّئُونَهُ ۚ بِمَا لَا يَعْلَمُ فِى ٱلْأَرْضِ أَم بِظَٰهِرٍ
مِّنَ ٱلْقَوْلِ ۗ بَلْ زُيِّنَ لِلَّذِينَ كَفَرُواْ مَكْرُهُمْ وَصُدُّواْ عَنِ ٱلسَّبِيلِ ۗ
وَمَن يُضْلِلِ ٱللَّهُ فَمَا لَهُ ۚ مِنْ هَادٍ (٣٣)

Is then He (Allâh) Who takes charge
(guards, maintains, provides) of every
person and knows all that he has earned
(like any other deities who know
nothing)? Yet they ascribe partners to
Allâh. Say: "Name them! Is it that you will
inform Him of something He knows not in
the earth or is it (just) a show of false
words." Nay! To those who disbelieved,
their plotting is made fairseeming, and they
have been hindered from the Right Path, and
whom Allâh sends astray, for him, there is
no guide. (33)

Quran 14:9

أَلَمْ يَأْتِكُمْ نَبَؤُاْ ٱلَّذِينَ مِن قَبْلِكُمْ قَوْمِ نُوحٍ وَعَادٍ وَثَمُودَ
وَٱلَّذِينَ مِنۢ بَعْدِهِمْ ۚ لَا يَعْلَمُهُمْ إِلَّا ٱللَّهُ ۚ جَآءَتْهُمْ رُسُلُهُم بِٱلْبَيِّنَٰتِ
فَرَدُّواْ أَيْدِيَهُمْ فِىٓ أَفْوَٰهِهِمْ وَقَالُوٓاْ إِنَّا كَفَرْنَا بِمَآ أُرْسِلْتُم بِهِۦ
وَإِنَّا لَفِى شَكٍّ مِّمَّا تَدْعُونَنَآ إِلَيْهِ مُرِيبٍ (٩)

Has not the news reached you, of those before you, the people of Nûh (Noah), and 'Ad, and Thamud? And those after them? None knows them but Allâh. To them came their Messengers with clear proofs, but they put their hands in their mouths (biting them from anger) and said: "Verily, we disbelieve in that with which you have been sent, and we are really in grave doubt as to that to which you invite us (i.e. Islâmic Monotheism)." (9)

Quran 14:28

۞ أَلَمْ تَرَ إِلَى ٱلَّذِينَ بَدَّلُواْ نِعْمَتَ ٱللَّهِ كُفْرًا وَأَحَلُّواْ قَوْمَهُمْ دَارَ ٱلْبَوَارِ (٢٨)

Have you not seen those who have changed the Blessings of Allâh into disbelief (by denying Prophet Muhammad and his Message of Islâm), and caused their people to dwell in the house of destruction? (28)

Quran 15:32-35

قَالَ يَـٰٓإِبْلِيسُ مَا لَكَ أَلَّا تَكُونَ مَعَ ٱلسَّـٰجِدِينَ (٣٢) قَالَ لَمْ
أَكُن لِّأَسْجُدَ لِبَشَرٍ خَلَقْتَهُۥ مِن صَلْصَـٰلٍ مِّنْ حَمَإٍ مَّسْنُونٍ
(٣٣) قَالَ فَٱخْرُجْ مِنْهَا فَإِنَّكَ رَجِيمٌ (٣٤) وَإِنَّ عَلَيْكَ ٱللَّعْنَةَ
إِلَىٰ يَوْمِ ٱلدِّينِ (٣٥)

*(Allâh) said: "**O Iblîs (Satan)! What is
your reason for not being among the
prostrators?**" (32) [Iblîs (Satan)] said: "I
am not the one to prostrate myself to a
human being, whom You created from dried
(sounding) clay of altered mud."
(33) (Allâh) said: "Then, get out from here,
for verily, you are Rajîm (an outcast or a
cursed one)." (34) "And verily, the curse
shall be upon you till the Day of
Recompense (i.e. the Day of Resurrection)."
(35)*

Quran 16:17-20

أَفَمَن يَخْلُقُ كَمَن لَّا يَخْلُقُ أَفَلَا تَذَكَّرُونَ (١٧) وَإِن تَعُدُّواْ
نِعْمَةَ ٱللَّهِ لَا تُحْصُوهَآ إِنَّ ٱللَّهَ لَغَفُورٌ رَّحِيمٌ (١٨) وَٱللَّهُ يَعْلَمُ
مَا تُسِرُّونَ وَمَا تُعْلِنُونَ (١٩) وَٱلَّذِينَ يَدْعُونَ مِن دُونِ ٱللَّهِ
لَا يَخْلُقُونَ شَيْئًا وَهُمْ يُخْلَقُونَ (٢٠)

*Is then He, Who creates as one who
creates not? Will you not then
remember? (17) And if you would count
the favours of Allâh, never could you be able
to count them. Truly! Allâh is Oft-
Forgiving, Most Merciful. (18) And Allâh
knows what you conceal and what you
reveal. (19) Those whom they (Al-
Mushrikûn) invoke besides Allâh have not
created anything, but are themselves
created. (20)*

Quran 16:27

ثُمَّ يَوْمَ ٱلْقِيَـٰمَةِ يُخْزِيهِمْ وَيَقُولُ أَيْنَ شُرَكَآءِىَ ٱلَّذِينَ كُنتُمْ
تُشَـٰٓقُّونَ فِيهِمْ قَالَ ٱلَّذِينَ أُوتُواْ ٱلْعِلْمَ إِنَّ ٱلْخِزْىَ ٱلْيَوْمَ وَٱلسُّوٓءَ
عَلَى ٱلْكَـٰفِرِينَ (٢٧)

*Then, on the Day of Resurrection, He will
disgrace them and will say:* "**Where are My
(so called) 'partners' concerning whom
you used to disagree and dispute (with
the believers, by defying and disobeying
Allâh)?**" *Those who have been given the
knowledge (about the Torment of Allâh for*

the disbelievers) will say: "Verily! Disgrace this Day and misery this Day are upon the disbelievers. (27)

Quran 16:35

وَقَالَ ٱلَّذِينَ أَشْرَكُوا لَوْ شَاءَ ٱللَّهُ مَا عَبَدْنَا مِن دُونِهِ مِن شَيْءٍ نَّحْنُ وَلَاۤ ءَابَاؤُنَا وَلَا حَرَّمْنَا مِن دُونِهِ مِن شَيْءٍ كَذَٰلِكَ فَعَلَ ٱلَّذِينَ مِن قَبْلِهِمْ فَهَلْ عَلَى ٱلرُّسُلِ إِلَّا ٱلْبَلَٰغُ ٱلْمُبِينُ (٣٥)

And those who joined others in worship with Allâh say: "If Allâh had so willed, neither we nor our fathers would have worshipped aught but Him, nor would we have forbidden anything without (Command from) Him." So did those before them. Then! *Are the Messengers charged with anything but to convey clearly the Message?* (35)

Quran 16:45-48

أَفَأَمِنَ ٱلَّذِينَ مَكَرُوا ٱلسَّيِّئَاتِ أَن يَخْسِفَ ٱللَّهُ بِهِمُ ٱلْأَرْضَ أَوْ يَأْتِيَهُمُ ٱلْعَذَابُ مِنْ حَيْثُ لَا يَشْعُرُونَ (٤٥) أَوْ يَأْخُذَهُمْ فِى تَقَلُّبِهِمْ فَمَا هُم بِمُعْجِزِينَ (٤٦) أَوْ يَأْخُذَهُمْ عَلَىٰ تَخَوُّفٍ فَإِنَّ

رَبَّكُمْ لَرَءُوفٌ رَّحِيمٌ (٤٧) أَوَلَمْ يَرَوْاْ إِلَىٰ مَا خَلَقَ ٱللَّهُ مِن شَىْءٍ يَتَفَيَّؤُاْ ظِلَـٰلُهُ ۥ عَنِ ٱلْيَمِينِ وَٱلشَّمَآئِلِ سُجَّدًا لِّلَّهِ وَهُمْ دَٰخِرُونَ (٤٨)

Do then those who devise evil plots feel secure that Allâh will not sink them into the earth, or that the torment will not seize them from directions they perceive not? (45) Or that He may catch them in the midst of their going to and fro (in their jobs), so that there be no escape for them (from Allâh's Punishment)? (46) Or that He may catch them with gradual wasting (of their wealth and health)? Truly! Your Lord is indeed full of Kindness, Most Merciful? (47) **Have they not observed things that Allâh has created, (how) their shadows incline to the right and to the left, making prostration unto Allâh, and they are lowly? (48)**

Quran 16:52

وَلَهُ مَا فِى ٱلسَّمَـٰوَٰتِ وَٱلْأَرْضِ وَلَهُ ٱلدِّينُ وَاصِبًا أَفَغَيْرَ
ٱللَّهِ تَتَّقُونَ (٥٢)

*To Him belongs all that is in the heavens
and (all that is in) the earth and Ad-Din
Wasiba is His [(i.e. perpetual sincere
obedience to Allâh is obligatory). None has
the right to be worshipped but Allâh)].* **Will
you then fear any other than Allâh?** *(52)*

Quran 16:71-72

وَٱللَّهُ فَضَّلَ بَعْضَكُمْ عَلَىٰ بَعْضٍ فِى ٱلرِّزْقِ فَمَا ٱلَّذِينَ فُضِّلُواْ
بِرَآدِّى رِزْقِهِمْ عَلَىٰ مَا مَلَكَتْ أَيْمَـٰنُهُمْ فَهُمْ فِيهِ سَوَآءٌ
أَفَبِنِعْمَةِ ٱللَّهِ يَجْحَدُونَ (٧١) وَٱللَّهُ جَعَلَ لَكُم مِّنْ أَنفُسِكُمْ
أَزْوَٰجًا وَجَعَلَ لَكُم مِّنْ أَزْوَٰجِكُم بَنِينَ وَحَفَدَةً وَرَزَقَكُم مِّنَ
ٱلطَّيِّبَـٰتِ أَفَبِٱلْبَـٰطِلِ يُؤْمِنُونَ وَبِنِعْمَتِ ٱللَّهِ هُمْ يَكْفُرُونَ (٧٢)

*And Allâh has preferred some of you above
others in wealth and properties. Then, those
who are preferred will by no means hand
over their wealth and properties to those
(slaves) whom their right hands possess, so
that they may be equal with them in respect
thereof.* **Do they then deny the Favour of
Allâh?** *(71) And Allâh has made for you*

Azwaj (makes or wives) of your own kind, and has made for you, from your wives, sons and grandsons, and has bestowed on you good provision. **Do they then believe in false deities and deny the Favour of Allâh (by not worshipping Allâh Alone)?** *(72)*

Quran 16:75-76

﴿۞ ضَرَبَ ٱللَّهُ مَثَلًا عَبۡدًا مَّمۡلُوكًا لَّا يَقۡدِرُ عَلَىٰ شَىۡءٍ وَمَن رَّزَقۡنَـٰهُ مِنَّا رِزۡقًا حَسَنًا فَهُوَ يُنفِقُ مِنۡهُ سِرًّا وَجَهۡرًا هَلۡ يَسۡتَوُۥنَّ ٱلۡحَمۡدُ لِلَّهِ بَلۡ أَكۡثَرُهُمۡ لَا يَعۡلَمُونَ (٧٥) وَضَرَبَ ٱللَّهُ مَثَلًا رَّجُلَيۡنِ أَحَدُهُمَآ أَبۡكَمُ لَا يَقۡدِرُ عَلَىٰ شَىۡءٍ وَهُوَ كَلٌّ عَلَىٰ مَوۡلَىٰهُ أَيۡنَمَا يُوَجِّههُّ لَا يَأۡتِ بِخَيۡرٍ هَلۡ يَسۡتَوِى هُوَ وَمَن يَأۡمُرُ بِٱلۡعَدۡلِ وَهُوَ عَلَىٰ صِرَٰطٍ مُّسۡتَقِيمٍ (٧٦)﴾

Allâh puts forward the example (of two men — a believer and a disbeliever); a slave (disbeliever) under the possession of another, he has no power of any sort, and (the other), a man (believer) on whom We have bestowed a good provision from Us, and he spends thereof secretly and openly. **Can they be equal?** *(By no means). All the praises and* *thanks are to Allâh. Nay! (But) most of them know not. (75) And Allâh puts forward (another) example of two men, one of them dumb, who has no power over anything (disbeliever), and he is a burden on his master, whichever way he directs him, he brings no good.* **Is such a man equal to one (believer in the Islâmic Monotheism) who commands justice, and is himself on a Straight Path? (76)**

Quran 16:79

أَلَمْ يَرَوْاْ إِلَى ٱلطَّيْرِ مُسَخَّرَٰتٍ فِى جَوِّ ٱلسَّمَآءِ مَا يُمْسِكُهُنَّ إِلَّا ٱللَّهُ إِنَّ فِى ذَٰلِكَ لَأَيَٰتٍ لِّقَوْمٍ يُؤْمِنُونَ (٧٩)

Do they not see the birds held (flying) in the midst of the sky? *None holds them but Allâh [none gave them the ability to fly but Allâh]. Verily, in this are clear Ayat (proofs and signs) for people who believe (in the Oneness of Allâh). (79)*

Quran 17:40

أَفَأَصْفَلَكُمْ رَبُّكُم بِٱلْبَنِينَ وَٱتَّخَذَ مِنَ ٱلْمَلَٰٓئِكَةِ إِنَٰثًا إِنَّكُمْ
لَتَقُولُونَ قَوْلًا عَظِيمًا (٤٠)

*Has then your Lord (O pagans of
Makkah) preferred for you sons, and
taken for Himself from among the
angels daughters? Verily! You indeed
utter an awful saying. (40)*

Quran 17:67-69

وَإِذَا مَسَّكُمُ ٱلضُّرُّ فِى ٱلْبَحْرِ ضَلَّ مَن تَدْعُونَ إِلَّا إِيَّاهُ فَلَمَّا
نَجَّىٰكُمْ إِلَى ٱلْبَرِّ أَعْرَضْتُمْ وَكَانَ ٱلْإِنسَٰنُ كَفُورًا
(٦٧) أَفَأَمِنتُمْ أَن يَخْسِفَ بِكُمْ جَانِبَ ٱلْبَرِّ أَوْ يُرْسِلَ عَلَيْكُمْ
حَاصِبًا ثُمَّ لَا تَجِدُواْ لَكُمْ وَكِيلًا (٦٨) أَمْ أَمِنتُمْ أَن يُعِيدَكُمْ
فِيهِ تَارَةً أُخْرَىٰ فَيُرْسِلَ عَلَيْكُمْ قَاصِفًا مِّنَ ٱلرِّيحِ فَيُغْرِقَكُم بِمَا
كَفَرْتُمْ ثُمَّ لَا تَجِدُواْ لَكُمْ عَلَيْنَا بِهِۦ تَبِيعًا (٦٩)

*And when harm touches you upon the sea,
those that you call upon vanish from you
except Him (Allâh Alone). But when He
brings you safe to land, you turn away
(from Him). And man is ever ungrateful.
(67)* **Do you then feel secure that He will
not cause a side of the land to swallow
you up, or that He will not send against**

you a violent sand-storm? Then, you shall find no Wakîl (guardian — one to guard you from the torment). (68) **Or do you feel secure that He will not send you back a second time to sea and send against you a hurricane of wind and drown you because of your disbelief?** *Then you will not find any avenger therein against Us. (69)*

Quran 17:88-93

قُل لَّئِنِ ٱجْتَمَعَتِ ٱلْإِنسُ وَٱلْجِنُّ عَلَىٰ أَن يَأْتُواْ بِمِثْلِ هَـٰذَا
ٱلْقُرْءَانِ لَا يَأْتُونَ بِمِثْلِهِۦ وَلَوْ كَانَ بَعْضُهُمْ لِبَعْضٍ ظَهِيرًا
(٨٨) وَلَقَدْ صَرَّفْنَا لِلنَّاسِ فِى هَـٰذَا ٱلْقُرْءَانِ مِن كُلِّ مَثَلٍ
فَأَبَىٰٓ أَكْثَرُ ٱلنَّاسِ إِلَّا كُفُورًا (٨٩) وَقَالُواْ لَن نُّؤْمِنَ لَكَ
حَتَّىٰ تَفْجُرَ لَنَا مِنَ ٱلْأَرْضِ يَنبُوعًا (٩٠) أَوْ تَكُونَ لَكَ جَنَّةٌ
مِّن نَّخِيلٍ وَعِنَبٍ فَتُفَجِّرَ ٱلْأَنْهَـٰرَ خِلَـٰلَهَا تَفْجِيرًا (٩١) أَوْ
تُسْقِطَ ٱلسَّمَآءَ كَمَا زَعَمْتَ عَلَيْنَا كِسَفًا أَوْ تَأْتِىَ بِٱللَّهِ
وَٱلْمَلَـٰٓئِكَةِ قَبِيلاً (٩٢) أَوْ يَكُونَ لَكَ بَيْتٌ مِّن زُخْرُفٍ أَوْ
تَرْقَىٰ فِى ٱلسَّمَآءِ وَلَن نُّؤْمِنَ لِرُقِيِّكَ حَتَّىٰ تُنَزِّلَ عَلَيْنَا كِتَـٰبًا
نَّقْرَؤُهُۥ قُلْ سُبْحَانَ رَبِّى هَلْ كُنتُ إِلَّا بَشَرًا رَّسُولاً (٩٣)

Say: "If the mankind and the jinn were together to produce the like of this Qur'ân, they could not produce the like thereof, even if they helped one another." (88) And indeed We have fully explained to mankind, in this Qur'ân, every kind of similitude, but most of mankind refuse (the truth and accept nothing) but disbelief. (89) And they say: "We shall not believe in you (O Muhammad), until you cause a spring to gush forth from the earth for us; (90) "Or you have a garden of date-palms and grapes, and cause rivers to gush forth in their midst abundantly; (91) "Or you cause the heaven to fall upon us in pieces, as you have pretended, or you bring Allâh and the angels before (us) face to face; (92) "Or you have a house of Zukhruf (like silver and pure gold), or you ascend up into the sky, and even then we will put no faith in your ascension until you bring down for us a Book that we would read." Say (O Muhammad): "Glorified (and Exalted) is my Lord [(Allâh) above all that evil they (polytheists) associate with Him]!

Am I anything but a man, sent as a Messenger?" (93)

Quran 18:9

أَمْ حَسِبْتَ أَنَّ أَصْحَٰبَ ٱلْكَهْفِ وَٱلرَّقِيمِ كَانُوا۟ مِنْ ءَايَٰتِنَا عَجَبًا (٩)

Do you think that the people of the Cave and the Inscription (the news or the names of the people of the Cave) were a wonder among Our Signs? (9)

Quran 18:50

وَإِذْ قُلْنَا لِلْمَلَٰٓئِكَةِ ٱسْجُدُوا۟ لِءَادَمَ فَسَجَدُوٓا۟ إِلَّآ إِبْلِيسَ كَانَ مِنَ ٱلْجِنِّ فَفَسَقَ عَنْ أَمْرِ رَبِّهِۦٓ أَفَتَتَّخِذُونَهُۥ وَذُرِّيَّتَهُۥٓ أَوْلِيَآءَ مِن دُونِى وَهُمْ لَكُمْ عَدُوٌّۢ بِئْسَ لِلظَّٰلِمِينَ بَدَلًا (٥٠)

And (remember) when We said to the angels;"Prostrate yourselves unto Adam." So they prostrated themselves except Iblîs (Satan). He was one of the jinn; he disobeyed the Command of his Lord. **Will you then take him (Iblîs) and his offspring as protectors and helpers rather than Me while they are enemies to you?** *What an*

evil is the exchange for the Zâlimûn
(polytheists, and wrong-doers). (50)

Quran 18:57

وَمَنْ أَظْلَمُ مِمَّن ذُكِّرَ بِـَٔايَٰتِ رَبِّهِۦ فَأَعْرَضَ عَنْهَا وَنَسِىَ مَا
قَدَّمَتْ يَدَاهُ إِنَّا جَعَلْنَا عَلَىٰ قُلُوبِهِمْ أَكِنَّةً أَن يَفْقَهُوهُ وَفِىٓ
ءَاذَانِهِمْ وَقْرًا وَإِن تَدْعُهُمْ إِلَى ٱلْهُدَىٰ فَلَن يَهْتَدُوٓاْ إِذًا أَبَدًا
(٥٧)

*And who does more wrong than he who
is reminded of the Ayât (proofs,
evidences, verses, lessons, signs,
revelations, etc.) of his Lord, but turns
away from them forgetting what (deeds)
his hands have sent forth?* Truly, We
have set veils over their hearts lest they
should understand this (the Qur'ân), and in
their ears, deafness. And if you (O
Muhammad) call them to guidance, even
then they will never be guided. (57)

Quran 18:102-106

أَفَحَسِبَ ٱلَّذِينَ كَفَرُوٓاْ أَن يَتَّخِذُواْ عِبَادِى مِن دُونِىٓ أَوْلِيَآءَ إِنَّآ
أَعْتَدْنَا جَهَنَّمَ لِلْكَٰفِرِينَ نُزُلاً (١٠٢) قُلْ هَلْ نُنَبِّئُكُم

بِٱلۡأَخۡسَرِينَ أَعۡمَٰلاً (١٠٣) ٱلَّذِينَ ضَلَّ سَعۡيُهُمۡ فِى ٱلۡحَيَوٰةِ ٱلدُّنۡيَا وَهُمۡ يَحۡسَبُونَ أَنَّهُمۡ يُحۡسِنُونَ صُنۡعًا (١٠٤) أُوْلَٰئِكَ ٱلَّذِينَ كَفَرُواْ بِٔايَٰتِ رَبِّهِمۡ وَلِقَآئِهِۦ فَحَبِطَتۡ أَعۡمَٰلُهُمۡ فَلَا نُقِيمُ لَهُمۡ يَوۡمَ ٱلۡقِيَٰمَةِ وَزۡنًا (١٠٥) ذَٰلِكَ جَزَآؤُهُمۡ جَهَنَّمُ بِمَا كَفَرُواْ وَٱتَّخَذُوٓاْ ءَايَٰتِى وَرُسُلِى هُزُوًا (١٠٦)

Do then those who disbelieved think that they can take My slaves [i.e., the angels, Allâh's Messengers, 'Īsā (Jesus), son of Maryam (Mary)] as Auliyâ' (lords, gods, protectors) besides Me? Verily, We have prepared Hell as an entertainment for the disbelievers (in the Oneness of Allâh Islâmic Monotheism). (102) Say (O Muhammad): "**Shall We tell you the greatest losers in respect of (their) deeds?** (103) "Those whose efforts have been wasted in this life while they thought that they were acquiring good by their deeds! (104) "They are those who deny the Ayât (proofs, evidences, verses, lessons, signs, revelations, etc.) of their Lord and the Meeting with Him (in the Hereafter). So their works are in vain, and on the Day of*

Resurrection, We shall assign not weight for them. (105) "That shall be their recompense, Hell; because they disbelieved and took My Ayât (proofs, evidences, verses, lessons, signs, revelations, etc.) and My Messengers by way of jest and mockery. (106)

Quran 19:73-75

وَإِذَا تُتْلَىٰ عَلَيْهِمْ ءَايَـٰتُنَا بَيِّنَـٰتٍ قَالَ ٱلَّذِينَ كَفَرُواْ لِلَّذِينَ ءَامَنُوٓاْ أَىُّ ٱلْفَرِيقَيْنِ خَيْرٌ مَّقَامًا وَأَحْسَنُ نَدِيًّا (٧٣) وَكَمْ أَهْلَكْنَا قَبْلَهُم مِّن قَرْنٍ هُمْ أَحْسَنُ أَثَـٰثًا وَرِءْيًا (٧٤) قُلْ مَن كَانَ فِى ٱلضَّلَـٰلَةِ فَلْيَمْدُدْ لَهُ ٱلرَّحْمَـٰنُ مَدًّا حَتَّىٰٓ إِذَا رَأَوْاْ مَا يُوعَدُونَ إِمَّا ٱلْعَذَابَ وَإِمَّا ٱلسَّاعَةَ فَسَيَعْلَمُونَ مَنْ هُوَ شَرٌّ مَّكَانًا وَأَضْعَفُ جُندًا (٧٥)

And when Our Clear Verses are recited to them, those who disbelieve (the rich and strong among the pagans of Quraish who live a life of luxury) say to those who believe (the weak, poor companions of Prophet Muhammad who have a hard life): "Which of the two groups (i.e. believers or disbelievers) is best in (point of) position and as regards station (place of council for *consultation)." (73)* **And how many a generation (past nations) have We destroyed before them, who were better in wealth, goods and outward appearance?** *(74) Say (O Muhammad) whoever is in error, the Most Gracious (Allâh) will extend (the rope) to him, until, when they see that which they were promised, either the torment or the Hour, they will come to know who is worst in position, and who is weaker in forces. (75)*

Quran 19:77-80

أَفَرَءَيْتَ ٱلَّذِى كَفَرَ بِـَٔايَـٰتِنَا وَقَالَ لَأُوتَيَنَّ مَالاً وَوَلَدًا (٧٧) أَطَّلَعَ ٱلْغَيْبَ أَمِ ٱتَّخَذَ عِندَ ٱلرَّحْمَـٰنِ عَهْدًا (٧٨) كَلَّا سَنَكْتُبُ مَا يَقُولُ وَنَمُدُّ لَهُ ۥ مِنَ ٱلْعَذَابِ مَدًّا (٧٩) وَنَرِثُهُ ۥ مَا يَقُولُ وَيَأْتِينَا فَرْدًا (٨٠)

Have you seen him who disbelieved in Our Ayât (this Qur'ân and Muhammad) and said: "I shall certainly be given wealth and children [if I will be alive (again)],"
(77) **Has he known the unseen or has he taken a covenant from the Most**

Gracious (Allâh)? (78) Nay! We shall record what he says, and We shall increase his torment (in the Hell); (79) And We shall inherit from him (at his death) all that he talks of (i.e. wealth and children which We have bestowed upon him in this world), and he shall come to Us alone (80)

Quran 19:98

وَكَمْ أَهْلَكْنَا قَبْلَهُم مِّن قَرْنٍ هَلْ تُحِسُّ مِنْهُم مِّنْ أَحَدٍ أَوْ تَسْمَعُ لَهُمْ رِكْزًا (٩٨)

And how many a generation before them have We destroyed! **Can you find a single one of them or hear even a whisper of them? (98)**

Quran 20:9

وَهَلْ أَتَنكَ حَدِيثُ مُوسَىٰ (٩)

And has there come to you the story of Mûsa (Moses)? (9)

Quran 20:17-24

وَمَا تِلْكَ بِيَمِينِكَ يَٰمُوسَىٰ (١٧) قَالَ هِىَ عَصَاىَ أَتَوَكَّؤُاْ عَلَيْهَا وَأَهُشُّ بِهَا عَلَىٰ غَنَمِى وَلِىَ فِيهَا مَآرِبُ أُخْرَىٰ (١٨) قَالَ أَلْقِهَا يَٰمُوسَىٰ (١٩) فَأَلْقَىٰهَا فَإِذَا هِىَ حَيَّةٌ تَسْعَىٰ (٢٠) قَالَ خُذْهَا وَلَا تَخَفْ سَنُعِيدُهَا سِيرَتَهَا ٱلْأُولَىٰ (٢١) وَٱضْمُمْ يَدَكَ إِلَىٰ جَنَاحِكَ تَخْرُجْ بَيْضَآءَ مِنْ غَيْرِ سُوٓءٍ ءَايَةً أُخْرَىٰ (٢٢) لِنُرِيَكَ مِنْ ءَايَٰتِنَا ٱلْكُبْرَى (٢٣) ٱذْهَبْ إِلَىٰ فِرْعَوْنَ إِنَّهُۥ طَغَىٰ (٢٤)

"And what is that in your right hand, O Mûsa (Moses)?" (17) *He said: "This is my stick, whereon I lean, and wherewith I beat down branches for my sheep, and wherein I find other uses."* (18) *(Allâh) said: "Cast it down, O Mûsa (Moses)!"* (19) *He cast it down, and behold! It was a snake, moving quickly.* (20) *Allâh said:" Grasp it, and fear not, We shall return it to its former state,* (21) *"And press your (right) hand to your (left) side, it will come forth white (and shining), without any disease as another sign, —* (22) *"That We may show you (some) of Our Greater Signs,* (23) *"Go to Fir'aun (Pharaoh)! Verily, he has transgressed (all bounds in disbelief and*

disobedience, and has behaved as an arrogant, and as a tyrant)." (24)

Quran 20:83-85

۞ وَمَآ أَعْجَلَكَ عَن قَوْمِكَ يَٰمُوسَىٰ (٨٣) قَالَ هُمْ أُوْلَآءِ عَلَىٰٓ أَثَرِى وَعَجِلْتُ إِلَيْكَ رَبِّ لِتَرْضَىٰ (٨٤) قَالَ فَإِنَّا قَدْ فَتَنَّا قَوْمَكَ مِنۢ بَعْدِكَ وَأَضَلَّهُمُ ٱلسَّامِرِىُّ (٨٥)

"And what made you hasten from your people, O Mûsa (Moses)?" (83) *He said: "They are close on my footsteps, and I hastened to You, O my Lord, that You might be pleased." (84) (Allâh) said: "Verily! we have tried your people in your absence, and As-Samiri has led them astray." (85)*

Quran 20:89-90

أَفَلَا يَرَوْنَ أَلَّا يَرْجِعُ إِلَيْهِمْ قَوْلاً وَلَا يَمْلِكُ لَهُمْ ضَرًّا وَلَا نَفْعًا (٨٩) وَلَقَدْ قَالَ لَهُمْ هَٰرُونُ مِن قَبْلُ يَٰقَوْمِ إِنَّمَا فُتِنتُم بِهِۦ وَإِنَّ رَبَّكُمُ ٱلرَّحْمَٰنُ فَٱتَّبِعُونِى وَأَطِيعُوٓاْ أَمْرِى (٩٠)

Did they not see that it could not return them a word (for answer), and that it had no power either to harm them or to do them good? (89) *And Hârûn (Aaron) indeed had said to them beforehand: "O my people! You are being tried in this, and verily, your Lord is (Allâh) the Most Gracious, so follow me and obey my order." (90)*

Quran 21:10-11

لَقَدْ أَنزَلْنَا إِلَيْكُمْ كِتَـٰبًا فِيهِ ذِكْرُكُمْ أَفَلَا تَعْقِلُونَ (١٠) وَكَمْ قَصَمْنَا مِن قَرْيَةٍ كَانَتْ ظَالِمَةً وَأَنشَأْنَا بَعْدَهَا قَوْمًا ءَاخَرِينَ (١١)

Indeed, We have sent down for you (O mankind) a Book, (the Qur'ân) in which there is Dhikrukum, (your Reminder or an honour for you i.e. honour for the one who follows the teaching of the Qur'ân and acts on its teachings). **Will you not then understand? (10) How many a town (community), given to wrong-doing, have We destroyed, and raised up after them another people?! (11)**

Quran 21:21

أَمِ ٱتَّخَذُوٓاْ ءَالِهَةً مِّنَ ٱلْأَرْضِ هُمْ يُنشِرُونَ (٢١)

Or have they taken (for worship) âlihah (gods) from the earth who raise the dead? (21)

Quran 21:24

أَمِ ٱتَّخَذُوٓاْ مِن دُونِهِۦٓ ءَالِهَةً قُلْ هَاتُواْ بُرْهَـٰنَكُمْ هَـٰذَا ذِكْرُ مَن مَّعِىَ وَذِكْرُ مَن قَبْلِى بَلْ أَكْثَرُهُمْ لَا يَعْلَمُونَ ٱلْحَقَّ فَهُم مُّعْرِضُونَ (٢٤)

Or have they taken for worship (other) âlihah (gods) besides Him? Say: "Bring your proof:" This (the Qur'ân) is the Reminder for those with me and the Reminder for those before me. But most of them know not the Truth, so they are averse. (24)

Quran 21:30

أَوَلَمْ يَرَ ٱلَّذِينَ كَفَرُوٓاْ أَنَّ ٱلسَّمَـٰوَٰتِ وَٱلْأَرْضَ كَانَتَا رَتْقًا فَفَتَقْنَـٰهُمَا وَجَعَلْنَا مِنَ ٱلْمَآءِ كُلَّ شَىْءٍ حَىٍّ أَفَلَا يُؤْمِنُونَ (٣٠)

Have not those who disbelieve known that the heavens and the earth were

joined together as one united piece, then
We parted them? *And We have made from*
water every living thing. **Will they not**
then believe? *(30)*

Quran 21:34

وَمَا جَعَلْنَا لِبَشَرٍ مِّن قَبْلِكَ ٱلْخُلْدَ أَفَإِيْن مِّتَّ فَهُمُ ٱلْخَٰلِدُونَ
(٣٤)

And We granted not to any human being
immortality before you (Muhammad),
then if you die, would they live forever?
(34)

Quran 21:42-44

قُلْ مَن يَكْلَؤُكُم بِٱلَّيْلِ وَٱلنَّهَارِ مِنَ ٱلرَّحْمَٰنِ بَلْ هُمْ عَن
ذِكْرِ رَبِّهِم مُّعْرِضُونَ (٤٢) أَمْ لَهُمْ ءَالِهَةٌ تَمْنَعُهُم مِّن
دُونِنَآ لَا يَسْتَطِيعُونَ نَصْرَ أَنفُسِهِمْ وَلَا هُم مِّنَّا يُصْحَبُونَ
(٤٣) بَلْ مَتَّعْنَا هَٰؤُلَآءِ وَءَابَآءَهُمْ حَتَّىٰ طَالَ عَلَيْهِمُ ٱلْعُمُرُ
أَفَلَا يَرَوْنَ أَنَّا نَأْتِى ٱلْأَرْضَ نَنقُصُهَا مِنْ أَطْرَافِهَآ أَفَهُمُ
ٱلْغَٰلِبُونَ (٤٤)

*Say: "**Who can guard and protect you in**
the night or in the day from the
(punishment of the) Most Gracious*

(Allâh)?" Nay, but they turn away from the remembrance of their Lord. (42) **Or have they âlihah (gods) who can guard them from Us?** They have no power to help themselves, nor can they be protected from Us (i.e. from Our Torment). (43) Nay, We gave the luxuries of this life to these men and their fathers until the period grew long for them. **See they not that We gradually reduce the land (in their control) from its outlying borders?** Is it then they who will overcome. (44)

Quran 21:50

وَهَٰذَا ذِكْرٌ مُّبَارَكٌ أَنزَلْنَـٰهُ أَفَأَنتُمْ لَهُ ۥ مُنكِرُونَ (٥٠)

And this is a blessed Reminder (the Qur'ân) which We have sent down, will you then (dare to) deny it? (50)

Quran 21:79-80

فَفَهَّمْنَـٰهَا سُلَيْمَـٰنَ وَكُلاًّ ءَاتَيْنَا حُكْمًا وَعِلْمًا وَسَخَّرْنَا مَعَ دَاوُ ۥ دَ ٱلْجِبَالَ يُسَبِّحْنَ وَٱلطَّيْرَ وَكُنَّا فَـٰعِلِينَ (٧٩) وَعَلَّمْنَـٰهُ

صَنْعَةَ لَبُوسٍ لَّكُمْ لِتُحْصِنَكُم مِّنْ بَأْسِكُمْ فَهَلْ أَنتُمْ شَاكِرُونَ (٨٠)

And We made Sulaimân (Solomon) to
understand (the case), and to each of them
We gave Hukm (right judgement of the
affairs and Prophethood) and knowledge.
And We subjected the mountains and the
birds to glorify Our Praises along with
Dawûd (David), And it was We Who were
the doers (of all these things), (79) And We
taught him the making of metal coats of mail
(for battles), to protect you in your fighting.
Are you then grateful? (80)

Quran 21:108

قُلْ إِنَّمَا يُوحَىٰ إِلَيَّ أَنَّمَا إِلَـٰهُكُمْ إِلَـٰهٌ وَٰحِدٌ فَهَلْ أَنتُم مُّسْلِمُونَ (١٠٨)

Say (O Muhammad): "It is revealed to me
that your Ilâh (God) is only one Ilâh (God -
Allâh). ***Will you then submit to His Will***
(become Muslims and stop worshipping
others besides Allâh)?" *(108)*

Quran 22:18

أَلَمْ تَرَ أَنَّ ٱللَّهَ يَسْجُدُ لَهُ مَن فِى ٱلسَّمَٰوَٰتِ وَمَن فِى ٱلْأَرْضِ وَٱلشَّمْسُ وَٱلْقَمَرُ وَٱلنُّجُومُ وَٱلْجِبَالُ وَٱلشَّجَرُ وَٱلدَّوَآبُّ وَكَثِيرٌ مِّنَ ٱلنَّاسِ ۖ وَكَثِيرٌ حَقَّ عَلَيْهِ ٱلْعَذَابُ ۗ وَمَن يُهِنِ ٱللَّهُ فَمَا لَهُ مِن مُّكْرِمٍ ۚ إِنَّ ٱللَّهَ يَفْعَلُ مَا يَشَآءُ ۩ (١٨)

See you not that whoever is in the heavens and whoever is on the earth, and the sun, and the moon, and the stars, and the mountains, and the trees, and Ad-Dawâb moving (living creatures, beasts), and many of mankind prostrate themselves to Allah? But there are many (men) on whom the punishment is justified. And whomsoever Allâh disgraces, none can honour him. Verily! Allâh does what He wills. (18)

Quran 22:46

أَفَلَمْ يَسِيرُواْ فِى ٱلْأَرْضِ فَتَكُونَ لَهُمْ قُلُوبٌ يَعْقِلُونَ بِهَآ أَوْ ءَاذَانٌ يَسْمَعُونَ بِهَا ۖ فَإِنَّهَا لَا تَعْمَى ٱلْأَبْصَٰرُ وَلَٰكِن تَعْمَى ٱلْقُلُوبُ ٱلَّتِى فِى ٱلصُّدُورِ (٤٦)

*Have they not travelled through the
land, and have they hearts wherewith to
understand and ears wherewith to hear?*
*Verily, it is not the eyes that grow blind, but
it is the hearts which are in the breasts that
grow blind. (46)*

Quran 22:63

أَلَمْ تَرَ أَنَّ ٱللَّهَ أَنزَلَ مِنَ ٱلسَّمَاءِ مَاءً فَتُصْبِحُ ٱلْأَرْضُ
مُخْضَرَّةً إِنَّ ٱللَّهَ لَطِيفٌ خَبِيرٌ (٦٣)

*See you not that Allâh sends down
water (rain) from the sky, and then the
earth becomes green?* *Verily, Allâh is the
Most Kind and Courteous, Well-Acquainted
with all things. (63)*

Quran 22:5

أَلَمْ تَرَ أَنَّ ٱللَّهَ سَخَّرَ لَكُم مَّا فِى ٱلْأَرْضِ وَٱلْفُلْكَ تَجْرِى فِى
ٱلْبَحْرِ بِأَمْرِهِ وَيُمْسِكُ ٱلسَّمَاءَ أَن تَقَعَ عَلَى ٱلْأَرْضِ إِلَّا
بِإِذْنِهِ إِنَّ ٱللَّهَ بِٱلنَّاسِ لَرَءُوفٌ رَّحِيمٌ (٦٥)

*See you not that Allâh has subjected to
you (mankind) all that is on the earth,
and the ships that sail through the sea*

by His Command? He withholds the heaven from falling on the earth except by His Leave. Verily, Allâh is, for mankind, full of Kindness, Most Merciful. (65)

Quran 22:70

أَلَمْ تَعْلَمْ أَنَّ ٱللَّهَ يَعْلَمُ مَا فِى ٱلسَّمَآءِ وَٱلْأَرْضِ إِنَّ ذَٰلِكَ فِى كِتَٰبٍ إِنَّ ذَٰلِكَ عَلَى ٱللَّهِ يَسِيرٌ (٧٠)

Know you not that Allâh knows all that is in heaven and on earth? *Verily, it is (all) in the Book (Al-Lauh al-Mahfûz). Verily! that is easy for Allâh. (70)*

Quran 22:72

وَإِذَا تُتْلَىٰ عَلَيْهِمْ ءَايَٰتُنَا بَيِّنَٰتٍ تَعْرِفُ فِى وُجُوهِ ٱلَّذِينَ كَفَرُواْ ٱلْمُنكَرَ يَكَادُونَ يَسْطُونَ بِٱلَّذِينَ يَتْلُونَ عَلَيْهِمْ ءَايَٰتِنَا قُلْ أَفَأُنَبِّئُكُم بِشَرٍّ مِّن ذَٰلِكُمُ ٱلنَّارُ وَعَدَهَا ٱللَّهُ ٱلَّذِينَ كَفَرُواْ وَبِئْسَ ٱلْمَصِيرُ (٧٢)

*And when Our Clear Verses are recited to them, you will notice a denial on the faces of the disbelievers! They are nearly ready to attack with violence those who recite Our Verses to them. Say: "**Shall I tell you of*** *something worse than that?* The Fire (of Hell) which Allâh has promised to those who disbelieved, and worst indeed is that destination!" (72)

Quran 23:55-56

أَيَحْسَبُونَ أَنَّمَا نُمِدُّهُم بِهِۦ مِن مَّالٍ وَبَنِينَ (٥٥) نُسَارِعُ لَهُمْ فِى ٱلْخَيْرَٰتِ بَل لَّا يَشْعُرُونَ (٥٦)

Do they think that in wealth and children with which We enlarge them (55) We hasten unto them with good things? (Nay it is Fitnah (trail) in this worldly life so that they will have no share of good things in the Hereafter) but they perceive not. (56)

Quran 23:68-72

أَفَلَمْ يَدَّبَّرُواْ ٱلْقَوْلَ أَمْ جَاءَهُم مَّا لَمْ يَأْتِ ءَابَاءَهُمُ ٱلْأَوَّلِينَ (٦٨) أَمْ لَمْ يَعْرِفُواْ رَسُولَهُمْ فَهُمْ لَهُۥ مُنكِرُونَ (٦٩) أَمْ يَقُولُونَ بِهِۦ جِنَّةٌ بَلْ جَاءَهُم بِٱلْحَقِّ وَأَكْثَرُهُمْ لِلْحَقِّ كَٰرِهُونَ (٧٠) وَلَوِ ٱتَّبَعَ ٱلْحَقُّ أَهْوَاءَهُمْ لَفَسَدَتِ ٱلسَّمَٰوَٰتُ وَٱلْأَرْضُ وَمَن فِيهِنَّ بَلْ أَتَيْنَٰهُم بِذِكْرِهِمْ فَهُمْ عَن ذِكْرِهِم مُّعْرِضُونَ (٧١) أَمْ تَسْـَٔلُهُمْ خَرْجًا فَخَرَاجُ رَبِّكَ خَيْرٌ وَهُوَ خَيْرُ ٱلرَّٰزِقِينَ (٧٢)

Have they not pondered over the Word (of Allâh, i.e. what is sent down to the Prophet), or has there come to them what had not come to their fathers of old? (68) Or is it that they did not recognize their Messenger (Muhammad) so they deny him? (69) Or say they: "There is madness in him?" Nay, but he brought them the truth [i.e. "Tauhîd: Worshipping Allâh Alone in all aspects The Qur'ân and the religion of Islâm,"] but most of them (the disbelievers) are averse to the truth. (70) And if the truth had been in accordance with their desires, verily, the heavens and the earth, and whosoever is therein would have been corrupted! Nay, We have brought them their reminder, but they turn away from their reminder.

(71) *Or is it that you (Muhammad) ask them for some wages?* But the recompense of your Lord is better, and He is the Best of those who give sustenance. (72)

Quran 23:80-89

وَهُوَ ٱلَّذِى يُحۡىِۦ وَيُمِيتُ وَلَهُ ٱخۡتِلَٰفُ ٱلَّيۡلِ وَٱلنَّهَارِۚ أَفَلَا
تَعۡقِلُونَ (٨٠) بَلۡ قَالُواْ مِثۡلَ مَا قَالَ ٱلۡأَوَّلُونَ (٨١) قَالُوٓاْ
أَءِذَا مِتۡنَا وَكُنَّا تُرَابًا وَعِظَٰمًا أَءِنَّا لَمَبۡعُوثُونَ (٨٢) لَقَدۡ
وُعِدۡنَا نَحۡنُ وَءَابَآؤُنَا هَٰذَا مِن قَبۡلُ إِنۡ هَٰذَآ إِلَّآ أَسَٰطِيرُ
ٱلۡأَوَّلِينَ (٨٣) قُل لِّمَنِ ٱلۡأَرۡضُ وَمَن فِيهَآ إِن كُنتُمۡ تَعۡلَمُونَ
(٨٤) سَيَقُولُونَ لِلَّهِۚ قُلۡ أَفَلَا تَذَكَّرُونَ (٨٥) قُلۡ مَن رَّبُّ
ٱلسَّمَٰوَٰتِ ٱلسَّبۡعِ وَرَبُّ ٱلۡعَرۡشِ ٱلۡعَظِيمِ (٨٦) سَيَقُولُونَ لِلَّهِۚ
قُلۡ أَفَلَا تَتَّقُونَ (٨٧) قُلۡ مَنۢ بِيَدِهِۦ مَلَكُوتُ كُلِّ شَىۡءٍ وَهُوَ
يُجِيرُ وَلَا يُجَارُ عَلَيۡهِ إِن كُنتُمۡ تَعۡلَمُونَ (٨٨) سَيَقُولُونَ لِلَّهِۚ قُلۡ
فَأَنَّىٰ تُسۡحَرُونَ (٨٩)

And it is He Who gives life and causes
death, and His is the alternation of night
and day. **Will you not then understand?**
(80) Nay, but they say the like of what the
men of old said. (81) They said: "When we
are dead and have become dust and bones,
shall we be resurrected indeed? (82) "Verily,
this we have been promised, - we and our
fathers before (us)! This is only the tales of
the ancients!" (83) Say: "**Whose is the
earth and whosoever is therein? If you
know!**" (84) They will say: "It is Allâh's!"
Say: "**Will you not then remember?**"

(85) Say: "Who is (the) Lord of the seven heavens, and (the) Lord of the Great Throne?" (86) They will say: "Allâh." Say: "Will you not then fear Allâh (believe in His Oneness, obey Him, believe in the Resurrection and Recompense for every good or bad deed)?" (87) Say "In Whose Hand is the sovereignty of everything (i.e. treasures of each and everything)? And He protects (all), while against Whom there is no protector, if you know?" (88) They will say: "(All that belongs) to Allâh." Say: "How then are you deceived and turn away from the truth?" (89)

Quran 23:105

أَلَمْ تَكُنْ ءَايَـٰتِى تُتْلَىٰ عَلَيْكُمْ فَكُنتُم بِهَا تُكَذِّبُونَ (١٠٥)

"Were not My Verses (this Qur'ân) recited to you, and then you used to deny them?" (105)

Quran 23:112-115

قَلَ كَمْ لَبِثْتُمْ فِى ٱلْأَرْضِ عَدَدَ سِنِينَ (١١٢) قَالُوا۟ لَبِثْنَا
يَوْمًا أَوْ بَعْضَ يَوْمٍ فَسْـَٔلِ ٱلْعَآدِّينَ (١١٣) قَلَ إِن لَّبِثْتُمْ إِلَّا
قَلِيلًا ۖ لَّوْ أَنَّكُمْ كُنتُمْ تَعْلَمُونَ (١١٤) أَفَحَسِبْتُمْ أَنَّمَا خَلَقْنَـٰكُمْ
عَبَثًا وَأَنَّكُمْ إِلَيْنَا لَا تُرْجَعُونَ (١١٥)

He (Allâh) will say: **"What number of years did you stay on earth?"** (112) They will say: "We stayed a day or part of a day. Ask of those who keep account." (113) He (Allâh) will say: "You stayed not but a little, if you had only known! (114) **"Did you think that We had created you in play (without any purpose), and that you would not be brought back to Us?"** (115)

Quran 24:11-13

إِنَّ ٱلَّذِينَ جَآءُو بِٱلْإِفْكِ عُصْبَةٌ مِّنكُمْ ۚ لَا تَحْسَبُوهُ شَرًّا لَّكُم ۖ بَلْ
هُوَ خَيْرٌ لَّكُمْ ۚ لِكُلِّ ٱمْرِئٍ مِّنْهُم مَّا ٱكْتَسَبَ مِنَ ٱلْإِثْمِ ۚ وَٱلَّذِى
تَوَلَّىٰ كِبْرَهُۥ مِنْهُمْ لَهُۥ عَذَابٌ عَظِيمٌ (١١) لَّوْلَآ إِذْ سَمِعْتُمُوهُ
ظَنَّ ٱلْمُؤْمِنُونَ وَٱلْمُؤْمِنَـٰتُ بِأَنفُسِهِمْ خَيْرًا وَقَالُوا۟ هَـٰذَآ إِفْكٌ
مُّبِينٌ (١٢) لَّوْلَا جَآءُو عَلَيْهِ بِأَرْبَعَةِ شُهَدَآءَ ۚ فَإِذْ لَمْ يَأْتُوا۟
بِٱلشُّهَدَآءِ فَأُو۟لَـٰٓئِكَ عِندَ ٱللَّهِ هُمُ ٱلْكَـٰذِبُونَ (١٣)

Verily! those who brought forth the slander (against 'Aishah the wife of the Prophet) are a group among you. Consider it not a bad thing for you. Nay, it is good for you. Unto every man among them will be paid that which he had earned of the sin, and as for him among them who had the greater share therein, his will be a great torment.
(11) Why then, did not the believers, men and women, when you heard it (the slander) think good of their own people and say: "This (charge) is an obvious lie."? (12) Why did they not produce four witnesses? *Since they (the slanderers) have not produced witnesses! Then with Allâh they are the liars. (13)*

Quran 24:22

وَلَا يَأْتَلِ أُوْلُواْ ٱلْفَضْلِ مِنكُمْ وَٱلسَّعَةِ أَن يُؤْتُواْ أُوْلِى ٱلْقُرْبَىٰ وَٱلْمَسَٰكِينَ وَٱلْمُهَٰجِرِينَ فِى سَبِيلِ ٱللَّهِ وَلْيَعْفُواْ وَلْيَصْفَحُواْ أَلَا تُحِبُّونَ أَن يَغْفِرَ ٱللَّهُ لَكُمْ وَٱللَّهُ غَفُورٌ رَّحِيمٌ (٢٢)

And let not those among you who are blessed with graces and wealth swear not to give (any sort of help) to their kinsmen, Al-Masâkîn (the poor), and those who left their homes for Allâh's Cause. Let them pardon and forgive. **Do you not love that Allâh should forgive you?** And Allâh is Oft-Forgiving, Most Merciful. (22)

Quran 24:41

أَلَمْ تَرَ أَنَّ ٱللَّهَ يُسَبِّحُ لَهُ ۥ مَن فِى ٱلسَّمَـٰوَٰتِ وَٱلْأَرْضِ وَٱلطَّيْرُ صَـٰٓفَّـٰتٍ ۖ كُلٌّ قَدْ عَلِمَ صَلَاتَهُ ۥ وَتَسْبِيحَهُ ۥ ۗ وَٱللَّهُ عَلِيمٌ بِمَا يَفْعَلُونَ (٤١)

See you not that Allâh, He it is Whom glorify whosoever is in the heavens and the earth, and the birds with wings outspread (in their flight)? Of each one He (Allâh) knows indeed his Salât (prayer) and his glorification, [or everyone knows his Salât (prayer) and his glorification], and Allâh is All-Aware of what they do. (41)

Quran 24:50

أَفِى قُلُوبِهِم مَّرَضٌ أَمِ ٱرْتَابُوٓاْ أَمْ يَخَافُونَ أَن يَحِيفَ ٱللَّهُ عَلَيْهِمْ وَرَسُولُهُ ۚ بَلْ أُوْلَـٰٓئِكَ هُمُ ٱلظَّـٰلِمُونَ (٥٠)

Is there a disease in their hearts? Or do they doubt or fear lest Allâh and His Messenger should wrong them in judgement. Nay, it is they themselves who are the Zâlimûn (polytheists, hypocrites and wrong-doers). (50)

Quran 25:15

قُلْ أَذَٰلِكَ خَيْرٌ أَمْ جَنَّةُ ٱلْخُلْدِ ٱلَّتِى وُعِدَ ٱلْمُتَّقُونَ كَانَتْ لَهُمْ جَزَآءً وَمَصِيرًا (١٥)

Say: (O Muhammad) "Is that (torment) better or the Paradise of Eternity which is promised to the Muttaqûn (pious and righteous persons)?" It will be theirs as a reward and as a final destination. (15)

Quran 25:17-20

وَيَوْمَ يَحْشُرُهُمْ وَمَا يَعْبُدُونَ مِن دُونِ ٱللَّهِ فَيَقُولُ ءَأَنتُمْ أَضْلَلْتُمْ عِبَادِى هَٰؤُلَآءِ أَمْ هُمْ ضَلُّواْ ٱلسَّبِيلَ (١٧) قَالُواْ سُبْحَٰنَكَ مَا كَانَ يَنۢبَغِى لَنَآ أَن نَّتَّخِذَ مِن دُونِكَ مِنْ أَوْلِيَآءَ وَلَٰكِن مَّتَّعْتَهُمْ وَءَابَآءَهُمْ حَتَّىٰ نَسُواْ ٱلذِّكْرَ وَكَانُواْ قَوْمًۢا بُورًا (١٨) فَقَدْ كَذَّبُوكُم بِمَا تَقُولُونَ فَمَا تَسْتَطِيعُونَ صَرْفًا وَلَا نَصْرًا وَمَن يَظْلِم مِّنكُمْ نُذِقْهُ عَذَابًا كَبِيرًا (١٩) وَمَآ أَرْسَلْنَا قَبْلَكَ مِنَ ٱلْمُرْسَلِينَ إِلَّآ إِنَّهُمْ لَيَأْكُلُونَ ٱلطَّعَامَ وَيَمْشُونَ

فِى ٱلْأَسْوَاقِ وَجَعَلْنَا بَعْضَكُمْ لِبَعْضٍ فِتْنَةً أَتَصْبِرُونَ وَكَانَ رَبُّكَ بَصِيرًا (٢٠)

*And on the Day when He will gather them together and that which they worship besides Allâh [idols, angels, pious men, saints, 'Īsā (Jesus) son of Maryam (Mary), etc.]. He will say: "**Was it you who misled these My slaves or did they (themselves) stray from the (Right) Path?**" (17) They will say: "Glorified are You! It was not for us to take any Auliyâ' (Protectors, Helpers) besides You, but You gave them and their fathers comfort till they forgot the warning, and became a lost people (doomed to total loss). (18) Thus they (false gods — all deities other than Allâh) will belie you (polytheists) regarding what you say (that they are gods besides Allâh), then you can neither avert (the punishment), nor get help. And whoever among you does wrong (i.e. sets up rivals to Allâh), We shall make him taste a great torment. (19) And We never sent before you (O Muhammad) any* of the Messengers but verily, they ate food and walked in the markets. And We have made some of you as a trial for others: *will you have patience?* And your Lord is Ever All-Seer (of everything). (20)

Quran 25:43-44

أَرَءَيْتَ مَنِ ٱتَّخَذَ إِلَـٰهَهُ هَوَىٰهُ أَفَأَنتَ تَكُونُ عَلَيْهِ وَكِيلاً (٤٣) أَمْ تَحْسَبُ أَنَّ أَكْثَرَهُمْ يَسْمَعُونَ أَوْ يَعْقِلُونَ إِنْ هُمْ إِلَّا كَٱلْأَنْعَـٰمِ بَلْ هُمْ أَضَلُّ سَبِيلاً (٤٤)

Have you seen him who has taken as his ilâh (god) his own vain desire? Would you then be a Wakîl (a disposer of his affairs or a watcher) over him? (43) Or do you think that most of them hear or understand? They are only like cattle; nay, — they are even farther astray from the Path. (i.e. even worst than cattle). (44)

Quran 25:60

وَإِذَا قِيلَ لَهُمُ ٱسْجُدُواْ لِلرَّحْمَـٰنِ قَالُواْ وَمَا ٱلرَّحْمَـٰنُ أَنَسْجُدُ لِمَا تَأْمُرُنَا وَزَادَهُمْ نُفُورًا ۩ (٦٠)

And when it is said to them: "Prostrate yourserves to the Most Gracious (Allâh)! they say: **"And what is the Most Gracious? Shall we fall down in prostration to that which you (O Muhammad) command us?"** *And it increases in them only aversion.* (60)

Quran 26:7-8

أَوَلَمْ يَرَوْاْ إِلَى ٱلْأَرْضِ كَمْ أَنۢبَتْنَا فِيهَا مِن كُلِّ زَوْجٍ كَرِيمٍ (٧) إِنَّ فِى ذَٰلِكَ لَأَيَةًۖ وَمَا كَانَ أَكْثَرُهُم مُّؤْمِنِينَ (٨)

Do they not observe the earth, — how much of every good kind We cause to grow therein? *(7) Verily, in this is an Ayâh (proof or sign), yet most of them (polytheists, pagans, who do not believe in Resurrection) are not believers.* (8)

Quran 26:91-95

وَبُرِّزَتِ ٱلْجَحِيمُ لِلْغَاوِينَ (٩١) وَقِيلَ لَهُمْ أَيْنَ مَا كُنتُمْ تَعْبُدُونَ (٩٢) مِن دُونِ ٱللَّهِ هَلْ يَنصُرُونَكُمْ أَوْ يَنتَصِرُونَ (٩٣) فَكُبْكِبُواْ فِيهَا هُمْ وَٱلْغَاوُ ۫نَ (٩٤) وَجُنُودُ إِبْلِيسَ أَجْمَعُونَ (٩٥)

And the (Hell) Fire will be placed in full
view of the erring. (91) And it will be said to
them: "**Where are those (the false gods
whom you used to set up as rivals with
Allâh) that you used to worship,
(92) "Instead of Allâh? Can they help
you or (even) help themselves?"**
(93) Then they will be thrown on their faces
into the (Fire), They and the Ghâwûn
(devils, and those who were in error).
(94) And the whole hosts of Iblîs (Satan)
together. (95)

Quran 26:192-197

وَإِنَّهُ ٗ لَتَنزِيلُ رَبِّ ٱلْعَٰلَمِينَ (١٩٢) نَزَلَ بِهِ ٱلرُّوحُ ٱلْأَمِينُ
(١٩٣) عَلَىٰ قَلْبِكَ لِتَكُونَ مِنَ ٱلْمُنذِرِينَ (١٩٤) بِلِسَانٍ
عَرَبِىٍّ مُّبِينٍ (١٩٥) وَإِنَّهُ ٗ لَفِى زُبُرِ ٱلْأَوَّلِينَ (١٩٦) أَوَلَمْ
يَكُن لَّهُمْ ءَايَةً أَن يَعْلَمَهُ ٗ عُلَمَٰٓؤُاْ بَنِىٓ إِسْرَٰٓءِيلَ (١٩٧)

And truly, this (the Qur'ân) is a revelation
from the Lord of the 'Alamîn (mankind, jinn
and all that exists), (192) Which the
trustworthy Rûh [Jibril (Gabriel)] has
brought down; (193) Upon your heart (O

Muhammad) that you may be (one) of the warners, (194) In the plain Arabic language. (195) And verily, it (the Qur'ân, and its revelation to Prophet Muhammad) is (announced) in the Scriptures [i.e. the Taurât (Torah) and the Injeel] of former people. (196) **Is it not a sign to them that the learned scholars (like 'Abdullâh bin Salâm who embraced Islâm) of the Children of Israel knew it (as true)? (197)**

Quran 26:221-227

هَلْ أُنَبِّئُكُمْ عَلَىٰ مَن تَنَزَّلُ ٱلشَّيَـٰطِينُ (٢٢١) تَنَزَّلُ عَلَىٰ كُلِّ أَفَّاكٍ أَثِيمٍ (٢٢٢) يُلْقُونَ ٱلسَّمْعَ وَأَكْثَرُهُمْ كَـٰذِبُونَ (٢٢٣) وَٱلشُّعَرَآءُ يَتَّبِعُهُمُ ٱلْغَاوُۥنَ (٢٢٤) أَلَمْ تَرَ أَنَّهُمْ فِى كُلِّ وَادٍ يَهِيمُونَ (٢٢٥) وَأَنَّهُمْ يَقُولُونَ مَا لَا يَفْعَلُونَ (٢٢٦) إِلَّا ٱلَّذِينَ ءَامَنُوا۟ وَعَمِلُوا۟ ٱلصَّـٰلِحَـٰتِ وَذَكَرُوا۟ ٱللَّهَ كَثِيرًا وَٱنتَصَرُوا۟ مِنۢ بَعْدِ مَا ظُلِمُوا۟ ۗ وَسَيَعْلَمُ ٱلَّذِينَ ظَلَمُوٓا۟ أَىَّ مُنقَلَبٍ يَنقَلِبُونَ (٢٢٧)

Shall I inform you (O people!) upon whom the Shayâtin (devils) descend? (221) They descend on every lying, sinful

person. (222) *Who gives ear (to the devils
and they pour what they may have heard of
the unseen from the angels), and most of
them are liars. (223)* **As for the poets, the
erring ones follow them, (224) See you
not that they speak about every subject
in their poetry?** *(225) And that they say
what they do not do. (226) Except those who
believe (in the Oneness of Allâh — Islâmic
Monotheism), and do righteous deeds, and
remember Allâh much and vindicate
themselves after they have been wronged [by
replying back in the poetry to the unjust
poetry (which the pagan poets utter against
the Muslims)]. And those who do wrong
will come to know by what overturning they
will be overturned. (227)*

Quran 27:59-64

قُلِ ٱلْحَمْدُ لِلَّهِ وَسَلَـٰمٌ عَلَىٰ عِبَادِهِ ٱلَّذِينَ ٱصْطَفَىٰٓ ءَآللَّهُ خَيْرٌ أَمَّا
يُشْرِكُونَ (٥٩) أَمَّنْ خَلَقَ ٱلسَّمَـٰوَٰتِ وَٱلْأَرْضَ وَأَنزَلَ لَكُم
مِّنَ ٱلسَّمَآءِ مَآءً فَأَنۢبَتْنَا بِهِۦ حَدَآئِقَ ذَاتَ بَهْجَةٍ مَّا كَانَ لَكُمْ
أَن تُنۢبِتُواْ شَجَرَهَآ أَءِلَـٰهٌ مَّعَ ٱللَّهِ بَلْ هُمْ قَوْمٌ يَعْدِلُونَ
(٦٠) أَمَّن جَعَلَ ٱلْأَرْضَ قَرَارًا وَجَعَلَ خِلَـٰلَهَآ أَنْهَـٰرًا وَجَعَلَ

لَهَا رَوَاسِيَ وَجَعَلَ بَيْنَ ٱلْبَحْرَيْنِ حَاجِزًا ۗ أَءِلَٰهٌ مَّعَ ٱللَّهِ ۚ بَلْ أَكْثَرُهُمْ لَا يَعْلَمُونَ (٦١) أَمَّن يُجِيبُ ٱلْمُضْطَرَّ إِذَا دَعَاهُ وَيَكْشِفُ ٱلسُّوءَ وَيَجْعَلُكُمْ خُلَفَاءَ ٱلْأَرْضِ ۗ أَءِلَٰهٌ مَّعَ ٱللَّهِ ۚ قَلِيلًا مَّا تَذَكَّرُونَ (٦٢) أَمَّن يَهْدِيكُمْ فِى ظُلُمَٰتِ ٱلْبَرِّ وَٱلْبَحْرِ وَمَن يُرْسِلُ ٱلرِّيَٰحَ بُشْرًا بَيْنَ يَدَىْ رَحْمَتِهِ ۗ أَءِلَٰهٌ مَّعَ ٱللَّهِ ۚ تَعَٰلَى ٱللَّهُ عَمَّا يُشْرِكُونَ (٦٣) أَمَّن يَبْدَؤُاْ ٱلْخَلْقَ ثُمَّ يُعِيدُهُ وَمَن يَرْزُقُكُم مِّنَ ٱلسَّمَاءِ وَٱلْأَرْضِ ۗ أَءِلَٰهٌ مَّعَ ٱللَّهِ ۚ قُلْ هَاتُواْ بُرْهَٰنَكُمْ إِن كُنتُمْ صَٰدِقِينَ (٦٤)

Say (O Muhammad): "Praise and thanks are to Allâh, and peace be on His slaves whom He has chosen (for His Message)! **Is Allâh better, or (all) that you ascribe as partners (to Him)?**" (Of course, Allâh is Better). (59) **Is not He (better than your gods) Who created the heavens and the earth, and sends down for you water (rain) from the sky, whereby We cause to grow wonderful gardens full of beauty and delight?** It is not in your ability to cause the growth of their trees. **Is there any ilâh (god) with Allâh?** Nay, but they are a people who ascribe equals (to Him)! (60) **Is not He (better than your** *gods) Who has made the earth as a fixed abode, and has placed rivers in its midst, and has placed firm mountains therein, and has set a barrier between the two seas (of salt and sweet water)? Is there any ilâh (god) with Allâh?* Nay, but most of them know not! (61) *Is not He (better than your gods) Who responds to the distressed one, when he calls on Him, and Who removes the evil, and makes you inheritors of the earth, generations after generations? Is there any ilâh (god) with Allâh?* Little is that you remember! (62) *Is not He (better than your gods) Who guides you in the darkness of the land and the sea, and Who sends the winds as heralds of glad tidings, going before His Mercy (rain)? Is there any ilâh (god) with Allâh?* High Exalted is Allâh above all that they associate as partners (to Him)! (63) *Is not He (better than your so-called gods) Who originates creation, and shall thereafter*

repeat it, and Who provides for you
from heaven and earth? Is there any ilâh
(god) with Allâh? Say, "Bring forth your
proofs, if you are truthful." (64)

Quran 27:83-86

وَيَوْمَ نَحْشُرُ مِن كُلِّ أُمَّةٍ فَوْجًا مِّمَّن يُكَذِّبُ بِـَٔايَـٰتِنَا فَهُمْ
يُوزَعُونَ (٨٣) حَتَّىٰٓ إِذَا جَآءُو قَالَ أَكَذَّبْتُم بِـَٔايَـٰتِى وَلَمْ
تُحِيطُوا بِهَا عِلْمًا أَمَّاذَا كُنتُمْ تَعْمَلُونَ (٨٤) وَوَقَعَ ٱلْقَوْلُ
عَلَيْهِم بِمَا ظَلَمُوا فَهُمْ لَا يَنطِقُونَ (٨٥) أَلَمْ يَرَوْا أَنَّا جَعَلْنَا
ٱلَّيْلَ لِيَسْكُنُوا فِيهِ وَٱلنَّهَارَ مُبْصِرًا إِنَّ فِى ذَٰلِكَ لَأَيَـٰتٍ لِّقَوْمٍ
يُؤْمِنُونَ (٨٦)

And (remember) the Day when We shall
gather out of every nation a troop of those
who denied Our Ayât (proofs, evidences,
verses, lessons, signs, revelations, etc.), and
(then) they (all) shall be set in array
(gathered and driven to the place of
reckoning), (83) Till, when they come (before
their Lord at the place of reckoning), He will
*say: "**Did you deny My Ayât (proofs,***
evidences, verses, lessons, signs,
revelations, etc.) where as you

comprehended them not by knowledge (of their truth or falsehood), or what (else) was it that you used to do?" (84) *And the Word (of torment) will be fulfilled against them, because they have done wrong, and they will be unable to speak (in order to defend themselves).* (85) **See they not that We have made the night for them to rest therein, and the day sight-giving?** *Verily, in this are Ayât (proofs, evidences, verses, lessons, signs, revelations, etc.) for the people who believe.* (86)

Quran 27:89-90

مَن جَآءَ بِٱلۡحَسَنَةِ فَلَهُۥ خَيۡرٌ مِّنۡهَا وَهُم مِّن فَزَعٍ يَوۡمَئِذٍ ءَامِنُونَ (٨٩) وَمَن جَآءَ بِٱلسَّيِّئَةِ فَكُبَّتۡ وُجُوهُهُمۡ فِى ٱلنَّارِ هَلۡ تُجۡزَوۡنَ إِلَّا مَا كُنتُمۡ تَعۡمَلُونَ (٩٠)

Whoever brings a good deed (i.e. Belief in the Oneness of Allâh along with every deed of righteousness), will have better than its worth, and they will be safe from the terror on that Day. (89) And whoever brings an

evil deed (i.e. Shirk — polytheism, disbelief
in the Oneness of Allâh and every evil sinful
deed), they will be cast down (prone) on
their faces in the Fire. (And it will be said to
them) "**Are you being recompensed
anything except what you used to do?**"
(90)

Quran 28:47-50

وَلَوْلَآ أَن تُصِيبَهُم مُّصِيبَةٌۢ بِمَا قَدَّمَتْ أَيْدِيهِمْ فَيَقُولُواْ رَبَّنَا
لَوْلَآ أَرْسَلْتَ إِلَيْنَا رَسُولاً فَنَتَّبِعَ ءَايَـٰتِكَ وَنَكُونَ مِنَ ٱلْمُؤْمِنِينَ
(٤٧) فَلَمَّا جَآءَهُمُ ٱلْحَقُّ مِنْ عِندِنَا قَالُواْ لَوْلَآ أُوتِىَ مِثْلَ مَآ
أُوتِىَ مُوسَىٰٓ أَوَلَمْ يَكْفُرُواْ بِمَآ أُوتِىَ مُوسَىٰ مِن قَبْلُ قَالُواْ
سِحْرَانِ تَظَـٰهَرَا وَقَالُوٓاْ إِنَّا بِكُلٍّ كَـٰفِرُونَ (٤٨) قُلْ فَأْتُواْ
بِكِتَـٰبٍ مِّنْ عِندِ ٱللَّهِ هُوَ أَهْدَىٰ مِنْهُمَآ أَتَّبِعْهُ إِن كُنتُمْ صَـٰدِقِينَ
(٤٩) فَإِن لَّمْ يَسْتَجِيبُواْ لَكَ فَٱعْلَمْ أَنَّمَا يَتَّبِعُونَ أَهْوَآءَهُمْۚ وَمَنْ
أَضَلُّ مِمَّنِ ٱتَّبَعَ هَوَىٰهُ بِغَيْرِ هُدًى مِّنَ ٱللَّهِۚ إِنَّ ٱللَّهَ لَا يَهْدِى
ٱلْقَوْمَ ٱلظَّـٰلِمِينَ (٥٠)

And if (We had) not (sent you to the people
of Makkah) - in case a calamity should seize
them for (the deeds) that their hands have
sent forth, they would have said: "Our Lord!
Why did You not send us a Messenger? We

would then have followed Your Ayât (Verses of the Qur'ân) and would have been among the believers." (47) But when the truth (i.e. Muhammad with his Message) has come to them from Us, they say: "Why is he not given the like of what was given to Mûsa (Moses)? **Did they not disbelieve in that which was given to Mûsa (Moses) of old?** *They say: "Two kinds of magic [the Taurât (Torah) and the Qur'ân] each helping the other!" And they say: "Verily! In both we are disbelievers." (48) Say (to them, O Muhammad): "Then bring a Book from Allâh, which is a better guide than these two [the Taurât (Torah) and the Qur'ân], that I may follow it, if you are truthful." (49) But if they answer you not (i.e. do not bring the book nor believe in your doctrine of Islâmic Monotheism), then know that they only follow their own lusts.* **And who is more astray than one who follows his own lusts, without guidance from Allâh?** *Verily! Allâh guides not the*

people who are Zâlimûn (wrong-doers,
disobedient to Allâh, and polytheists) (50)

Quran 28:60-67

وَمَآ أُوتِيتُم مِّن شَىْءٍ فَمَتَـٰعُ ٱلْحَيَوٰةِ ٱلدُّنْيَا وَزِينَتُهَاۚ وَمَا عِندَ
ٱللَّهِ خَيْرٌ وَأَبْقَىٰٓ أَفَلَا تَعْقِلُونَ (٦٠) أَفَمَن وَعَدْنَـٰهُ وَعْدًا حَسَنًا
فَهُوَ لَـٰقِيهِ كَمَن مَّتَّعْنَـٰهُ مَتَـٰعَ ٱلْحَيَوٰةِ ٱلدُّنْيَا ثُمَّ هُوَ يَوْمَ ٱلْقِيَـٰمَةِ
مِنَ ٱلْمُحْضَرِينَ (٦١) وَيَوْمَ يُنَادِيهِمْ فَيَقُولُ أَيْنَ شُرَكَآءِىَ
ٱلَّذِينَ كُنتُمْ تَزْعُمُونَ (٦٢) قَالَ ٱلَّذِينَ حَقَّ عَلَيْهِمُ ٱلْقَوْلُ رَبَّنَا
هَـٰٓؤُلَآءِ ٱلَّذِينَ أَغْوَيْنَآ أَغْوَيْنَـٰهُمْ كَمَا غَوَيْنَاۖ تَبَرَّأْنَآ إِلَيْكَۖ مَا
كَانُوٓا۟ إِيَّانَا يَعْبُدُونَ (٦٣) وَقِيلَ ٱدْعُوا۟ شُرَكَآءَكُمْ فَدَعَوْهُمْ فَلَمْ
يَسْتَجِيبُوا۟ لَهُمْ وَرَأَوُا۟ ٱلْعَذَابَۚ لَوْ أَنَّهُمْ كَانُوا۟ يَهْتَدُونَ
(٦٤) وَيَوْمَ يُنَادِيهِمْ فَيَقُولُ مَاذَآ أَجَبْتُمُ ٱلْمُرْسَلِينَ
(٦٥) فَعَمِيَتْ عَلَيْهِمُ ٱلْأَنۢبَآءُ يَوْمَئِذٍ فَهُمْ لَا يَتَسَآءَلُونَ
(٦٦) فَأَمَّا مَن تَابَ وَءَامَنَ وَعَمِلَ صَـٰلِحًا فَعَسَىٰٓ أَن يَكُونَ
مِنَ ٱلْمُفْلِحِينَ (٦٧)

And whatever you have been given is an
enjoyment of the life of (this) world and its
adornment, and that (Hereafter) which is
with Allâh is better and will remain forever.
*Have you then no sense? (60) Is he
whom We have promised an excellent
promise (Paradise), — which he will find
true, - like him whom We have made to*

enjoy the luxuries of the life of (this)
world, then on the Day of Resurrection,
he will be among those brought up (to
be punished in the Hell-fire)? (61) *And*
(remember) the Day when He will call to
*them, and say: "**Where are My (so-called)***
partners whom you used to assert?"
(62) Those about whom the Word will have
come true (to be punished) will say: "Our
Lord! These are they whom we led astray.
We led them astray, as we were astray
ourselves. We declare our innocence (from
them) before You. It was not us they
worshipped." (63) *And it will be said (to*
them): "Call upon your (so-called) partners
(of Allâh), and they will call upon them, but
they will give no answer to them, and they
will see the torment. (They will then wish) if
only they had been guided! (64) *And*
(remember) the Day (Allâh) will call to
*them, and say: "**What answer gave you to***
the Messengers?" (65) *Then the news of a*
good answer will be obscured to them on

that day, and they will not be able to ask one another. *(66) But as for him who repented (from polytheism and sins), believed (in the Oneness of Allâh, and in His Messenger), and did righteous deeds (in the life of this world), then he will be among those who are successful. (67)*

Quran 28:71-75

قُلْ أَرَءَيْتُمْ إِن جَعَلَ ٱللَّهُ عَلَيْكُمُ ٱلَّيْلَ سَرْمَدًا إِلَىٰ يَوْمِ ٱلْقِيَٰمَةِ مَنْ إِلَٰهٌ غَيْرُ ٱللَّهِ يَأْتِيكُم بِضِيَآءٍ أَفَلَا تَسْمَعُونَ (٧١) قُلْ أَرَءَيْتُمْ إِن جَعَلَ ٱللَّهُ عَلَيْكُمُ ٱلنَّهَارَ سَرْمَدًا إِلَىٰ يَوْمِ ٱلْقِيَٰمَةِ مَنْ إِلَٰهٌ غَيْرُ ٱللَّهِ يَأْتِيكُم بِلَيْلٍ تَسْكُنُونَ فِيهِ أَفَلَا تُبْصِرُونَ (٧٢) وَمِن رَّحْمَتِهِ جَعَلَ لَكُمُ ٱلَّيْلَ وَٱلنَّهَارَ لِتَسْكُنُواْ فِيهِ وَلِتَبْتَغُواْ مِن فَضْلِهِ وَلَعَلَّكُمْ تَشْكُرُونَ (٧٣) وَيَوْمَ يُنَادِيهِمْ فَيَقُولُ أَيْنَ شُرَكَآءِىَ ٱلَّذِينَ كُنتُمْ تَزْعُمُونَ (٧٤) وَنَزَعْنَا مِن كُلِّ أُمَّةٍ شَهِيدًا فَقُلْنَا هَاتُواْ بُرْهَٰنَكُمْ فَعَلِمُوٓاْ أَنَّ ٱلْحَقَّ لِلَّهِ وَضَلَّ عَنْهُم مَّا كَانُواْ يَفْتَرُونَ (٧٥)

Say: "Tell me! If Allâh made the night continuous for you till the Day of Resurrection, which ilâh (god) besides Allâh could bring you light? Will you not then hear?" (71) Say: "Tell me! If

Allâh made the day continuous for you till the Day of Resurrection, which ilâh (god) besides Allâh could bring you night wherein you rest? Will you not then see?" (72) *It is out of His Mercy that He has made for you the night and the day, that you may rest therein (i.e. during the night) and that you may seek of His Bounty (i.e. during the day), and in order that you may be grateful.* (73) *And (remember) the Day when He (your Lord — Allâh) will call to them (those who worshipped others along with Allâh), and will say: "**Where are My (so-called) partners, whom you used to assert?"*** (74) *And We shall take out from every nation a witness, and We shall say: "Bring your proof." Then they shall know that the truth is with Allâh (Alone), and the lies (false gods) which they invented will disappear from them.* (75)

Quran 28:78

قَالَ إِنَّمَا أُوتِيتُهُ عَلَىٰ عِلْمٍ عِندِيٓ أَوَلَمْ يَعْلَمْ أَنَّ ٱللَّهَ قَدْ أَهْلَكَ مِن قَبْلِهِۦ مِنَ ٱلْقُرُونِ مَنْ هُوَ أَشَدُّ مِنْهُ قُوَّةً وَأَكْثَرُ جَمْعًا وَلَا يُسْـَٔلُ عَن ذُنُوبِهِمُ ٱلْمُجْرِمُونَ (٧٨)

He said: "This has been given to me only because of knowledge I possess." **Did he not know that Allâh had destroyed before him generations, men who were stronger than him in might and greater in the amount (of riches) they had collected?** But the Mujrimûn (criminals, disbelievers, polytheists, sinners) will not be questioned of their sins (because Allâh knows them well, so they will be punished without being called to account). (78)

Quran 29:2-4

أَحَسِبَ ٱلنَّاسُ أَن يُتْرَكُوٓاْ أَن يَقُولُوٓاْ ءَامَنَّا وَهُمْ لَا يُفْتَنُونَ (٢) وَلَقَدْ فَتَنَّا ٱلَّذِينَ مِن قَبْلِهِمْ فَلَيَعْلَمَنَّ ٱللَّهُ ٱلَّذِينَ صَدَقُواْ وَلَيَعْلَمَنَّ ٱلْكَٰذِبِينَ (٣) أَمْ حَسِبَ ٱلَّذِينَ يَعْمَلُونَ ٱلسَّيِّـَٔاتِ أَن يَسْبِقُونَآ سَآءَ مَا يَحْكُمُونَ (٤)

Do people think that they will be left alone because they say: "We believe," and will not be tested? (2) And We indeed

tested those who were before them. And
Allâh will certainly make (it) known (the
truth of) those who are true, and will
certainly make (it) known (the falsehood of)
those who are liars, (although Allâh knows
all that before putting them to test). (3) **Or
think those who do evil deeds that they
can outstrip Us (i.e. escape Our
Punishment)?** Evil is that which they
judge! (4)

Quran 29:51

أَوَلَمْ يَكْفِهِمْ أَنَّا أَنزَلْنَا عَلَيْكَ ٱلْكِتَـٰبَ يُتْلَىٰ عَلَيْهِمْ إِنَّ فِى ذَٰلِكَ
لَرَحْمَةً وَذِكْرَىٰ لِقَوْمٍ يُؤْمِنُونَ (٥١)

**Is it not sufficient for them that We
have sent down to you the Book (the
Qur'ân) which is recited to them?** Verily,
herein is mercy and a reminder (or an
admonition) for a people who believe. (51)

Quran 29:61

وَلَئِن سَأَلْتَهُم مَّنْ خَلَقَ ٱلسَّمَـٰوَٰتِ وَٱلْأَرْضَ وَسَخَّرَ ٱلشَّمْسَ
وَٱلْقَمَرَ لَيَقُولُنَّ ٱللَّهُ فَأَنَّىٰ يُؤْفَكُونَ (٦١)

*And If you were to ask them: '***Who has created the heavens and the earth and subjected the sun and the moon?"** *They will surely reply: "Allâh."* **How then are they deviating (as polytheists and disbelievers)?** *(61)*

Quran 29:63

وَلَئِن سَأَلْتَهُم مَّن نَّزَّلَ مِنَ ٱلسَّمَآءِ مَآءً فَأَحْيَا بِهِ ٱلْأَرْضَ مِنْ بَعْدِ مَوْتِهَا لَيَقُولُنَّ ٱللَّهُ قُلِ ٱلْحَمْدُ لِلَّهِ بَلْ أَكْثَرُهُمْ لَا يَعْقِلُونَ (٦٣)

*And If you were to ask them: "***Who sends down water (rain) from the sky, and gives life therewith to the earth after its death?"** *they will surely reply: "Allâh." Say: "All the praises and thanks are to Allâh!" Nay! Most of them have no sense.* *(63)*

Quran 29:67-68

أَوَلَمْ يَرَوْاْ أَنَّا جَعَلْنَا حَرَمًا ءَامِنًا وَيُتَخَطَّفُ ٱلنَّاسُ مِنْ حَوْلِهِمْ أَفَبِٱلْبَـٰطِلِ يُؤْمِنُونَ وَبِنِعْمَةِ ٱللَّهِ يَكْفُرُونَ (٦٧) وَمَنْ أَظْلَمُ

مِمَّنِ ٱفْتَرَىٰ عَلَى ٱللَّهِ كَذِبًا أَوْ كَذَّبَ بِٱلْحَقِّ لَمَّا جَآءَهُ ۚ أَلَيْسَ فِى جَهَنَّمَ مَثْوًى لِّلْكَٰفِرِينَ (٦٨)

Have they not seen that We have made (Makkah) a secure sanctuary, while men are being snatched away from all around them? Then do they believe in Bâtil (falsehood - polytheism, idols and all deities other than Allâh), and deny (become ingrate for) the Graces of Allâh? (67) And who does more wrong than he who invents a lie against Allâh or denies the truth (Muhammad and his doctrine of Islâmic Monotheism and this Qur'ân), when it comes to him? Is there not a dwelling in Hell for disbelievers? (68)

Quran 30:8-9

أَوَلَمْ يَتَفَكَّرُوا۟ فِىٓ أَنفُسِهِم ۗ مَّا خَلَقَ ٱللَّهُ ٱلسَّمَٰوَٰتِ وَٱلْأَرْضَ وَمَا بَيْنَهُمَآ إِلَّا بِٱلْحَقِّ وَأَجَلٍ مُّسَمًّى ۗ وَإِنَّ كَثِيرًا مِّنَ ٱلنَّاسِ بِلِقَآىِٕ رَبِّهِمْ لَكَٰفِرُونَ (٨) أَوَلَمْ يَسِيرُوا۟ فِى ٱلْأَرْضِ فَيَنظُرُوا۟ كَيْفَ كَانَ عَٰقِبَةُ ٱلَّذِينَ مِن قَبْلِهِمْ ۚ كَانُوٓا۟ أَشَدَّ مِنْهُمْ قُوَّةً وَأَثَارُوا۟ ٱلْأَرْضَ وَعَمَرُوهَآ أَكْثَرَ مِمَّا عَمَرُوهَا وَجَآءَتْهُمْ

رُسُلُهُم بِٱلْبَيِّنَـٰتِ فَمَا كَانَ ٱللَّهُ لِيَظْلِمَهُمْ وَلَـٰكِن كَانُوٓاْ أَنفُسَهُمْ يَظْلِمُونَ (٩)

Do they not think deeply (in their ownselves) about themselves (how Allâh created them from nothing, and similarly He will resurrect them)? Allâh has created not the heavens and the earth, and all that is between them, except with truth and for an appointed term. And indeed many of mankind deny the Meeting with their Lord. (8) *Do they not travel in the land, and see what was the end of those before them?* They were superior to them in strength, and they tilled the earth and populated it in greater numbers than these (pagans) have done, and there came to them their Messengers with clear proofs. Surely, Allâh wronged them not, but they used to wrong themselves. (9)

Quran 30:28-29

ضَرَبَ لَكُم مَّثَلاً مِّنْ أَنفُسِكُمْ هَل لَّكُم مِّن مَّا مَلَكَتْ أَيْمَـٰنُكُم مِّن شُرَكَآءَ فِى مَا رَزَقْنَـٰكُمْ فَأَنتُمْ فِيهِ سَوَآءٌ تَخَافُونَهُمْ

كَخِيفَتِكُمْ أَنفُسَكُمْ ۚ كَذَٰلِكَ نُفَصِّلُ ٱلْأَيَٰتِ لِقَوْمٍ يَعْقِلُونَ
(٢٨) بَلِ ٱتَّبَعَ ٱلَّذِينَ ظَلَمُوٓا۟ أَهْوَآءَهُم بِغَيْرِ عِلْمٍ ۖ فَمَن يَهْدِى
مَنْ أَضَلَّ ٱللَّهُ ۖ وَمَا لَهُم مِّن نَّٰصِرِينَ (٢٩)

He sets forth for you a parable from your
ownselves, - **Do you have partners among
those whom your right hands possess
(i.e your slaves) to share as equals in
the wealth We have bestowed on you
Whom you fear as you fear each other?**
Thus do We explain the signs in detail to a
people who have sense. (28) Nay, but those
who do wrong follow their own lusts
without knowledge. **Then who will guide
him whom Allâh has sent astray?** And
for such there will be no helpers. (29)

Quran 30:40

ٱللَّهُ ٱلَّذِى خَلَقَكُمْ ثُمَّ رَزَقَكُمْ ثُمَّ يُمِيتُكُمْ ثُمَّ يُحْيِيكُمْ ۖ هَلْ مِن
شُرَكَآئِكُم مَّن يَفْعَلُ مِن ذَٰلِكُم مِّن شَىْءٍ ۚ سُبْحَٰنَهُۥ وَتَعَٰلَىٰ
عَمَّا يُشْرِكُونَ (٤٠)

Allâh is He Who created you, then provided
food for you, then will cause you to die, then
(again) He will give you life (on the Day of

Resurrection). *Is there any of your (so¬called) partners (of Allâh) that do anything of that ?* Glory is to Him! And Exalted is He above all that (evil) they associate (with Him). (40)

Quran 31:20-21

أَلَمْ تَرَوْاْ أَنَّ ٱللَّهَ سَخَّرَ لَكُم مَّا فِى ٱلسَّمَـٰوَٰتِ وَمَا فِى ٱلْأَرْضِ وَأَسْبَغَ عَلَيْكُمْ نِعَمَهُ ظَـٰهِرَةً وَبَاطِنَةً وَمِنَ ٱلنَّاسِ مَن يُجَـٰدِلُ فِى ٱللَّهِ بِغَيْرِ عِلْمٍ وَلَا هُدًى وَلَا كِتَـٰبٍ مُّنِيرٍ (٢٠) وَإِذَا قِيلَ لَهُمُ ٱتَّبِعُواْ مَآ أَنزَلَ ٱللَّهُ قَالُواْ بَلْ نَتَّبِعُ مَا وَجَدْنَا عَلَيْهِ ءَابَآءَنَآ أَوَلَوْ كَانَ ٱلشَّيْطَـٰنُ يَدْعُوهُمْ إِلَىٰ عَذَابِ ٱلسَّعِيرِ (٢١)

See you not that Allâh has subjected for you whatsoever is in the heavens and whatsoever is in the earth, and has completed and perfected His Graces upon you, (both) apparent (i.e Islâmic Monotheism, and the lawful pleasures of this world, including health, good looks, etc.) and hidden [i.e. One's Faith in Allâh knowledge, wisdom, guidance for doing righteous deeds, and also the pleasures and delights of the Hereafter in Paradise]? Yet of mankind is he who disputes about Allâh without knowledge or guidance or a Book giving light! (20) And when it is said to them: "Follow that which Allâh has sent down", they say: "Nay, we shall follow that which we found our fathers (following)." **(Would they do so) even if Shaitân (Satan) invites them to the torment of the Fire? (21)**

Quran 31:31

أَلَمۡ تَرَ أَنَّ ٱلۡفُلۡكَ تَجۡرِى فِى ٱلۡبَحۡرِ بِنِعۡمَتِ ٱللَّهِ لِيُرِيَكُم مِّنۡ ءَايَٰتِهِۦٓ إِنَّ فِى ذَٰلِكَ لَأَيَٰتٍ لِّكُلِّ صَبَّارٍ شَكُورٍ (٣١)

See you not that the ships sail through the sea by Allâh's Grace that He may show you of His Signs? *Verily, in this are signs for every patient, grateful (person). (31)*

Quran 32:4

ٱللَّهُ ٱلَّذِى خَلَقَ ٱلسَّمَٰوَٰتِ وَٱلۡأَرۡضَ وَمَا بَيۡنَهُمَا فِى سِتَّةِ أَيَّامٍ ثُمَّ ٱسۡتَوَىٰ عَلَى ٱلۡعَرۡشِۖ مَا لَكُم مِّن دُونِهِۦ مِن وَلِيٍّ وَلَا شَفِيعٍ أَفَلَا تَتَذَكَّرُونَ (٤)

Allâh it is He Who has created the heavens and the earth, and all that is between them in six Days. Then He rose over (Istawâ) the Throne (in a manner that suits His Majesty). You (mankind) have none, besides Him, as a Walî (protector or helper) or an intercessor. **Will you not then remember (or receive admonition)?** *(4)*

Quran 32:18

أَفَمَن كَانَ مُؤْمِنًا كَمَن كَانَ فَاسِقًا لَّا يَسْتَوُ ُنَ (١٨)

Is then he who is a believer like him who is Fâsiq (disbeliever and disobedient to Allâh)? Not equal are they (18)

Quran 32:22

وَمَنْ أَظْلَمُ مِمَّن ذُكِّرَ بِـَايَـٰتِ رَبِّهِۦ ثُمَّ أَعْرَضَ عَنْهَآ إِنَّا مِنَ ٱلْمُجْرِمِينَ مُنتَقِمُونَ (٢٢)

And who does more wrong than he who is reminded of the Ayât (proofs, evidences, verses, lessons, signs, revelations, etc.) of his Lord, then turns aside therefrom? Verily, We shall exact retribution from the Mujrimûn (criminals, disbelievers, polytheists, sinners, etc.) (22)

Quran 32:26-27

أَوَلَمْ يَهْدِ لَهُمْ كَمْ أَهْلَكْنَا مِن قَبْلِهِم مِّنَ ٱلْقُرُونِ يَمْشُونَ فِى مَسَٰكِنِهِمْ إِنَّ فِى ذَٰلِكَ لَءَايَٰتٍ أَفَلَا يَسْمَعُونَ (٢٦) أَوَلَمْ يَرَوْاْ أَنَّا نَسُوقُ ٱلْمَآءَ إِلَى ٱلْأَرْضِ ٱلْجُرُزِ فَنُخْرِجُ بِهِۦ زَرْعًا تَأْكُلُ مِنْهُ أَنْعَٰمُهُمْ وَأَنفُسُهُمْ أَفَلَا يُبْصِرُونَ (٢٧)

Is it not a guidance for them, how many generations We have destroyed before them in whose dwellings they do walk about? Verily, therein indeed are signs. Would they not then listen? (26) Have they not seen how We drive water to the dry land that has no any vegetation, and therewith bring forth crops providing food for their cattle and themselves? Will they not then see? (27)

Quran 33:17

قُلْ مَن ذَا ٱلَّذِى يَعْصِمُكُم مِّنَ ٱللَّهِ إِنْ أَرَادَ بِكُمْ سُوٓءًا أَوْ أَرَادَ بِكُمْ رَحْمَةً وَلَا يَجِدُونَ لَهُم مِّن دُونِ ٱللَّهِ وَلِيًّا وَلَا نَصِيرًا (١٧)

*Say: "**Who is he who can protect you from Allâh if He intends to harm you, or intends mercy on you?**" And they will not find, besides Allâh, for themselves any Walî (protector, supporter) or any helper. (17)*

Quran 33:63

يَسْـَٔلُكَ ٱلنَّاسُ عَنِ ٱلسَّاعَةِ قُلْ إِنَّمَا عِلْمُهَا عِندَ ٱللَّهِ وَمَا يُدْرِيكَ لَعَلَّ ٱلسَّاعَةَ تَكُونُ قَرِيبًا (٦٣)

*People ask you concerning the Hour, say: "The knowledge of it is with Allâh only. **What do you know?** It may be that the Hour is near!" (63)*

Quran 34:9

أَفَلَمْ يَرَوْاْ إِلَىٰ مَا بَيْنَ أَيْدِيهِمْ وَمَا خَلْفَهُم مِّنَ ٱلسَّمَآءِ وَٱلْأَرْضِ إِن نَّشَأْ نَخْسِفْ بِهِمُ ٱلْأَرْضَ أَوْ نُسْقِطْ عَلَيْهِمْ كِسَفًا مِّنَ ٱلسَّمَآءِ إِنَّ فِى ذَٰلِكَ لَآيَةً لِّكُلِّ عَبْدٍ مُّنِيبٍ (٩)

See they not what is before them and what is behind them, of the heaven and the earth? *If We will, We shall sink the earth with them, or cause a piece of the heaven to fall upon them. Verily, in this is a sign for every slave who truns to Allah in repentance (i.e. the one who believes in the Oneness of Allah and performs deeds of His obedience and always begs His Pardon). (9)*

Quran 34:24

۞ قُلْ مَن يَرْزُقُكُم مِّنَ ٱلسَّمَـٰوَٰتِ وَٱلْأَرْضِ قُلِ ٱللَّهُ وَإِنَّآ أَوْ إِيَّاكُمْ لَعَلَىٰ هُدًى أَوْ فِى ضَلَـٰلٍ مُّبِينٍ (٢٤)

Say (O Muhammad to polytheists, pagans) **"Who gives you provision from the heavens and the earth?"** *Say: "Allâh, And verily, (either) we or you are rightly guided or in plain error." (24)*

Quran 34:33

وَقَالَ ٱلَّذِينَ ٱسْتُضْعِفُوا۟ لِلَّذِينَ ٱسْتَكْبَرُوٓا۟ بَلْ مَكْرُ ٱلَّيْلِ وَٱلنَّهَارِ إِذْ تَأْمُرُونَنَآ أَن نَّكْفُرَ بِٱللَّهِ وَنَجْعَلَ لَهُۥٓ أَندَادًا وَأَسَرُّوا۟ ٱلنَّدَامَةَ لَمَّا رَأَوُا۟ ٱلْعَذَابَ وَجَعَلْنَا ٱلْأَغْلَـٰلَ فِىٓ أَعْنَاقِ ٱلَّذِينَ كَفَرُوا۟ هَلْ يُجْزَوْنَ إِلَّا مَا كَانُوا۟ يَعْمَلُونَ (٣٣)

*Those who were deemed weak will say to those who were arrogant: "Nay, but it was your plotting by night and day, when you ordered us to disbelieve in Allâh and set up rivals to Him!" And each of them (parties) will conceal their own regrets (for disobeying Allâh during this worldly life), when they behold the torment. And We shall put iron collars round the necks of those who disbelieved. **Are they requited aught except what they used to do?** (33)*

Quran 34:40-42

وَيَوْمَ يَحْشُرُهُمْ جَمِيعًا ثُمَّ يَقُولُ لِلْمَلَٰئِكَةِ أَهَٰٓؤُلَآءِ إِيَّاكُمْ كَانُوا۟ يَعْبُدُونَ (٤٠) قَالُوا۟ سُبْحَٰنَكَ أَنتَ وَلِيُّنَا مِن دُونِهِمۖ بَلْ كَانُوا۟ يَعْبُدُونَ ٱلْجِنَّ أَكْثَرُهُم بِهِم مُّؤْمِنُونَ (٤١) فَٱلْيَوْمَ لَا يَمْلِكُ بَعْضُكُمْ لِبَعْضٍ نَّفْعًا وَلَا ضَرًّا وَنَقُولُ لِلَّذِينَ ظَلَمُوا۟ ذُوقُوا۟ عَذَابَ ٱلنَّارِ ٱلَّتِى كُنتُم بِهَا تُكَذِّبُونَ (٤٢)

*And (remember) the Day when He will gather them all together, then He will say to the angels: "**Was it you that these people used to worship?**" (40) They (the angels) will say: "Glorified are You! You are our*

Walî (Lord) instead of them. Nay, but they used to worship the jinn; most of them were believers in them." (41) So Today (i.e. the Day of Resurrection), none of you can profit or harm one another. And We shall say to those who did wrong [i.e. worshipped others (like angels, jinn, prophets, saints, righteous persons) along with Allâh]: "Taste the torment of the Fire which you used to belie. (42)

Quran 35:3

يَٰٓأَيُّهَا ٱلنَّاسُ ٱذۡكُرُواْ نِعۡمَتَ ٱللَّهِ عَلَيۡكُمۡۚ هَلۡ مِنۡ خَٰلِقٍ غَيۡرُ ٱللَّهِ يَرۡزُقُكُم مِّنَ ٱلسَّمَآءِ وَٱلۡأَرۡضِۚ لَآ إِلَٰهَ إِلَّا هُوَۖ فَأَنَّىٰ تُؤۡفَكُونَ (٣)

O mankind! Remember the Grace of Allâh upon you! **Is there any creator other than Allâh who provides for you from the sky (rain) and the earth?** *Lâ ilâha illa Huwa (none has the right to be worshipped but He).* **How then are you turning away (from Him)?** *(3)*

Quran 35:8

أَفَمَن زُيِّنَ لَهُۥ سُوٓءُ عَمَلِهِۦ فَرَءَاهُ حَسَنًاۖ فَإِنَّ ٱللَّهَ يُضِلُّ مَن يَشَآءُ وَيَهْدِى مَن يَشَآءُۖ فَلَا تَذْهَبْ نَفْسُكَ عَلَيْهِمْ حَسَرَٰتٍۚ إِنَّ ٱللَّهَ عَلِيمٌۢ بِمَا يَصْنَعُونَ (٨)

Is he, then, to whom the evil of his deeds made fair¬seeming, so that he considers it as good (equal to one who is rightly guided)? Verily, Allâh sends astray whom He wills, and guides whom He wills. So destroy not yourself in sorrow for them. Truly, Allâh is the All¬Knower of what they do! (8)

Quran 35:37

وَهُمْ يَصْطَرِخُونَ فِيهَا رَبَّنَآ أَخْرِجْنَا نَعْمَلْ صَٰلِحًا غَيْرَ ٱلَّذِى كُنَّا نَعْمَلُۚ أَوَلَمْ نُعَمِّرْكُم مَّا يَتَذَكَّرُ فِيهِ مَن تَذَكَّرَ وَجَآءَكُمُ ٱلنَّذِيرُۖ فَذُوقُواْ فَمَا لِلظَّٰلِمِينَ مِن نَّصِيرٍ (٣٧)

*Therein they will cry: "Our Lord! Bring us out, we shall do righteous good deeds, not (the evil deeds) that we used to do." (Allâh will reply): "**Did We not give you lives long enough, so that whosoever would receive admonition, could receive it?** And the warner came to you. So taste you* *(the evil of your deeds). For the Zâlimûn (polytheists and wrong¬doers) there is no helper." (37)*

Quran 35:40

قُلْ أَرَءَيْتُمْ شُرَكَآءَكُمُ ٱلَّذِينَ تَدْعُونَ مِن دُونِ ٱللَّهِ أَرُونِى مَاذَا خَلَقُوا مِنَ ٱلْأَرْضِ أَمْ لَهُمْ شِرْكٌ فِى ٱلسَّمَٰوَٰتِ أَمْ ءَاتَيْنَٰهُمْ كِتَٰبًا فَهُمْ عَلَىٰ بَيِّنَتٍ مِّنْهُ بَلْ إِن يَعِدُ ٱلظَّٰلِمُونَ بَعْضُهُم بَعْضًا إِلَّا غُرُورًا ﴿٤٠﴾

Say (O Muhammad): "Tell me or inform me (what) do you think about your (so¬called) partner¬gods to whom you call upon besides Allâh? Show me, what they have created of the earth? Or have they any share in the heavens? Or have We given them a Book, so that they act on clear proof therefrom? *Nay, the Zâlimûn (polytheists and wrong¬doers) promise one another nothing but delusions."* *(40)*

Quran 35:43-44

ٱسْتِكْبَارًا فِى ٱلْأَرْضِ وَمَكْرَ ٱلسَّيِّئِ وَلَا يَحِيقُ ٱلْمَكْرُ ٱلسَّيِّئُ
إِلَّا بِأَهْلِهِۦ فَهَلْ يَنظُرُونَ إِلَّا سُنَّتَ ٱلْأَوَّلِينَ فَلَن تَجِدَ لِسُنَّتِ
ٱللَّهِ تَبْدِيلًا وَلَن تَجِدَ لِسُنَّتِ ٱللَّهِ تَحْوِيلًا (٤٣) أَوَلَمْ يَسِيرُواْ
فِى ٱلْأَرْضِ فَيَنظُرُواْ كَيْفَ كَانَ عَـٰقِبَةُ ٱلَّذِينَ مِن قَبْلِهِمْ
وَكَانُوٓاْ أَشَدَّ مِنْهُمْ قُوَّةً وَمَا كَانَ ٱللَّهُ لِيُعْجِزَهُۥ مِن شَىْءٍ فِى
ٱلسَّمَـٰوَٰتِ وَلَا فِى ٱلْأَرْضِ إِنَّهُۥ كَانَ عَلِيمًا قَدِيرًا (٤٤)

(They took to flight because of their)
arrogance in the land and their plotting of
evil. But the evil plot encompasses only him
who makes it. **Then, can they expect
anything (else), but the Sunnah (way of
dealing) of the peoples of old?** So no
change will you find in Allâh's Sunnah
(way of dealing), and no turning off will you
find in Allâh's Sunnah (way of dealing).
(43) **Have they not travelled in the land,
and seen what was the end of those
before them, though they were superior
to them in power?** Allâh is not such that
anything in the heavens or in the earth
escapes Him. Verily, He is All¬Knowing,
All¬Omnipotent. (44)

Quran 36:30-35

يَٰحَسْرَةً عَلَى ٱلْعِبَادِ مَا يَأْتِيهِم مِّن رَّسُولٍ إِلَّا كَانُوا۟ بِهِۦ
يَسْتَهْزِءُونَ (٣٠) أَلَمْ يَرَوْا۟ كَمْ أَهْلَكْنَا قَبْلَهُم مِّنَ ٱلْقُرُونِ أَنَّهُمْ
إِلَيْهِمْ لَا يَرْجِعُونَ (٣١) وَإِن كُلٌّ لَّمَّا جَمِيعٌ لَّدَيْنَا مُحْضَرُونَ
(٣٢) وَءَايَةٌ لَّهُمُ ٱلْأَرْضُ ٱلْمَيْتَةُ أَحْيَيْنَٰهَا وَأَخْرَجْنَا مِنْهَا حَبًّا
فَمِنْهُ يَأْكُلُونَ (٣٣) وَجَعَلْنَا فِيهَا جَنَّٰتٍ مِّن نَّخِيلٍ
وَأَعْنَٰبٍ وَفَجَّرْنَا فِيهَا مِنَ ٱلْعُيُونِ (٣٤) لِيَأْكُلُوا۟ مِن ثَمَرِهِۦ
وَمَا عَمِلَتْهُ أَيْدِيهِمْ أَفَلَا يَشْكُرُونَ (٣٥)

Alas for mankind! There never came a
Messenger to them but they used to mock at
him. (30) **Do they not see how many of
the generations We have destroyed
before them?** Verily, they will not return to
them. (31) And surely, all, – everyone of
them will be brought before Us. (32) And a
sign for them is the dead land. We gave it
life, and We bring forth from it grains, so
that they eat thereof. (33) And We have
made therein gardens of date-palms and
grapes, and We have caused springs of water
to gush forth therein. (34) So that they may
eat of the fruit thereof, – and their hands
made it not. **Will they not, then, give
thanks?** (35)

Quran 36:60-62

{۞} أَلَمْ أَعْهَدْ إِلَيْكُمْ يَٰبَنِىٓ ءَادَمَ أَن لَّا تَعْبُدُواْ ٱلشَّيْطَٰنَۖ إِنَّهُۥ لَكُمْ عَدُوٌّ مُّبِينٌ (٦٠) وَأَنِ ٱعْبُدُونِىۚ هَٰذَا صِرَٰطٌ مُّسْتَقِيمٌ (٦١) وَلَقَدْ أَضَلَّ مِنكُمْ جِبِلًّا كَثِيرًاۖ أَفَلَمْ تَكُونُواْ تَعْقِلُونَ (٦٢)

Did I not command for you, O Children of Adam, that you should not worship Shaitân (Satan)? Verily, he is a plain enemy to you. (60) And that you should worship Me [Alone — Islâmic Monotheism, and set up not rivals, associate-gods with Me]. That is the Straight Path. (61) And indeed he (Satan) did lead astray a great multitude of you. **Did you not, then, understand?** *(62)*

Quran 36:71-73

أَوَلَمْ يَرَوْاْ أَنَّا خَلَقْنَا لَهُم مِّمَّا عَمِلَتْ أَيْدِينَآ أَنْعَٰمًا فَهُمْ لَهَا مَٰلِكُونَ (٧١) وَذَلَّلْنَٰهَا لَهُمْ فَمِنْهَا رَكُوبُهُمْ وَمِنْهَا يَأْكُلُونَ (٧٢) وَلَهُمْ فِيهَا مَنَٰفِعُ وَمَشَارِبُۖ أَفَلَا يَشْكُرُونَ (٧٣)

Do they not see that We have created for them of what Our Hands have

created, the cattle, so that they are their
owners? (71) And We have subdued them
unto them so that some of them they have for
riding and some they eat. (72) And they
have (other) benefits from them, and they get
(milk) to drink. **Will they not then be**
grateful? *(73)*

Quran 36:77

أَوَلَمْ يَرَ ٱلْإِنسَـٰنُ أَنَّا خَلَقْنَـٰهُ مِن نُّطْفَةٍ فَإِذَا هُوَ خَصِيمٌ مُّبِينٌ
(٧٧)

Does not man see that We have created
him from Nutfah (mixed male and
female discharge — semen drops)? Yet
behold! he (stands forth) as an open
opponent. (77)

Quran 36:81

أَوَلَيْسَ ٱلَّذِى خَلَقَ ٱلسَّمَـٰوَٰتِ وَٱلْأَرْضَ بِقَـٰدِرٍ عَلَىٰٓ أَن يَخْلُقَ
مِثْلَهُم ۚ بَلَىٰ وَهُوَ ٱلْخَلَّـٰقُ ٱلْعَلِيمُ (٨١)

Is not He, Who created the heavens and
the earth Able to create the like of them?

Yes, indeed! He is the All-Knowing Supreme Creator. (81)

Quran 37:11

فَٱسْتَفْتِهِمْ أَهُمْ أَشَدُّ خَلْقًا أَم مَّنْ خَلَقْنَا ۚ إِنَّا خَلَقْنَـٰهُم مِّن طِينٍ لَّازِبٍ (١١)

Then ask them (i.e. these polytheists, O Muhammad): **"Are they stronger as creation, or those (others like the heavens and the earth and the mountains) whom We have created?"** *Verily, We created them of a sticky clay. (11)*

Quran 37:62-68

أَذَٰلِكَ خَيْرٌ نُّزُلاً أَمْ شَجَرَةُ ٱلزَّقُّومِ (٦٢) إِنَّا جَعَلْنَـٰهَا فِتْنَةً لِّلظَّـٰلِمِينَ (٦٣) إِنَّهَا شَجَرَةٌ تَخْرُجُ فِى أَصْلِ ٱلْجَحِيمِ (٦٤) طَلْعُهَا كَأَنَّهُ رُءُوسُ ٱلشَّيَـٰطِينِ (٦٥) فَإِنَّهُمْ لَأَكِلُونَ مِنْهَا فَمَالِـُٔونَ مِنْهَا ٱلْبُطُونَ (٦٦) ثُمَّ إِنَّ لَهُمْ عَلَيْهَا لَشَوْبًا مِّنْ حَمِيمٍ (٦٧) ثُمَّ إِنَّ مَرْجِعَهُمْ لَإِلَى ٱلْجَحِيمِ (٦٨)

Is that (Paradise) better entertainment or the tree of Zaqqûm (a horrible tree in Hell)? *(62) Truly We have made it (as) a*

*trial for the Zâlimûn (polytheists,
disbelievers, wrong-doers). (63) Verily, it is
a tree that springs out of the bottom of Hell-
fire, (64) The shoots of its fruit-stalks are
like the heads of Shayâtin (devils);
(65) Truly, they will eat thereof and fill their
bellies therewith. (66) Then on the top of
that they will be given boiling water to drink
so that it becomes a mixture (of boiling
water and Zaqqûm in their bellies).
(67) Then thereafter, verily, their return is
to the flaming fire of Hell. (68)*

Quran 37:136-138

ثُمَّ دَمَّرْنَا ٱلْأَخَرِينَ (١٣٦) وَإِنَّكُمْ لَتَمُرُّونَ عَلَيْهِم مُّصْبِحِينَ
(١٣٧) وَبِٱلَّيْلِ أَفَلَا تَعْقِلُونَ (١٣٨)

*Then We destroyed the rest [i.e. the town of
Sodom at the place of the Dead Sea now in
Palestine]. (136) Verily, you pass by them in
the morning. (137) And at night;* **will you
not then reflect?** *(138)*

Quran 37:149-159

فَٱسْتَفْتِهِمْ أَلِرَبِّكَ ٱلْبَنَاتُ وَلَهُمُ ٱلْبَنُونَ (١٤٩) أَمْ خَلَقْنَا ٱلْمَلَـٰئِكَةَ إِنَـٰثًا وَهُمْ شَـٰهِدُونَ (١٥٠) أَلَا إِنَّهُم مِّنْ إِفْكِهِمْ لَيَقُولُونَ (١٥١) وَلَدَ ٱللَّهُ وَإِنَّهُمْ لَكَـٰذِبُونَ (١٥٢) أَصْطَفَى ٱلْبَنَاتِ عَلَى ٱلْبَنِينَ (١٥٣) مَا لَكُمْ كَيْفَ تَحْكُمُونَ (١٥٤) أَفَلَا تَذَكَّرُونَ (١٥٥) أَمْ لَكُمْ سُلْطَـٰنٌ مُّبِينٌ (١٥٦) فَأْتُوا۟ بِكِتَـٰبِكُمْ إِن كُنتُمْ صَـٰدِقِينَ (١٥٧) وَجَعَلُوا۟ بَيْنَهُ وَبَيْنَ ٱلْجِنَّةِ نَسَبًا وَلَقَدْ عَلِمَتِ ٱلْجِنَّةُ إِنَّهُمْ لَمُحْضَرُونَ (١٥٨) سُبْحَـٰنَ ٱللَّهِ عَمَّا يَصِفُونَ (١٥٩)

Now ask them (O Muhammad): "**Are there (only) daughters for your Lord and sons for them?**" (149) **Or did We create the angels female while they were witnesses?** (150) Verily, it is of their falsehood that they (Quraish pagans) say: (151) "Allâh has begotten (off spring the angels being the daughters of Allâh)?" And, verily, they are liars! (152) **Has He (then) chosen daughters rather than sons? (153) What is the matter with you? How do you decide? (154) Will you not then remember? (155) Or is there for you a plain authority? (156)** Then bring your

Book if you are truthful! (157) And they have invented a kinship between Him and the jinn, but the jinn know well that they have indeed to appear (before Him) (i.e. they will be brought for account). (158) Glorified is Allâh! (He is Free) from what they attribute unto Him! (159)

Quran 38:9-10

أَمْ عِندَهُمْ خَزَآئِنُ رَحْمَةِ رَبِّكَ ٱلْعَزِيزِ ٱلْوَهَّابِ (٩) أَمْ لَهُم مُّلْكُ ٱلسَّمَـٰوَٰتِ وَٱلْأَرْضِ وَمَا بَيْنَهُمَاۖ فَلْيَرْتَقُواْ فِى ٱلْأَسْبَـٰبِ (١٠)

Or have they the treasures of the Mercy of your Lord, the All-Mighty, the Real Bestower? (9) Or is it that the dominion of the heavens and the earth and all that is between them is theirs? *If so, let them ascend up with means (to the heavens)! (10)*

Quran 38:28

أَمْ نَجْعَلُ ٱلَّذِينَ ءَامَنُواْ وَعَمِلُواْ ٱلصَّـٰلِحَـٰتِ كَٱلْمُفْسِدِينَ فِى ٱلْأَرْضِ أَمْ نَجْعَلُ ٱلْمُتَّقِينَ كَٱلْفُجَّارِ (٢٨)

Shall We treat those who believe (in the Oneness of Allâh — Islâmic Monotheism) and do righteous good deeds, as Mufsidûn (those who associate partners in worship with Allâh and commit crimes) on earth? Or shall We treat the Muttaqûn (pious), as the Fujjâr (criminals, disbelievers, the wicked)? (28)

Quran 38:75-85

قَالَ يَٰٓإِبْلِيسُ مَا مَنَعَكَ أَن تَسْجُدَ لِمَا خَلَقْتُ بِيَدَىَّ أَسْتَكْبَرْتَ أَمْ كُنتَ مِنَ ٱلْعَالِينَ (٧٥) قَالَ أَنَا۠ خَيْرٌ مِّنْهُ خَلَقْتَنِى مِن نَّارٍ وَخَلَقْتَهُۥ مِن طِينٍ (٧٦) قَالَ فَٱخْرُجْ مِنْهَا فَإِنَّكَ رَجِيمٌ (٧٧) وَإِنَّ عَلَيْكَ لَعْنَتِىٓ إِلَىٰ يَوْمِ ٱلدِّينِ (٧٨) قَالَ رَبِّ فَأَنظِرْنِىٓ إِلَىٰ يَوْمِ يُبْعَثُونَ (٧٩) قَالَ فَإِنَّكَ مِنَ ٱلْمُنظَرِينَ (٨٠) إِلَىٰ يَوْمِ ٱلْوَقْتِ ٱلْمَعْلُومِ (٨١) قَالَ فَبِعِزَّتِكَ لَأُغْوِيَنَّهُمْ أَجْمَعِينَ (٨٢) إِلَّا عِبَادَكَ مِنْهُمُ ٱلْمُخْلَصِينَ (٨٣) قَالَ فَٱلْحَقُّ وَٱلْحَقَّ أَقُولُ (٨٤) لَأَمْلَأَنَّ جَهَنَّمَ مِنكَ وَمِمَّن تَبِعَكَ مِنْهُمْ أَجْمَعِينَ (٨٥)

(Allâh) said: "O Iblîs (Satan)! What prevents you from prostrating yourself to one whom I have created with Both

My Hands? Are you too proud (to fall prostrate to Adam) or are you one of the high exalted?" *(75) [Iblîs (Satan)] said: "I am better than he, You created me from fire, and You created him from clay." (76) (Allâh) said: "Then get out from here, for verily, you are outcast. (77) "And verily!, My Curse is on you till the Day of Recompense." (78) [Iblîs (Satan)] said: "My Lord! Give me then respite till the Day the (dead) are resurrected." (79) (Allâh) said: "Verily! You are of those allowed respite (80) "Till the Day of the time appointed." (81) [Iblîs (Satan)] said: "By Your Might, then I will surely mislead them all, (82) "Except Your chosen slaves amongst them (faithful, obedient, true believers of Islâmic Monotheism)." (83) (Allâh) said: "The Truth is, – and the Truth I say, – (84) That I will fill Hell with you [Iblîs (Satan)] and those of them (mankind) that follow you, together." (85)*

Quran 39:6

خَلَقَكُم مِّن نَّفْسٍ وَاحِدَةٍ ثُمَّ جَعَلَ مِنْهَا زَوْجَهَا وَأَنزَلَ لَكُم مِّنَ الْأَنْعَامِ ثَمَانِيَةَ أَزْوَاجٍ يَخْلُقُكُمْ فِى بُطُونِ أُمَّهَاتِكُمْ خَلْقًا مِّنْ بَعْدِ خَلْقٍ فِى ظُلُمَاتٍ ثَلَاثٍ ذَالِكُمُ اللَّهُ رَبُّكُمْ لَهُ الْمُلْكُ لَا إِلَهَ إِلَّا هُوَ فَأَنَّىٰ تُصْرَفُونَ (٦)

He created you (all) from a single person (Adam); then made from him his wife [Hawwa' (Eve)]. And He has sent down for you of cattle eight pairs (of the sheep, two, male and female; of the goats, two, male and female; of the oxen, two, male and female; and of the camels, two, male and female). He creates you in the wombs of your mothers, creation after creation in three veils of darkness, such is Allâh your Lord. His is the kingdom, Lâ ilâha illa Huwa (none has the right to be worshipped but He). **How then are you turned away?** (6)

Quran 39:9

أَمَّنْ هُوَ قَانِتٌ ءَانَاءَ اللَّيْلِ سَاجِدًا وَقَائِمًا يَحْذَرُ الْأَخِرَةَ وَيَرْجُواْ رَحْمَةَ رَبِّهِ قُلْ هَلْ يَسْتَوِى الَّذِينَ يَعْلَمُونَ وَالَّذِينَ لَا يَعْلَمُونَ إِنَّمَا يَتَذَكَّرُ أُوْلُواْ الْأَلْبَابِ (٩)

Is one who is obedient to Allâh, prostrating himself or standing (in prayer) during the hours of the night, fearing the Hereafter and hoping for the Mercy of his Lord (like one who disbelieves)? Say: "Are those who know equal to those who know not?" It is only men of understanding who will remember (i.e. get a lesson from Allâh's Signs and Verses). (9)

Quran 39:19

أَفَمَنْ حَقَّ عَلَيْهِ كَلِمَةُ ٱلْعَذَابِ أَفَأَنتَ تُنقِذُ مَن فِى ٱلنَّارِ (١٩)

Is, then one against whom the Word of punishment is justified (equal to the one who avoids evil)? Will you rescue him who is in the Fire? (19)

Quran 39:22-24

أَفَمَن شَرَحَ ٱللَّهُ صَدْرَهُ لِلْإِسْلَٰمِ فَهُوَ عَلَىٰ نُورٍ مِّن رَّبِّهِۦ فَوَيْلٌ لِّلْقَٰسِيَةِ قُلُوبُهُم مِّن ذِكْرِ ٱللَّهِ أُوْلَٰٓئِكَ فِى ضَلَٰلٍ مُّبِينٍ (٢٢) ٱللَّهُ نَزَّلَ أَحْسَنَ ٱلْحَدِيثِ كِتَٰبًا مُّتَشَٰبِهًا مَّثَانِىَ تَقْشَعِرُّ مِنْهُ جُلُودُ ٱلَّذِينَ يَخْشَوْنَ رَبَّهُمْ ثُمَّ تَلِينُ جُلُودُهُمْ وَقُلُوبُهُمْ إِلَىٰ

ذِكْرِ ٱللَّهِ ذَٰلِكَ هُدَى ٱللَّهِ يَهْدِى بِهِۦ مَن يَشَآءُ وَمَن يُضْلِلِ ٱللَّهُ فَمَا لَهُۥ مِنْ هَادٍ (٢٣) أَفَمَن يَتَّقِى بِوَجْهِهِۦ سُوٓءَ ٱلْعَذَابِ يَوْمَ ٱلْقِيَٰمَةِ وَقِيلَ لِلظَّٰلِمِينَ ذُوقُواْ مَا كُنتُمْ تَكْسِبُونَ (٢٤)

Is he whose breast Allâh has opened to Islâm, so that he is in light from His Lord (as he who is non-Muslim)? So, woe to those whose hearts are hardened against remembrance of Allâh! They are in plain error! (22) Allâh has sent down the Best statement, a Book (this Qur'ân), its parts resembling each other (in goodness and truth), and oft-repeated. The skins of those who fear their Lord shiver from it (when they recite it or hear it). Then their skin and their heart soften to the remembrance of Allâh. That is the guidance of Allâh. He Guides therewith whom He wills and whomever Allâh sends astray, for him there is no guide. (23) **Is he then, who will confront with his face the awful torment on the Day of Resurrection (as he who enters peacefully in Paradise)?** And it will be said to the Zâlimûn (polytheists and wrong-doers): "Taste what you used to earn!" (24)

Quran 39:32

۞ فَمَنْ أَظْلَمُ مِمَّن كَذَبَ عَلَى ٱللَّهِ وَكَذَّبَ بِٱلصِّدْقِ إِذْ جَآءَهُ ۚ أَلَيْسَ فِى جَهَنَّمَ مَثْوًى لِّلْكَٰفِرِينَ (٣٢)

Then, who does more wrong than one who utters a lie against Allâh, and denies the truth [this Qur'ân, the Prophet (Muhammad), and the Islâmic Monotheism] when it comes to him! **Is there not in Hell an abode for the disbelievers?** *(32)*

Quran 39:36-38

أَلَيْسَ ٱللَّهُ بِكَافٍ عَبْدَهُ ۖ وَيُخَوِّفُونَكَ بِٱلَّذِينَ مِن دُونِهِ ۚ وَمَن يُضْلِلِ ٱللَّهُ فَمَا لَهُ ۥ مِنْ هَادٍ (٣٦) وَمَن يَهْدِ ٱللَّهُ فَمَا لَهُ ۥ مِن مُّضِلٍّ ۗ أَلَيْسَ ٱللَّهُ بِعَزِيزٍ ذِى ٱنتِقَامٍ (٣٧) وَلَئِن سَأَلْتَهُم مَّنْ خَلَقَ ٱلسَّمَٰوَٰتِ وَٱلْأَرْضَ لَيَقُولُنَّ ٱللَّهُ ۚ قُلْ أَفَرَءَيْتُم مَّا تَدْعُونَ مِن دُونِ ٱللَّهِ إِنْ أَرَادَنِىَ ٱللَّهُ بِضُرٍّ هَلْ هُنَّ كَٰشِفَٰتُ ضُرِّهِ ۦ أَوْ أَرَادَنِى بِرَحْمَةٍ هَلْ هُنَّ مُمْسِكَٰتُ رَحْمَتِهِ ۚ قُلْ حَسْبِىَ ٱللَّهُ ۖ عَلَيْهِ يَتَوَكَّلُ ٱلْمُتَوَكِّلُونَ (٣٨)

Is not Allâh Sufficient for His slave? *Yet they try to frighten you with those (whom*

they worship) besides Him! And whom
Allâh sends astray, for him there will be no
guide. (36) And whomsoever Allâh guides,
for him there will be no misleader. **Is not
Allâh All-Mighty, Possessor of
Retribution?** (37) And verily, if you ask
them: "**Who created the heavens and the
earth?**" Surely, they will say: "Allâh (has
created them)." Say: "**Tell me then, the
things that you invoke besides Allâh, if
Allâh intended some harm for me, could
they remove His harm, or if He (Allâh)
intended some mercy for me, could they
withhold His Mercy?**" Say : "Sufficient
for me is Allâh; in Him those who trust (i.e.
believers) must put their trust." (38)

Quran 39:43-45

أَمِ ٱتَّخَذُواْ مِن دُونِ ٱللَّهِ شُفَعَآءَ قُلْ أَوَلَوْ كَانُواْ لَا يَمْلِكُونَ
شَيْـًٔا وَلَا يَعْقِلُونَ (٤٣) قُل لِّلَّهِ ٱلشَّفَٰعَةُ جَمِيعًا ۖ لَّهُۥ مُلْكُ
ٱلسَّمَٰوَٰتِ وَٱلْأَرْضِ ۖ ثُمَّ إِلَيْهِ تُرْجَعُونَ (٤٤) وَإِذَا ذُكِرَ ٱللَّهُ
وَحْدَهُ ٱشْمَأَزَّتْ قُلُوبُ ٱلَّذِينَ لَا يُؤْمِنُونَ بِٱلْأَخِرَةِ ۖ وَإِذَا ذُكِرَ
ٱلَّذِينَ مِن دُونِهِۦ إِذَا هُمْ يَسْتَبْشِرُونَ (٤٥)

Have they taken (others) as intercessors besides Allâh? Say: "Even if they have power over nothing whatever and have no intelligence?" (43) Say: "To Allâh belongs all intercession. His is the Sovereignty of the heavens and the earth, Then to Him you shall be brought back." (44) And when Allâh Alone is mentioned, the hearts of those who believe not in the Hereafter are filled with disgust (from the Oneness of Allâh and when those (whom they obey or worship) besides Him [like all false deities other than Allâh, it may be a Messenger, an angel, a pious man, a jinn, or any other creature even idols, graves of religious people, saints, priests, monks and others] are mentioned, behold, they rejoice! (45)

Quran 39:60

وَيَوْمَ ٱلْقِيَٰمَةِ تَرَى ٱلَّذِينَ كَذَبُوا۟ عَلَى ٱللَّهِ وُجُوهُهُم مُّسْوَدَّةٌ أَلَيْسَ فِى جَهَنَّمَ مَثْوًى لِّلْمُتَكَبِّرِينَ (٦٠)

And on the Day of Resurrection you will see those who lied against Allâh (i.e. attributed to Him sons, partners) — their faces will be black. **Is there not in Hell an abode for the arrogant?** *(60)*

Quran 39:64-65

قُلْ أَفَغَيْرَ ٱللَّهِ تَأْمُرُوٓنِّىٓ أَعْبُدُ أَيُّهَا ٱلْجَٰهِلُونَ (٦٤) وَلَقَدْ أُوحِىَ إِلَيْكَ وَإِلَى ٱلَّذِينَ مِن قَبْلِكَ لَئِنْ أَشْرَكْتَ لَيَحْبَطَنَّ عَمَلُكَ وَلَتَكُونَنَّ مِنَ ٱلْخَٰسِرِينَ (٦٥)

Say: **"Do you order me to worship other than Allâh?** *O you fools!" (64) And indeed it has been revealed to you (O Muhammad), as it was to those (Allâh's Messengers) before you: "If you join others in worship with Allâh, (then) surely (all) your deeds will be in vain, and you will certainly be among the losers." (65)*

Quran 40:69

أَلَمْ تَرَ إِلَى ٱلَّذِينَ يُجَٰدِلُونَ فِىٓ ءَايَٰتِ ٱللَّهِ أَنَّىٰ يُصْرَفُونَ (٦٩)

See you not those who dispute about the Ayât (proofs, evidences, verses, lessons, signs, revelations, etc.) of Allâh? How are they turning away (from the truth, i.e. Islâmic Monotheism to the falsehood (i.e. polytheism))? (69)

Quran 40:73-74

ثُمَّ قِيلَ لَهُمْ أَيْنَ مَا كُنتُمْ تُشْرِكُونَ (٧٣) مِن دُونِ ٱللَّهِ قَالُواْ ضَلُّواْ عَنَّا بَل لَّمْ نَكُن نَّدْعُواْ مِن قَبْلُ شَيْـًٔا كَذَٰلِكَ يُضِلُّ ٱللَّهُ ٱلْكَٰفِرِينَ (٧٤)

*Then it will be said to them: **"Where are (all) those whom you used to join in worship as partners (73) besides Allâh"?** They will say: "They have vanished from us: Nay, we did not invoke (worship) anything before." Thus Allâh leads astray the disbelievers. (74)*

Quran 40:81-82

وَيُرِيكُمْ ءَايَٰتِهِۦ فَأَىَّ ءَايَٰتِ ٱللَّهِ تُنكِرُونَ (٨١) أَفَلَمْ يَسِيرُواْ فِى ٱلْأَرْضِ فَيَنظُرُواْ كَيْفَ كَانَ عَٰقِبَةُ ٱلَّذِينَ مِن قَبْلِهِمْ كَانُوٓاْ

أَكْثَرَ مِنْهُمْ وَأَشَدَّ قُوَّةً وَءَاثَارًا فِى ٱلْأَرْضِ فَمَآ أَغْنَىٰ عَنْهُم مَّا كَانُواْ يَكْسِبُونَ (٨٢)

And He shows you His Ayat, (Signs and Proofs) (of His Oneness in all the above mentioned things). **Which, then of the Ayat (Signs and Proofs) of Allâh do you deny? (81) Have they not travelled through the earth and seen what was the end of those before them?** *They were more in number than them and mightier in strength, and in the traces (they have left behind them) in the land, yet all that they used to earn availed them not. (82)*

Quran 41:9

﴾ قُلْ أَئِنَّكُمْ لَتَكْفُرُونَ بِٱلَّذِى خَلَقَ ٱلْأَرْضَ فِى يَوْمَيْنِ وَتَجْعَلُونَ لَهُۥ أَندَادًا ذَٰلِكَ رَبُّ ٱلْعَـٰلَمِينَ (٩)

Say (O Muhammad): **"Do you verily disbelieve in Him Who created the earth in two Days and you set up rivals (in worship) with Him?** *That is the Lord of the 'Alamîn (mankind, jinn and all that exists). (9)*

Quran 41:47-48

۞ إِلَيْهِ يُرَدُّ عِلْمُ ٱلسَّاعَةِۚ وَمَا تَخْرُجُ مِن ثَمَرَٰتٍ مِّنْ أَكْمَامِهَا وَمَا تَحْمِلُ مِنْ أُنثَىٰ وَلَا تَضَعُ إِلَّا بِعِلْمِهِۦۚ وَيَوْمَ يُنَادِيهِمْ أَيْنَ شُرَكَآءِى قَالُوٓاْ ءَاذَنَّٰكَ مَا مِنَّا مِن شَهِيدٍ (٤٧) وَضَلَّ عَنْهُم مَّا كَانُواْ يَدْعُونَ مِن قَبْلُۖ وَظَنُّواْ مَا لَهُم مِّن مَّحِيصٍ (٤٨)

*To Him (Alone) is referred the knowledge of the Hour. No fruit comes out of its sheath, nor does a female conceive, nor brings forth (young), except by His Knowledge. And on the Day when He will call unto them (polytheists) (saying): "**Where are My (so-called) partners (whom you did invent)?**" They will say: "We inform You that none of us bears witness to it (that they are Your partners)!" (47) And those whom they used to invoke before before (in this world) shall disappear from them, and they will perceive that they have no place of refuge (from Allâh's punishment). (48)*

Quran 41:52-53

قُلْ أَرَءَيْتُمْ إِن كَانَ مِنْ عِندِ ٱللَّهِ ثُمَّ كَفَرْتُم بِهِۦ مَنْ أَضَلُّ مِمَّنْ هُوَ فِى شِقَاقٍۭ بَعِيدٍ (٥٢) سَنُرِيهِمْ ءَايَـٰتِنَا فِى ٱلْءَافَاقِ وَفِىٓ أَنفُسِهِمْ حَتَّىٰ يَتَبَيَّنَ لَهُمْ أَنَّهُ ٱلْحَقُّ أَوَلَمْ يَكْفِ بِرَبِّكَ أَنَّهُۥ عَلَىٰ كُلِّ شَىْءٍ شَهِيدٌ (٥٣)

Say: "Tell me, if it (the Qur'ân) is from Allâh, and you disbelieve in it, who is more astray than one who is in opposition far away (from Allâh's Right Path and His obedience)? (52) We will show them Our Signs in the universe, and in their own selves, until it becomes manifest to them that this (the Qur'ân) is the truth. **Is it not sufficient in regard to your Lord that He is a Witness over all things?** *(53)*

Quran 42:9

أَمِ ٱتَّخَذُوا۟ مِن دُونِهِۦٓ أَوْلِيَآءَ فَٱللَّهُ هُوَ ٱلْوَلِىُّ وَهُوَ يُحْىِ ٱلْمَوْتَىٰ وَهُوَ عَلَىٰ كُلِّ شَىْءٍ قَدِيرٌ (٩)

Or have they taken (for worship) Auliyâ' (guardians, supporters, helpers, protectors, lords, gods) besides Him? But Allâh, He Alone is the Walî (Lord, God,

Protector). And it is He Who gives life to the dead, and He is Able to do all things. (9)

Quran 42:17-18

اَللَّهُ ٱلَّذِىٓ أَنزَلَ ٱلْكِتَـٰبَ بِٱلْحَقِّ وَٱلْمِيزَانَّ وَمَا يُدْرِيكَ لَعَلَّ ٱلسَّاعَةَ قَرِيبٌ (١٧) يَسْتَعْجِلُ بِهَا ٱلَّذِينَ لَا يُؤْمِنُونَ بِهَا وَٱلَّذِينَ ءَامَنُواْ مُشْفِقُونَ مِنْهَا وَيَعْلَمُونَ أَنَّهَا ٱلْحَقُّ أَلَآ إِنَّ ٱلَّذِينَ يُمَارُونَ فِى ٱلسَّاعَةِ لَفِى ضَلَـٰلٍ بَعِيدٍ (١٨)

It is Allâh Who has sent down the Book (the Qur'ân) in truth, and the Balance (i.e. to act justly). **And what can make you know that perhaps the Hour is close at hand?** *(17) Those who believe not therein seek to hasten it, while those who believe are fearful of it, and know that it is the very truth. Verily, those who dispute concerning the Hour are certainly in error far away. (18)*

Quran 42:21

أَمْ لَهُمْ شُرَكَـٰٓؤُاْ شَرَعُواْ لَهُم مِّنَ ٱلدِّينِ مَا لَمْ يَأْذَنۢ بِهِ ٱللَّهُ وَلَوْلَا كَلِمَةُ ٱلْفَصْلِ لَقُضِىَ بَيْنَهُمْ وَإِنَّ ٱلظَّـٰلِمِينَ لَهُمْ عَذَابٌ أَلِيمٌ (٢١)

Or have they partners with Allâh (false gods), who have instituted for them a religion which Allâh has not ordained? And had it not been for a decisive Word (gone forth already), the matter would have been judged between them. And verily, for the Zâlimûn (polytheists and wrong-doers), there is a painful torment. (21)

Quran 43:9-23

وَلَئِن سَأَلْتَهُم مَّنْ خَلَقَ ٱلسَّمَـٰوَٰتِ وَٱلْأَرْضَ لَيَقُولُنَّ خَلَقَهُنَّ ٱلْعَزِيزُ ٱلْعَلِيمُ (٩) ٱلَّذِى جَعَلَ لَكُمُ ٱلْأَرْضَ مَهْدًا وَجَعَلَ لَكُمْ فِيهَا سُبُلًا لَّعَلَّكُمْ تَهْتَدُونَ (١٠) وَٱلَّذِى نَزَّلَ مِنَ ٱلسَّمَآءِ مَآءً بِقَدَرٍ فَأَنشَرْنَا بِهِۦ بَلْدَةً مَّيْتًا كَذَٰلِكَ تُخْرَجُونَ (١١) وَٱلَّذِى خَلَقَ ٱلْأَزْوَٰجَ كُلَّهَا وَجَعَلَ لَكُم مِّنَ ٱلْفُلْكِ وَٱلْأَنْعَـٰمِ مَا تَرْكَبُونَ (١٢) لِتَسْتَوُۥا۟ عَلَىٰ ظُهُورِهِۦ ثُمَّ تَذْكُرُوا۟ نِعْمَةَ رَبِّكُمْ إِذَا ٱسْتَوَيْتُمْ عَلَيْهِ وَتَقُولُوا۟ سُبْحَـٰنَ ٱلَّذِى سَخَّرَ لَنَا هَـٰذَا وَمَا كُنَّا لَهُۥ مُقْرِنِينَ (١٣) وَإِنَّآ إِلَىٰ رَبِّنَا لَمُنقَلِبُونَ (١٤) وَجَعَلُوا۟ لَهُۥ مِنْ عِبَادِهِۦ جُزْءًا إِنَّ ٱلْإِنسَـٰنَ لَكَفُورٌ مُّبِينٌ (١٥) أَمِ ٱتَّخَذَ مِمَّا يَخْلُقُ بَنَاتٍ وَأَصْفَىٰكُم بِٱلْبَنِينَ (١٦) وَإِذَا بُشِّرَ أَحَدُهُم بِمَا ضَرَبَ لِلرَّحْمَـٰنِ مَثَلًا ظَلَّ وَجْهُهُۥ مُسْوَدًّا وَهُوَ كَظِيمٌ (١٧) أَوَمَن يُنَشَّؤُا۟ فِى ٱلْحِلْيَةِ وَهُوَ فِى ٱلْخِصَامِ غَيْرُ مُبِينٍ (١٨) وَجَعَلُوا۟ ٱلْمَلَـٰٓئِكَةَ ٱلَّذِينَ هُمْ عِبَـٰدُ ٱلرَّحْمَـٰنِ إِنَـٰثًا أَشَهِدُوا۟ خَلْقَهُمْ سَتُكْتَبُ شَهَـٰدَتُهُمْ

وَيُسْـَٔلُونَ (١٩) وَقَالُواْ لَوْ شَآءَ ٱلرَّحْمَـٰنُ مَا عَبَدْنَـٰهُمَّ مَّا لَهُم بِذَٰلِكَ مِنْ عِلْمٍ إِنْ هُمْ إِلَّا يَخْرُصُونَ (٢٠) أَمْ ءَاتَيْنَـٰهُمْ كِتَـٰبًا مِّن قَبْلِهِ فَهُم بِهِ مُسْتَمْسِكُونَ (٢١) بَلْ قَالُوٓاْ إِنَّا وَجَدْنَآ ءَابَآءَنَا عَلَىٰٓ أُمَّةٍ وَإِنَّا عَلَىٰٓ ءَاثَـٰرِهِم مُّهْتَدُونَ (٢٢) وَكَذَٰلِكَ مَآ أَرْسَلْنَا مِن قَبْلِكَ فِى قَرْيَةٍ مِّن نَّذِيرٍ إِلَّا قَالَ مُتْرَفُوهَآ إِنَّا وَجَدْنَآ ءَابَآءَنَا عَلَىٰٓ أُمَّةٍ وَإِنَّا عَلَىٰٓ ءَاثَـٰرِهِم مُّقْتَدُونَ (٢٣)

And indeed if you ask them, "**Who has created the heavens and the earth?**" They will surely say: "The All-Mighty, the All-Knower created them." (9) Who has made for you the earth like a bed, and has made for you roads therein, in order that you may find your way, (10) And Who sends down water (rain) from the sky in due measure. then We revive a dead land therewith, and even so you will be brought forth (from the graves), (11) And Who has created all the pairs and has appointed for you ships and cattle on which you ride; (12) In order that you may mount on their backs, and then may remember the Favour of your Lord when you mount thereon, and say: "Glory to Him who has subjected this to us, and we could never have it (by our efforts)." (13) And verily, to Our Lord we indeed are to return! (14) Yet they assign to some of His slaves a share with Him (by pretending that He has children, and considering them as equals or co-partners in worship with Him). Verily, man is indeed a manifest ingrate! (15) **Or has He taken daughters out of what He has created, and He has selected for you sons?** (16) And if one of them is informed of the news of (the birth of a girl) that which he set forth as a parable to the Most Gracious (Allâh) (i.e. of a girl), his face becomes dark, gloomy, and he is filled with grief! (17) **(Like they then for Allâh) a creature who is brought up in adornments (wearing silk and gold ornaments, i.e. women), and who in dispute cannot make herself clear? (18) And they make the angels who themselves are slaves of the Most Gracious (Allâh) females. Did** *they witness their creation? Their testimony will be recorded, and they will be questioned! (19) And they said: "If it had been the Will of the Most Gracious (Allâh), we should not have worshipped them (false deities)." They have no knowledge whatsoever of that. They do nothing but lie! (20)* **Or have We given them any Book before this (the Qur'ân), to which they are holding fast? (21)** *Nay! They say: "We found our fathers following a certain way and religion, and we guide ourselves by their footsteps." (22) And similarly, We sent not a warner before you (O Muhammad) to any town (people) but the luxurious ones among them said: "We found our fathers following a certain way and religion, and we will indeed follow their footsteps." (23)*

Quran 43:40

أَفَأَنتَ تُسْمِعُ ٱلصُّمَّ أَوْ تَهْدِى ٱلْعُمْىَ وَمَن كَانَ فِى ضَلَلٍ مُّبِينٍ (٤٠)

Can you make the deaf to hear, or can you guide the blind or him who is in manifest error? (40)

Quran 43:45

وَسْئَلْ مَنْ أَرْسَلْنَا مِن قَبْلِكَ مِن رُّسُلِنَآ أَجَعَلْنَا مِن دُونِ
ٱلرَّحْمَـٰنِ ءَالِهَةً يُعْبَدُونَ (٤٥)

*And ask (O Muhammad) those of Our Messengers whom We sent before you: "**Did We ever appoint âlihah (gods) to be worshipped besides the Most Gracious (Allâh)?**" (45)*

Quran 43:66

هَلْ يَنظُرُونَ إِلَّا ٱلسَّاعَةَ أَن تَأْتِيَهُم بَغْتَةً وَهُمْ لَا يَشْعُرُونَ
(٦٦)

Do they only wait for the Hour that it shall come upon them suddenly, while they perceive not? *(66)*

Quran 43:78-80

لَقَدْ جِئْنَـٰكُم بِٱلْحَقِّ وَلَـٰكِنَّ أَكْثَرَكُمْ لِلْحَقِّ كَـٰرِهُونَ (٧٨) أَمْ أَبْرَمُوٓا۟ أَمْرًۭا فَإِنَّا مُبْرِمُونَ (٧٩) أَمْ يَحْسَبُونَ أَنَّا لَا نَسْمَعُ سِرَّهُمْ وَنَجْوَىٰهُم ۚ بَلَىٰ وَرُسُلُنَا لَدَيْهِمْ يَكْتُبُونَ (٨٠)

Indeed We have brought the truth (Muhammad with the Qur'ân), to you, but most of you have a hatred for the truth. (78) **Or have they plotted some plan? Then We too are planning.** (79) **Or do they think that We hear not their secrets and their private counsel?** *(Yes We do) and Our Messengers (appointed angels in charge of mankind) are by them, to record.* (80)

Quran 43:87

وَلَئِن سَأَلْتَهُم مَّنْ خَلَقَهُمْ لَيَقُولُنَّ ٱللَّهُ ۖ فَأَنَّىٰ يُؤْفَكُونَ (٨٧)

And if you ask them who created them, they will surely say: "Allâh". **How then are they turned away (from the worship of Allâh, Who created them)?** *(87)*

Quran 44:10-13

فَٱرْتَقِبْ يَوْمَ تَأْتِى ٱلسَّمَاءُ بِدُخَانٍ مُّبِينٍ (١٠) يَغْشَى ٱلنَّاسَ ۖ
هَٰذَا عَذَابٌ أَلِيمٌ (١١) رَّبَّنَا ٱكْشِفْ عَنَّا ٱلْعَذَابَ إِنَّا مُؤْمِنُونَ
(١٢) أَنَّىٰ لَهُمُ ٱلذِّكْرَىٰ وَقَدْ جَاءَهُمْ رَسُولٌ مُّبِينٌ (١٣)

Then wait you for the Day when the sky will bring forth a visible smoke, (10)covering the people? this is a painful torment. (11) (They will say): "Our Lord! Remove the torment from us, really we shall become believers!" (12) How can there be for them an admonition (at the time when the torment has reached them), when a Messenger explaining things clearly has already come to them? (13)

Quran 44:34-39

إِنَّ هَٰؤُلَاءِ لَيَقُولُونَ (٣٤) إِنْ هِيَ إِلَّا مَوْتَتُنَا ٱلْأُولَىٰ وَمَا
نَحْنُ بِمُنشَرِينَ (٣٥) فَأْتُوا۟ بِآبَائِنَآ إِن كُنتُمْ صَٰدِقِينَ
(٣٦) أَهُمْ خَيْرٌ أَمْ قَوْمُ تُبَّعٍ وَٱلَّذِينَ مِن قَبْلِهِمْ ۚ أَهْلَكْنَٰهُمْ ۖ إِنَّهُمْ
كَانُوا۟ مُجْرِمِينَ (٣٧) وَمَا خَلَقْنَا ٱلسَّمَٰوَٰتِ وَٱلْأَرْضَ وَمَا
بَيْنَهُمَا لَٰعِبِينَ (٣٨) مَا خَلَقْنَٰهُمَآ إِلَّا بِٱلْحَقِّ وَلَٰكِنَّ أَكْثَرَهُمْ
لَا يَعْلَمُونَ (٣٩)

Verily, these (Quraish) people are saying: (34) "There is nothing but our first death, and we shall not be resurrected. (35) "Then bring back our forefathers, if you speak the truth!" (36) **Are they better or the people of Tubba' and those before them?** We destroyed them because they were indeed Mujrimûn (disbelievers, polytheists, sinners, criminals). (37) And We created not the heavens and the earth, and all that is between them, for mere play, (38) We created them not except with truth (i.e. to examine and test those who are obedient and those who are disobedient and then reward the obedient ones and punish the disobedient ones), but most of them know not. (39)

Quran 45:6-9

تِلْكَ ءَايَـٰتُ ٱللَّهِ نَتْلُوهَا عَلَيْكَ بِٱلْحَقِّ فَبِأَيِّ حَدِيثٍ بَعْدَ ٱللَّهِ وَءَايَـٰتِهِۦ يُؤْمِنُونَ (٦) وَيْلٌ لِّكُلِّ أَفَّاكٍ أَثِيمٍ (٧) يَسْمَعُ ءَايَـٰتِ ٱللَّهِ تُتْلَىٰ عَلَيْهِ ثُمَّ يُصِرُّ مُسْتَكْبِرًا كَأَن لَّمْ يَسْمَعْهَا فَبَشِّرْهُ بِعَذَابٍ أَلِيمٍ (٨) وَإِذَا عَلِمَ مِنْ ءَايَـٰتِنَا شَيْئًا ٱتَّخَذَهَا هُزُوًا أُوْلَـٰئِكَ لَهُمْ عَذَابٌ مُّهِينٌ (٩)

These are the Ayât (proofs, evidences, verses, lessons, revelations, etc.) of Allâh, which We recite to you (O Muhammad) with truth. **Then in which speech after Allâh and His Ayât will they believe?** (6) Woe to every sinful liar, (7) Who hears the Verses of Allâh (being) recited to him, yet persists with pride as if he heard them not. So announce to him a painful torment! (8) And when he learns something of Our Verses (this Qur'ân), he makes them a jest. For such there will be a humiliating torment. (9)

Quran 45:21-23

أَمْ حَسِبَ ٱلَّذِينَ ٱجْتَرَحُوا۟ ٱلسَّيِّـَٔاتِ أَن نَّجْعَلَهُمْ كَٱلَّذِينَ ءَامَنُوا۟ وَعَمِلُوا۟ ٱلصَّٰلِحَٰتِ سَوَآءً مَّحْيَاهُمْ وَمَمَاتُهُمْ سَآءَ مَا يَحْكُمُونَ (٢١) وَخَلَقَ ٱللَّهُ ٱلسَّمَٰوَٰتِ وَٱلْأَرْضَ بِٱلْحَقِّ وَلِتُجْزَىٰ كُلُّ نَفْسٍ بِمَا كَسَبَتْ وَهُمْ لَا يُظْلَمُونَ (٢٢) أَفَرَءَيْتَ مَنِ ٱتَّخَذَ إِلَٰهَهُۥ هَوَىٰهُ وَأَضَلَّهُ ٱللَّهُ عَلَىٰ عِلْمٍ وَخَتَمَ عَلَىٰ سَمْعِهِۦ وَقَلْبِهِۦ وَجَعَلَ عَلَىٰ بَصَرِهِۦ غِشَٰوَةً فَمَن يَهْدِيهِ مِنۢ بَعْدِ ٱللَّهِ أَفَلَا تَذَكَّرُونَ (٢٣)

Or do those who earn evil deeds think that We shall hold them equal with those who believe (in the Oneness of Allâh — Islâmic Monotheism) and do

righteous good deeds, in their present life and after their death? Worst is the judgement that they make. (21) And Allâh has created the heavens and the earth with truth, in order that each person may be recompensed what he has earned, and they will not be wronged. (22) **Have you seen him who takes his own lust (vain desires) as his ilâh (god)?** *and Allâh knowing (him as such), left him astray, and sealed his hearing and his heart, and put a cover on his sight.* **Who then will guide him after Allâh? Will you not then remember?** (23)

Quran 45:31

وَأَمَّا ٱلَّذِينَ كَفَرُواْ أَفَلَمْ تَكُنْ ءَايَـٰتِى تُتْلَىٰ عَلَيْكُمْ فَٱسْتَكْبَرْتُمْ وَكُنتُمْ قَوْمًا مُّجْرِمِينَ (٣١)

But as for those who disbelieved (it will be said to them): "**Were not Our Verses recited to you?** *But you were proud, and you were a people who were Mujrimûn* *(polytheists, disbelievers, sinners, criminals)." (31)*

Quran 46:4-5

قُلْ أَرَءَيْتُم مَّا تَدْعُونَ مِن دُونِ ٱللَّهِ أَرُونِى مَاذَا خَلَقُواْ مِنَ
ٱلْأَرْضِ أَمْ لَهُمْ شِرْكٌ فِى ٱلسَّمَـٰوَٰتِ ٱئْتُونِى بِكِتَـٰبٍ مِّن قَبْلِ
هَـٰذَآ أَوْ أَثَـٰرَةٍ مِّنْ عِلْمٍ إِن كُنتُمْ صَـٰدِقِينَ (٤) وَمَنْ أَضَلُّ
مِمَّن يَدْعُواْ مِن دُونِ ٱللَّهِ مَن لَّا يَسْتَجِيبُ لَهُ ۥ إِلَىٰ يَوْمِ
ٱلْقِيَـٰمَةِ وَهُمْ عَن دُعَآئِهِمْ غَـٰفِلُونَ (٥)

Say (O Muhammad to these pagans):
"Think you about all that you invoke besides Allâh? Show me. What have they created of the earth? Or have they a share in (the creation of) the heavens? *Bring me a Book (revealed before this), or some trace of knowledge (in support of your claims), if you are truthful!" (4)* **And who is more astray than one who calls on (invokes) besides Allâh, such as will not answer him till the Day of Resurrection, and who are (even) unaware of their calls (invocations) to them?(5)**

Quran 46:10

قُلْ أَرَءَيْتُمْ إِن كَانَ مِنْ عِندِ ٱللَّهِ وَكَفَرْتُم بِهِۦ وَشَهِدَ شَاهِدٌ مِّنۢ بَنِىٓ إِسْرَٰٓءِيلَ عَلَىٰ مِثْلِهِۦ فَـَٔامَنَ وَٱسْتَكْبَرْتُمْ إِنَّ ٱللَّهَ لَا يَهْدِى ٱلْقَوْمَ ٱلظَّٰلِمِينَ (١٠)

Say: "Tell me! If this (Qur'ân) is from Allâh and you deny it, and a witness from among the Children of Israel ('Abdullâh bin Salâm) testifies that [this Qur'ân is from Allâh (like the Taurât (Torah)], and he believed (embraced Islâm) while you are too proud (to believe)?" Verily, Allâh guides not the people who are Zâlimûn (polytheists, disbelievers and wrong-doers). (10)

Quran 46:33-35

أَوَلَمْ يَرَوْا۟ أَنَّ ٱللَّهَ ٱلَّذِى خَلَقَ ٱلسَّمَٰوَٰتِ وَٱلْأَرْضَ وَلَمْ يَعْىَ بِخَلْقِهِنَّ بِقَٰدِرٍ عَلَىٰٓ أَن يُحْۦِىَ ٱلْمَوْتَىٰ بَلَىٰٓ إِنَّهُۥ عَلَىٰ كُلِّ شَىْءٍ قَدِيرٌ (٣٣) وَيَوْمَ يُعْرَضُ ٱلَّذِينَ كَفَرُوا۟ عَلَى ٱلنَّارِ أَلَيْسَ هَٰذَا بِٱلْحَقِّ قَالُوا۟ بَلَىٰ وَرَبِّنَا قَالَ فَذُوقُوا۟ ٱلْعَذَابَ بِمَا كُنتُمْ تَكْفُرُونَ (٣٤) فَٱصْبِرْ كَمَا صَبَرَ أُو۟لُوا۟ ٱلْعَزْمِ مِنَ ٱلرُّسُلِ وَلَا تَسْتَعْجِل لَّهُمْ كَأَنَّهُمْ يَوْمَ يَرَوْنَ مَا يُوعَدُونَ لَمْ يَلْبَثُوٓا۟ إِلَّا سَاعَةً مِّن نَّهَارٍ بَلَٰغٌ فَهَلْ يُهْلَكُ إِلَّا ٱلْقَوْمُ ٱلْفَٰسِقُونَ (٣٥)

Do they not see that Allâh, Who created the heavens and the earth, and was not wearied by their creation, is Able to give life to the dead? Yes, He surely is Able to do all things. (33) And on the Day when those who disbelieve will be exposed to the Fire (it will be said to them): *"Is this not the truth?"* They will say: "Yes, By our Lord!" He will say: "Then taste the torment, because you used to disbelieve!"
(34) Therefore be patient (O Muhammad) as did the Messengers of strong will and be in no haste about them (disbelievers). On the Day when they will see that (torment) with which they are promised (i.e. threatened, it will be) as if they had not stayed more than an hour in a single day. (O mankind, this Qur'ân is sufficient as) a clear Message (or proclamation to save yourself from destruction). *But shall any be destroyed except the people who are Al-Fâsiqûn (the rebellious against Allâh's*

Command, the disobedient to Allâh)?
(35)

Quran 47:10

أَفَلَمْ يَسِيرُوا۟ فِى ٱلْأَرْضِ فَيَنظُرُوا۟ كَيْفَ كَانَ عَـٰقِبَةُ ٱلَّذِينَ مِن قَبْلِهِمْ دَمَّرَ ٱللَّهُ عَلَيْهِمْ وَلِلْكَـٰفِرِينَ أَمْثَـٰلُهَا (١٠)

Have they not travelled through the earth, and seen what was the end of those before them? Allâh destroyed them completely and a similar (fate awaits) the disbelievers. (10)

Quran 47:14-15

أَفَمَن كَانَ عَلَىٰ بَيِّنَةٍ مِّن رَّبِّهِۦ كَمَن زُيِّنَ لَهُۥ سُوٓءُ عَمَلِهِۦ وَٱتَّبَعُوٓا۟ أَهْوَآءَهُم (١٤) مَّثَلُ ٱلْجَنَّةِ ٱلَّتِى وُعِدَ ٱلْمُتَّقُونَ فِيهَآ أَنْهَـٰرٌ مِّن مَّآءٍ غَيْرِ ءَاسِنٍ وَأَنْهَـٰرٌ مِّن لَّبَنٍ لَّمْ يَتَغَيَّرْ طَعْمُهُۥ وَأَنْهَـٰرٌ مِّنْ خَمْرٍ لَّذَّةٍ لِّلشَّـٰرِبِينَ وَأَنْهَـٰرٌ مِّنْ عَسَلٍ مُّصَفًّى وَلَهُمْ فِيهَا مِن كُلِّ ٱلثَّمَرَٰتِ وَمَغْفِرَةٌ مِّن رَّبِّهِمْ كَمَنْ هُوَ خَـٰلِدٌ فِى ٱلنَّارِ وَسُقُوا۟ مَآءً حَمِيمًا فَقَطَّعَ أَمْعَآءَهُمْ (١٥)

Is he who is on a clear proof from his Lord, like those for whom their evil deeds that they do are beautified for them, while they follow their own lusts (evil desires)? (14) The description of Paradise which the Muttaqûn (pious) have been promised (is that) in it are rivers of water the taste and smell of which are not changed, rivers of milk of which the taste never changes, rivers of wine delicious to those who drink; and rivers of clarified honey (clear and pure) therein for them is every kind of fruit; and forgiveness from their Lord. **(Are these) like those who shall dwell for ever in the Fire, and be given, to drink, boiling water, so that it cuts up their bowels? (15)**

Quran 47:18

فَهَلْ يَنظُرُونَ إِلَّا ٱلسَّاعَةَ أَن تَأْتِيَهُم بَغْتَةً ۖ فَقَدْ جَآءَ أَشْرَاطُهَا ۚ فَأَنَّىٰ لَهُمْ إِذَا جَآءَتْهُمْ ذِكْرَىٰهُمْ (١٨)

Do they then await (anything) other than the Hour, that it should come upon them suddenly? But some of its portents (indications and signs) have already come, and when it (actually) is on them,

how can they benefit then by their reminder?(18)

Quran 47:22-29

فَهَلْ عَسَيْتُمْ إِن تَوَلَّيْتُمْ أَن تُفْسِدُواْ فِى ٱلْأَرْضِ وَتُقَطِّعُوٓاْ
أَرْحَامَكُمْ (٢٢) أُوْلَٰٓئِكَ ٱلَّذِينَ لَعَنَهُمُ ٱللَّهُ فَأَصَمَّهُمْ وَأَعْمَىٰٓ
أَبْصَٰرَهُمْ (٢٣) أَفَلَا يَتَدَبَّرُونَ ٱلْقُرْءَانَ أَمْ عَلَىٰ قُلُوبٍ أَقْفَالُهَآ
(٢٤) إِنَّ ٱلَّذِينَ ٱرْتَدُّواْ عَلَىٰٓ أَدْبَٰرِهِم مِّنۢ بَعْدِ مَا تَبَيَّنَ لَهُمُ
ٱلْهُدَى ٱلشَّيْطَٰنُ سَوَّلَ لَهُمْ وَأَمْلَىٰ لَهُمْ (٢٥) ذَٰلِكَ بِأَنَّهُمْ قَالُواْ
لِلَّذِينَ كَرِهُواْ مَا نَزَّلَ ٱللَّهُ سَنُطِيعُكُمْ فِى بَعْضِ ٱلْأَمْرِ وَٱللَّهُ
يَعْلَمُ إِسْرَارَهُمْ (٢٦) فَكَيْفَ إِذَا تَوَفَّتْهُمُ ٱلْمَلَٰٓئِكَةُ يَضْرِبُونَ
وُجُوهَهُمْ وَأَدْبَٰرَهُمْ (٢٧) ذَٰلِكَ بِأَنَّهُمُ ٱتَّبَعُواْ مَآ أَسْخَطَ ٱللَّهَ
وَكَرِهُواْ رِضْوَٰنَهُ فَأَحْبَطَ أَعْمَٰلَهُمْ (٢٨) أَمْ حَسِبَ ٱلَّذِينَ
فِى قُلُوبِهِم مَّرَضٌ أَن لَّن يُخْرِجَ ٱللَّهُ أَضْغَٰنَهُمْ (٢٩)

Would you then, if you were given the authority, do mischief in the land, and sever your ties of kinship? (22) Such are they whom Allâh has cursed, so that He has made them deaf and blinded their sight. *(23) Do they not then think deeply in the Qur'ân, or are their hearts locked up (from understanding it)? (24)* Verily, those who have turned back as disbelievers

~ 194 ~

after the guidance has been manifested to them — Shaitân (Satan) has beautified for them (their false hopes), and (Allâh) prolonged their term (age). (25) This is because they said to those who hate what Allâh has sent down: "We will obey you in part of the matter," but Allâh knows their secrets. (26) **Then how (will it be) when the angels will take their souls at death, smiting their faces and their backs?** (27) That is because they followed that which angered Allâh, and hated that which pleased Him. So He made their deeds fruitless. (28) **Or do those in whose hearts is a disease (of hypocrisy), think that Allâh will not bring to light all their hidden ill-wills?** (29)

Quran 48:11

سَيَقُولُ لَكَ ٱلْمُخَلَّفُونَ مِنَ ٱلْأَعْرَابِ شَغَلَتْنَا أَمْوَٰلُنَا وَأَهْلُونَا فَٱسْتَغْفِرْ لَنَا يَقُولُونَ بِأَلْسِنَتِهِم مَّا لَيْسَ فِى قُلُوبِهِمْ قُلْ فَمَن يَمْلِكُ لَكُم مِّنَ ٱللَّهِ شَيْئًا إِنْ أَرَادَ بِكُمْ ضَرًّا أَوْ أَرَادَ بِكُمْ نَفْعًا بَلْ كَانَ ٱللَّهُ بِمَا تَعْمَلُونَ خَبِيرًا (١١)

*Those of the bedouins who lagged behind
will say to you: "Our possessions and our
families occupied us, so ask forgiveness for
us." They say with their tongues what is not
in their hearts. Say: "**Who then has any
power at all (to intervene) on your
behalf with Allâh, if He intends you
hurt or intends you benefit?** Nay, but
Allâh is Ever All-Aware of what you do.
(11)*

Quran 49:12

يَٰٓأَيُّهَا ٱلَّذِينَ ءَامَنُواْ ٱجْتَنِبُواْ كَثِيرًا مِّنَ ٱلظَّنِّ إِنَّ بَعْضَ ٱلظَّنِّ
إِثْمٌ وَلَا تَجَسَّسُواْ وَلَا يَغْتَب بَّعْضُكُم بَعْضًا أَيُحِبُّ أَحَدُكُمْ أَن
يَأْكُلَ لَحْمَ أَخِيهِ مَيْتًا فَكَرِهْتُمُوهُ وَٱتَّقُواْ ٱللَّهَ إِنَّ ٱللَّهَ تَوَّابٌ
رَّحِيمٌ (١٢)

*O you who believe! Avoid much suspicion,
indeed some suspicions are sins. And spy
not, neither backbite one another. **Would
one of you like to eat the flesh of his
dead brother?** You would hate it (so hate
backbiting) . And fear Allâh. Verily, Allâh is*

the One Who forgives and accepts
repentance, Most Merciful. (12)

Quran 49:15-17

إِنَّمَا ٱلْمُؤْمِنُونَ ٱلَّذِينَ ءَامَنُواْ بِٱللَّهِ وَرَسُولِهِۦ ثُمَّ لَمْ يَرْتَابُواْ
وَجَٰهَدُواْ بِأَمْوَٰلِهِمْ وَأَنفُسِهِمْ فِى سَبِيلِ ٱللَّهِۚ أُوْلَٰٓئِكَ هُمُ
ٱلصَّٰدِقُونَ (١٥) قُلْ أَتُعَلِّمُونَ ٱللَّهَ بِدِينِكُمْ وَٱللَّهُ يَعْلَمُ مَا فِى
ٱلسَّمَٰوَٰتِ وَمَا فِى ٱلْأَرْضِۚ وَٱللَّهُ بِكُلِّ شَىْءٍ عَلِيمٌ
(١٦) يَمُنُّونَ عَلَيْكَ أَنْ أَسْلَمُواْۖ قُل لَّا تَمُنُّواْ عَلَىَّ إِسْلَٰمَكُمۖ بَلِ
ٱللَّهُ يَمُنُّ عَلَيْكُمْ أَنْ هَدَىٰكُمْ لِلْإِيمَٰنِ إِن كُنتُمْ صَٰدِقِينَ (١٧)

Only those are the believers who have
believed in Allâh and His Messenger, and
afterward doubt not but strive with their
wealth and their lives for the Cause of Allâh.
Those! They are the truthful. (15) Say:
**"Will you inform Allâh of your religion
While Allâh knows all that is in the
heavens and all that is in the earth, and
Allâh is All-Aware of everything?**
(16) They regard as favour to you (O
Muhammad) that they have embraced Islâm.
Say: "Count not your Islâm as a favour to
me. Nay, but Allâh has conferred a favour

upon you, that He has guided you to the Faith, if you indeed are true. (17)

Quran 50:6-7

أَفَلَمْ يَنظُرُوٓاْ إِلَى ٱلسَّمَآءِ فَوْقَهُمْ كَيْفَ بَنَيْنَٰهَا وَزَيَّنَّٰهَا وَمَا لَهَا مِن فُرُوجٍ (٦) وَٱلْأَرْضَ مَدَدْنَٰهَا وَأَلْقَيْنَا فِيهَا رَوَٰسِىَ وَأَنۢبَتْنَا فِيهَا مِن كُلِّ زَوْجٍ بَهِيجٍ (٧)

Have they not looked at the heaven above them, how We have made it and adorned it, and there are no rifts in it? (6) And the earth! We have spread it out, and set thereon mountains standing firm, and have produced therein every kind of lovely growth (plants). (7)

Quran 50:15

أَفَعَيِينَا بِٱلْخَلْقِ ٱلْأَوَّلِ بَلْ هُمْ فِى لَبْسٍ مِّنْ خَلْقٍ جَدِيدٍ (١٥)

Were We then tired with the first creation? Nay, they are in confused doubt about a new creation (i.e. Resurrection)? (15)

Quran 50:30

يَوْمَ نَقُولُ لِجَهَنَّمَ هَلِ ٱمْتَلَأْتِ وَتَقُولُ هَلْ مِن مَّزِيدٍ (٣٠)

*On the Day when **We will say to Hell:
"Are you filled?"** It will say: "Are there
any more (to come)?" (30)*

Quran 50:36

وَكَمْ أَهْلَكْنَا قَبْلَهُم مِّن قَرْنٍ هُمْ أَشَدُّ مِنْهُم بَطْشًا فَنَقَّبُواْ فِى
ٱلْبِلَٰدِ هَلْ مِن مَّحِيصٍ (٣٦)

*And how many a generation We have
destroyed before them, who were stronger in
power than they, and (when Our Torment
came) they ran for a refuge in the land!
**Could they find any place of refuge (for
them to save themselves from
destruction)?** (36)*

Quran 51:20-21

وَفِى ٱلْأَرْضِ ءَايَٰتٌ لِّلْمُوقِنِينَ (٢٠) وَفِىٓ أَنفُسِكُمْ أَفَلَا
تُبْصِرُونَ (٢١)

*And on the earth are signs for those who
have Faith with certainty, (20) And also in*

your ownselves. **Will you not then see?** *(21)*

Quran 51:24

هَلْ أَتَنكَ حَدِيثُ ضَيْفِ إِبْرَأهِيمَ ٱلْمُكْرَمِينَ (٢٤)

Has the story reached you, of the honoured guests [three angels; Jibril (Gabriel) along with another two] of Ibrahîm (Abraham)? (24)

Quran 51:52-53

كَذَٰلِكَ مَآ أَتَى ٱلَّذِينَ مِن قَبْلِهِم مِّن رَّسُولٍ إِلَّا قَالُوا۟ سَاحِرٌ أَوْ مَجْنُونٌ (٥٢) أَتَوَاصَوْا۟ بِهِۦ ۚ بَلْ هُمْ قَوْمٌ طَاغُونَ (٥٣)

Likewise, no Messenger came to those before them, but they said: "A sorcerer or a madman!" (52) **Have they (the people of the past) transmitted this saying to these (Quraish pagans)?** *Nay, they are themselves a people transgressing beyond bounds (in disbelief)! (53)*

Quran 52:7-16

إِنَّ عَذَابَ رَبِّكَ لَوَاقِعٌ (٧) مَّا لَهُ ۥ مِن دَافِعٍ (٨) يَوْمَ تَمُورُ
ٱلسَّمَآءُ مَوْرًا (٩) وَتَسِيرُ ٱلْجِبَالُ سَيْرًا (١٠) فَوَيْلٌ يَوْمَئِذٍ
لِّلْمُكَذِّبِينَ (١١) ٱلَّذِينَ هُمْ فِى خَوْضٍ يَلْعَبُونَ (١٢) يَوْمَ
يُدَعُّونَ إِلَىٰ نَارِ جَهَنَّمَ دَعًّا (١٣) هَٰذِهِ ٱلنَّارُ ٱلَّتِى كُنتُم بِهَا
تُكَذِّبُونَ (١٤) أَفَسِحْرٌ هَٰذَآ أَمْ أَنتُمْ لَا تُبْصِرُونَ
(١٥) ٱصْلَوْهَا فَٱصْبِرُوٓاْ أَوْ لَا تَصْبِرُواْ سَوَآءٌ عَلَيْكُمْ إِنَّمَا
تُجْزَوْنَ مَا كُنتُمْ تَعْمَلُونَ (١٦)

Verily, the Torment of your Lord will surely come to pass, (7) There is none that can avert it; (8) On the Day when the heaven will shake with a dreadful shaking, (9) And the mountains will move away with a (horrible) movement. (10) Then woe that Day to the beliers; (11) Who are playing in falsehood. (12) The Day when they will be pushed down by force to the Fire of Hell, with a horrible, forceful pushing. (13) This is the Fire which you used to belie. (14) **Is this magic, or do you not see?** *(15) Taste you therein its heat, and whether you are patient of it or impatient of it, it is all the same. You are only being requited for what you used to do. (16)*

Quran 52:34-47

فَلْيَأْتُواْ بِحَدِيثٍ مِّثْلِهِۦٓ إِن كَانُواْ صَٰدِقِينَ (٣٤) أَمْ خُلِقُواْ مِنْ
غَيْرِ شَىْءٍ أَمْ هُمُ ٱلْخَٰلِقُونَ (٣٥) أَمْ خَلَقُواْ ٱلسَّمَٰوَٰتِ
وَٱلْأَرْضَ بَل لَّا يُوقِنُونَ (٣٦) أَمْ عِندَهُمْ خَزَآئِنُ رَبِّكَ أَمْ هُمُ
ٱلْمُصَيْطِرُونَ (٣٧) أَمْ لَهُمْ سُلَّمٌ يَسْتَمِعُونَ فِيهِ ۖ فَلْيَأْتِ
مُسْتَمِعُهُم بِسُلْطَٰنٍ مُّبِينٍ (٣٨) أَمْ لَهُ ٱلْبَنَٰتُ وَلَكُمُ ٱلْبَنُونَ
(٣٩) أَمْ تَسْـَٔلُهُمْ أَجْرًا فَهُم مِّن مَّغْرَمٍ مُّثْقَلُونَ (٤٠) أَمْ
عِندَهُمُ ٱلْغَيْبُ فَهُمْ يَكْتُبُونَ (٤١) أَمْ يُرِيدُونَ كَيْدًا ۖ فَٱلَّذِينَ
كَفَرُواْ هُمُ ٱلْمَكِيدُونَ (٤٢) أَمْ لَهُمْ إِلَٰهٌ غَيْرُ ٱللَّهِ ۚ سُبْحَٰنَ ٱللَّهِ
عَمَّا يُشْرِكُونَ (٤٣) وَإِن يَرَوْاْ كِسْفًا مِّنَ ٱلسَّمَآءِ سَاقِطًا
يَقُولُواْ سَحَابٌ مَّرْكُومٌ (٤٤) فَذَرْهُمْ حَتَّىٰ يُلَٰقُواْ يَوْمَهُمُ ٱلَّذِى
فِيهِ يُصْعَقُونَ (٤٥) يَوْمَ لَا يُغْنِى عَنْهُمْ كَيْدُهُمْ شَيْـًٔا وَلَا هُمْ
يُنصَرُونَ (٤٦) وَإِنَّ لِلَّذِينَ ظَلَمُواْ عَذَابًا دُونَ ذَٰلِكَ وَلَٰكِنَّ
أَكْثَرَهُمْ لَا يَعْلَمُونَ (٤٧)

Let them then produce a recital like unto it (the Qur'ân) if they are truthful. (34) **Were they created by nothing? Or were they themselves the creators? (35) Or did they create the heavens and the earth?** *Nay, but they have no firm Belief. (36)* **Or are with them the treasures of your Lord? Or are they the tyrants with the authority to do as they like? (37) Or** *have they a stairway (to heaven), by means of which they listen (to the talks of the angels)?* Then let their listener produce some manifest proof. (38) **Or has He (Allâh) only daughters and you have sons? (39) Or is it that you (O Muhammad) ask a wage from them (for your preaching of Islâmic Monotheism) so that they are burdened with a load of debt? (40) Or that the Ghaib (unseen) is with them, and they write it down? (41) Or do they intend a plot (against you O Muhammad)?** But those who disbelieve (in the Oneness of Allâh – Islâmic Monotheism) are themselves plotted against! (42) **Or have they an ilâh (a god) other than Allâh?** Glorified is Allâh from all that they ascribe as partners (to Him) (43) And if they were to see a piece of the heaven falling down, they would say: "Clouds gathered in heaps!" (44) So leave them alone till they meet their Day, in which they will sink into a fainting (with horror).

(45) The Day when their plotting shall not avail them at all nor will they be helped (i.e. they will receive their torment in Hell). (46) And verily, for those who do wrong, there is another punishment (i.e. the torment in this world and in their graves) before this, but most of them know not. (47)

Quran 53:19-28

أَفَرَءَيْتُمُ ٱللَّٰتَ وَٱلْعُزَّىٰ (١٩) وَمَنَوٰةَ ٱلثَّالِثَةَ ٱلْأُخْرَىٰ (٢٠) أَلَكُمُ ٱلذَّكَرُ وَلَهُ ٱلْأُنثَىٰ (٢١) تِلْكَ إِذًا قِسْمَةٌ ضِيزَىٰٓ (٢٢) إِنْ هِيَ إِلَّآ أَسْمَآءٌ سَمَّيْتُمُوهَآ أَنتُمْ وَءَابَآؤُكُم مَّآ أَنزَلَ ٱللَّهُ بِهَا مِن سُلْطَٰنٍ إِن يَتَّبِعُونَ إِلَّا ٱلظَّنَّ وَمَا تَهْوَى ٱلْأَنفُسُ وَلَقَدْ جَآءَهُم مِّن رَّبِّهِمُ ٱلْهُدَىٰٓ (٢٣) أَمْ لِلْإِنسَٰنِ مَا تَمَنَّىٰ (٢٤) فَلِلَّهِ ٱلْأَخِرَةُ وَٱلْأُولَىٰ (٢٥) ۞ وَكَم مِّن مَّلَكٍ فِى ٱلسَّمَٰوَٰتِ لَا تُغْنِى شَفَٰعَتُهُمْ شَيْـًٔا إِلَّا مِنۢ بَعْدِ أَن يَأْذَنَ ٱللَّهُ لِمَن يَشَآءُ وَيَرْضَىٰٓ (٢٦) إِنَّ ٱلَّذِينَ لَا يُؤْمِنُونَ بِٱلْأَخِرَةِ لَيُسَمُّونَ ٱلْمَلَٰٓئِكَةَ تَسْمِيَةَ ٱلْأُنثَىٰ (٢٧) وَمَا لَهُم بِهِۦ مِنْ عِلْمٍ إِن يَتَّبِعُونَ إِلَّا ٱلظَّنَّ وَإِنَّ ٱلظَّنَّ لَا يُغْنِى مِنَ ٱلْحَقِّ شَيْـًٔا (٢٨)

Have you then considered Al-Lât, and Al-'Uzza (two idols of the pagan Arabs)? (19) And Manât (another idol of *the pagan Arabs), the other third? (20) **Is it for you the males and for Him the females?** (21)* That indeed is a division most unfair! (22) They are but names which you have named — you and your fathers — for which Allâh has sent down no authority. They follow but a guess and that which they themselves desire, whereas there has surely come to them the Guidance from their Lord! (23) **Or shall man have what he wishes?** (24) But to Allâh belongs the last (Hereafter) and the first (the world). (25) And there are many angels in the heavens, whose intercession will avail nothing except after Allâh has given leave for whom He wills and is pleased with. (26) Verily, those who believe not in the Hereafter, name the angels with female names. (27) But they have no knowledge thereof. They follow but a guess, and verily, guess is no substitute for the truth. (28)

Quran 53:33-62

أَفَرَءَيْتَ ٱلَّذِى تَوَلَّىٰ (٣٣) وَأَعْطَىٰ قَلِيلاً وَأَكْدَىٰ (٣٤) أَعِندَهُۥ عِلْمُ ٱلْغَيْبِ فَهُوَ يَرَىٰ (٣٥) أَمْ لَمْ يُنَبَّأْ بِمَا فِى صُحُفِ مُوسَىٰ (٣٦) وَإِبْرَٰهِيمَ ٱلَّذِى وَفَّىٰ (٣٧) أَلَّا تَزِرُ وَازِرَةٌ وِزْرَ أُخْرَىٰ (٣٨) وَأَن لَّيْسَ لِلْإِنسَٰنِ إِلَّا مَا سَعَىٰ (٣٩) وَأَنَّ سَعْيَهُۥ سَوْفَ يُرَىٰ (٤٠) ثُمَّ يُجْزَٰهُ ٱلْجَزَآءَ ٱلْأَوْفَىٰ (٤١) وَأَنَّ إِلَىٰ رَبِّكَ ٱلْمُنتَهَىٰ (٤٢) وَأَنَّهُۥ هُوَ أَضْحَكَ وَأَبْكَىٰ (٤٣) وَأَنَّهُۥ هُوَ أَمَاتَ وَأَحْيَا (٤٤) وَأَنَّهُۥ خَلَقَ ٱلزَّوْجَيْنِ ٱلذَّكَرَ وَٱلْأُنثَىٰ (٤٥) مِن نُّطْفَةٍ إِذَا تُمْنَىٰ (٤٦) وَأَنَّ عَلَيْهِ ٱلنَّشْأَةَ ٱلْأُخْرَىٰ (٤٧) وَأَنَّهُۥ هُوَ أَغْنَىٰ وَأَقْنَىٰ (٤٨) وَأَنَّهُۥ هُوَ رَبُّ ٱلشِّعْرَىٰ (٤٩) وَأَنَّهُۥ أَهْلَكَ عَادًا ٱلْأُولَىٰ (٥٠) وَثَمُودَا فَمَا أَبْقَىٰ (٥١) وَقَوْمَ نُوحٍ مِّن قَبْلُ إِنَّهُمْ كَانُوا۟ هُمْ أَظْلَمَ وَأَطْغَىٰ (٥٢) وَٱلْمُؤْتَفِكَةَ أَهْوَىٰ (٥٣) فَغَشَّىٰهَا مَا غَشَّىٰ (٥٤) فَبِأَىِّ ءَالَآءِ رَبِّكَ تَتَمَارَىٰ (٥٥) هَٰذَا نَذِيرٌ مِّنَ ٱلنُّذُرِ ٱلْأُولَىٰٓ (٥٦) أَزِفَتِ ٱلْأَزِفَةُ (٥٧) لَيْسَ لَهَا مِن دُونِ ٱللَّهِ كَاشِفَةٌ (٥٨) أَفَمِنْ هَٰذَا ٱلْحَدِيثِ تَعْجَبُونَ (٥٩) وَتَضْحَكُونَ وَلَا تَبْكُونَ (٦٠) وَأَنتُمْ سَٰمِدُونَ (٦١) فَٱسْجُدُوا۟ لِلَّهِ وَٱعْبُدُوا۟ ۩ (٦٢)

Did you (O Muhammad) observe him who turned away (from Islâm)? (33) And gave a little, then stopped (giving)? (34) Is with him the knowledge of the unseen so that he sees? (35) Or is he not informed with what is in the Pages (Scripture) of Mûsa (Moses),

*(36) **And of Ibrâhim (Abraham) who fulfilled (or conveyed) all that (Allâh ordered him to do or convey), (37) That no burdened person (with sins) shall bear the burden (sins) of another?*** *(38) And that man can have nothing but what he does (good or bad) , (39) And that his deeds will be seen, (40) Then he will be recompensed with a full and the best recompense (41) And that to your Lord (Allâh) is the End (Return of everything). (42) And that it is He (Allâh) Who makes (whom He wills) laugh, and makes (whom He wills) weep. (43) And that it is He (Allâh) Who causes death and gives life. (44) And that He (Allâh) creates the pairs, male and female. (45) From Nutfah (drops of semen — male and female discharges) when it is emitted. (46) And that upon Him (Allâh) is another bringing forth (Resurrection). (47) And that it is He (Allâh) Who gives much or a little (of wealth and contentment) (48) And that He (Allâh)*

is the Lord of Sirius (the star which the pagan Arabs used to worship); (49) And that it is He (Allâh) Who destroyed the former 'Ad (people), (50) And Thamûd (people). He spared none of them. (51) And the people of Nûh (Noah) aforetime, verily, they were more unjust and more rebellious and transgressing [in disobeying Allâh and His Messenger](52) And He destroyed the overthrown cities [of Sodom to which Prophet Lut (Lot) was sent]. (53) So there covered them that which did cover (i.e. torment with stones) (54) **Then which of the Graces of your Lord will you doubt?** (55) This (Muhammad) is a warner (Messenger) of the (series of) warners (Messengers) of old (56) The Day of Resurrection draws near, (57) None besides Allâh can avert it, (or advance it, or delay it). (58) **Do you then wonder at this recitation (the Qur'ân)?** (59) And you laugh at it and weep not, (60) Wasting your (precious) lifetime in pastime and amusements. (61) *So fall you down in prostration to Allâh, and worship Him (Alone). (62)*

Quran 54:9-22

﴿۞ كَذَّبَتْ قَبْلَهُمْ قَوْمُ نُوحٍ فَكَذَّبُواْ عَبْدَنَا وَقَالُواْ مَجْنُونٌ وَٱزْدُجِرَ (٩) فَدَعَا رَبَّهُۥٓ أَنِّى مَغْلُوبٌ فَٱنتَصِرْ (١٠) فَفَتَحْنَآ أَبْوَٰبَ ٱلسَّمَآءِ بِمَآءٍ مُّنْهَمِرٍ (١١) وَفَجَّرْنَا ٱلْأَرْضَ عُيُونًا فَٱلْتَقَى ٱلْمَآءُ عَلَىٰٓ أَمْرٍ قَدْ قُدِرَ (١٢) وَحَمَلْنَٰهُ عَلَىٰ ذَاتِ أَلْوَٰحٍ وَدُسُرٍ (١٣) تَجْرِى بِأَعْيُنِنَا جَزَآءً لِّمَن كَانَ كُفِرَ (١٤) وَلَقَد تَّرَكْنَٰهَآ ءَايَةً فَهَلْ مِن مُّدَّكِرٍ (١٥) فَكَيْفَ كَانَ عَذَابِى وَنُذُرِ (١٦) وَلَقَدْ يَسَّرْنَا ٱلْقُرْءَانَ لِلذِّكْرِ فَهَلْ مِن مُّدَّكِرٍ (١٧) كَذَّبَتْ عَادٌ فَكَيْفَ كَانَ عَذَابِى وَنُذُرِ (١٨) إِنَّآ أَرْسَلْنَا عَلَيْهِمْ رِيحًا صَرْصَرًا فِى يَوْمِ نَحْسٍ مُّسْتَمِرٍّ (١٩) تَنزِعُ ٱلنَّاسَ كَأَنَّهُمْ أَعْجَازُ نَخْلٍ مُّنقَعِرٍ (٢٠) فَكَيْفَ كَانَ عَذَابِى وَنُذُرِ (٢١) وَلَقَدْ يَسَّرْنَا ٱلْقُرْءَانَ لِلذِّكْرِ فَهَلْ مِن مُّدَّكِرٍ (٢٢)

The people of Nûh (Noah) denied (their Messenger) before them. They rejected Our slave, and said: "A madman!" and he was insolently rebuked and threatened. (9) Then he invoked his Lord (saying): "I have been overcome, so help (me)!" (10) So We opened the gates of heaven with water pouring forth. (11) And We caused the spring to gush forth from the earth. So the waters (of the heaven and the earth) met for a matter predestined (12) And We carried him on a (ship) made of planks and nails,

(13) Floating under Our Eyes, a reward for him who had been rejected! (14) And indeed, We have left this as a sign, Then is there any that will remember (or receive admonition)? (15) **Then how (terrible) was My Torment and My Warnings? (16) And We have indeed made the Qur'ân easy to understand and remember, then is there any one who will remember (or receive admonition)? (17)** 'Ad (people) **belied (their Prophet, Hûd), then how (terrible) was My Torment and My Warnings? (18)** Verily, We sent against them a furious wind of harsh voice on a day of evil omen and continuous calamity. (19) Plucking out men as if they were uprooted stems of date-palms. (20) **Then, how (terrible) was My Torment and My**

Warnings? (21) And We have indeed made the Qur'ân easy to understand and remember, then is there any that will remember (or receive admonition)? (22)

Quran 54:32

وَلَقَدْ يَسَّرْنَا ٱلْقُرْءَانَ لِلذِّكْرِ فَهَلْ مِن مُّدَّكِرٍ (٣٢)

And indeed, We have made the Qur'ân easy to understand and remember, then is there any that will remember (or receive admonition)? (32)

Quran 54:40-52

وَلَقَدْ يَسَّرْنَا ٱلْقُرْءَانَ لِلذِّكْرِ فَهَلْ مِن مُّدَّكِرٍ (٤٠) وَلَقَدْ جَآءَ ءَالَ فِرْعَوْنَ ٱلنُّذُرُ (٤١) كَذَّبُواْ بِـَٔايَتِنَا كُلِّهَا فَأَخَذْنَٰهُمْ أَخْذَ عَزِيزٍ مُّقْتَدِرٍ (٤٢) أَكُفَّارُكُمْ خَيْرٌ مِّنْ أُوْلَٰئِكُمْ أَمْ لَكُم بَرَآءَةٌ فِى ٱلزُّبُرِ (٤٣) أَمْ يَقُولُونَ نَحْنُ جَمِيعٌ مُّنتَصِرٌ (٤٤) سَيُهْزَمُ ٱلْجَمْعُ وَيُوَلُّونَ ٱلدُّبُرَ (٤٥) بَلِ ٱلسَّاعَةُ مَوْعِدُهُمْ وَٱلسَّاعَةُ أَدْهَىٰ وَأَمَرُّ (٤٦) إِنَّ ٱلْمُجْرِمِينَ فِى ضَلَٰلٍ وَسُعُرٍ (٤٧) يَوْمَ يُسْحَبُونَ فِى ٱلنَّارِ عَلَىٰ وُجُوهِهِمْ ذُوقُواْ مَسَّ سَقَرَ (٤٨) إِنَّا كُلَّ شَىْءٍ خَلَقْنَٰهُ بِقَدَرٍ (٤٩) وَمَآ أَمْرُنَآ إِلَّا وَٰحِدَةٌ كَلَمْحٍ بِٱلْبَصَرِ (٥٠) وَلَقَدْ أَهْلَكْنَآ أَشْيَاعَكُمْ فَهَلْ مِن مُّدَّكِرٍ (٥١) وَكُلُّ شَىْءٍ فَعَلُوهُ فِى ٱلزُّبُرِ (٥٢)

And indeed, We have made the Qur'ân easy to understand and remember, then is there any that will remember (or receive admonition)? (40) *And indeed, warnings came to the people of Fir'aun (Pharaoh) [through Mûsa (Moses) and Hârûn (Aaron)]. (41) (They) belied all Our Signs, so We seized them with a Seizure of the All-Mighty, All-Capable (Omnipotent). (42) **Are your disbelievers (O Quraish!) better than these [nations of Nûh (Noah), Lut (Lot), Sâlih, and the people of Fir'aun (Pharaoh), who were destroyed)? Or have you an immunity (against Our Torment) in the Divine Scriptures? (43) Or say they: "We are a great multitude, victorious.?"** (44) Their multitude will be put to flight, and they will show their backs. (45) Nay, but the Hour is their appointed time (for their full recompense), and the Hour will be more grievous and more bitter. (46) Verily, the Mujrimûn (polytheists, disbelievers,* sinners, criminals) are in error (in this world) and will burn (in the Hell-fire in the Hereafter). (47) The Day they will be dragged on their faces into the Fire (it will be said to them): "Taste you the touch of Hell!" (48) Verily, We have created all things with Qadar (Divine Preordainments of all things before their creation, as written in the Book of Decrees Al-Lauh Al-Mahfûz). (49) And Our Commandment is but one, as the twinkling of an eye. (50) **And indeed, We have destroyed your likes, then is there any that will remember (or receive admonition)?** (51) And everything they have done is noted in (their) Records (of deeds). (52)

Quran 55:1-78

ٱلرَّحۡمَـٰنُ (١) عَلَّمَ ٱلۡقُرۡءَانَ (٢) خَلَقَ ٱلۡإِنسَـٰنَ (٣) عَلَّمَهُ ٱلۡبَيَانَ (٤) ٱلشَّمۡسُ وَٱلۡقَمَرُ بِحُسۡبَانٍ (٥) وَٱلنَّجۡمُ وَٱلشَّجَرُ يَسۡجُدَانِ (٦) وَٱلسَّمَآءَ رَفَعَهَا وَوَضَعَ ٱلۡمِيزَانَ (٧) أَلَّا تَطۡغَوۡاْ فِى ٱلۡمِيزَانِ (٨) وَأَقِيمُواْ ٱلۡوَزۡنَ بِٱلۡقِسۡطِ وَلَا تُخۡسِرُواْ ٱلۡمِيزَانَ (٩) وَٱلۡأَرۡضَ وَضَعَهَا لِلۡأَنَامِ (١٠) فِيهَا فَـٰكِهَةٌ وَٱلنَّخۡلُ ذَاتُ ٱلۡأَكۡمَامِ (١١) وَٱلۡحَبُّ ذُو ٱلۡعَصۡفِ وَٱلرَّيۡحَانُ

(١٢) فَبِأَيِّ ءَالَآءِ رَبِّكُمَا تُكَذِّبَانِ (١٣) خَلَقَ ٱلْإِنسَٰنَ مِن صَلْصَٰلٍ كَٱلْفَخَّارِ (١٤) وَخَلَقَ ٱلْجَآنَّ مِن مَّارِجٍ مِّن نَّارٍ (١٥) فَبِأَيِّ ءَالَآءِ رَبِّكُمَا تُكَذِّبَانِ (١٦) رَبُّ ٱلْمَشْرِقَيْنِ وَرَبُّ ٱلْمَغْرِبَيْنِ (١٧) فَبِأَيِّ ءَالَآءِ رَبِّكُمَا تُكَذِّبَانِ (١٨) مَرَجَ ٱلْبَحْرَيْنِ يَلْتَقِيَانِ (١٩) بَيْنَهُمَا بَرْزَخٌ لَّا يَبْغِيَانِ (٢٠) فَبِأَيِّ ءَالَآءِ رَبِّكُمَا تُكَذِّبَانِ (٢١) يَخْرُجُ مِنْهُمَا ٱللُّؤْلُؤُ وَٱلْمَرْجَانُ (٢٢) فَبِأَيِّ ءَالَآءِ رَبِّكُمَا تُكَذِّبَانِ (٢٣) وَلَهُ ٱلْجَوَارِ ٱلْمُنشَئَاتُ فِى ٱلْبَحْرِ كَٱلْأَعْلَٰمِ (٢٤) فَبِأَيِّ ءَالَآءِ رَبِّكُمَا تُكَذِّبَانِ (٢٥) كُلُّ مَنْ عَلَيْهَا فَانٍ (٢٦) وَيَبْقَىٰ وَجْهُ رَبِّكَ ذُو ٱلْجَلَٰلِ وَٱلْإِكْرَامِ (٢٧) فَبِأَيِّ ءَالَآءِ رَبِّكُمَا تُكَذِّبَانِ (٢٨) يَسْـَٔلُهُ مَن فِى ٱلسَّمَٰوَٰتِ وَٱلْأَرْضِ كُلَّ يَوْمٍ هُوَ فِى شَأْنٍ (٢٩) فَبِأَيِّ ءَالَآءِ رَبِّكُمَا تُكَذِّبَانِ (٣٠) سَنَفْرُغُ لَكُمْ أَيُّهَ ٱلثَّقَلَانِ (٣١) فَبِأَيِّ ءَالَآءِ رَبِّكُمَا تُكَذِّبَانِ (٣٢) يَٰمَعْشَرَ ٱلْجِنِّ وَٱلْإِنسِ إِنِ ٱسْتَطَعْتُمْ أَن تَنفُذُوا۟ مِنْ أَقْطَارِ ٱلسَّمَٰوَٰتِ وَٱلْأَرْضِ فَٱنفُذُوا۟ لَا تَنفُذُونَ إِلَّا بِسُلْطَٰنٍ (٣٣) فَبِأَيِّ ءَالَآءِ رَبِّكُمَا تُكَذِّبَانِ (٣٤) يُرْسَلُ عَلَيْكُمَا شُوَاظٌ مِّن نَّارٍ وَنُحَاسٌ فَلَا تَنتَصِرَانِ (٣٥) فَبِأَيِّ ءَالَآءِ رَبِّكُمَا تُكَذِّبَانِ (٣٦) فَإِذَا ٱنشَقَّتِ ٱلسَّمَآءُ فَكَانَتْ وَرْدَةً كَٱلدِّهَانِ (٣٧) فَبِأَيِّ ءَالَآءِ رَبِّكُمَا تُكَذِّبَانِ (٣٨) فَيَوْمَئِذٍ لَّا يُسْـَٔلُ عَن ذَنۢبِهِ إِنسٌ وَلَا جَآنٌّ (٣٩) فَبِأَيِّ ءَالَآءِ رَبِّكُمَا تُكَذِّبَانِ (٤٠) يُعْرَفُ ٱلْمُجْرِمُونَ بِسِيمَٰهُمْ فَيُؤْخَذُ بِٱلنَّوَٰصِى وَٱلْأَقْدَامِ (٤١) فَبِأَيِّ ءَالَآءِ رَبِّكُمَا تُكَذِّبَانِ (٤٢) هَٰذِهِۦ جَهَنَّمُ ٱلَّتِى يُكَذِّبُ بِهَا ٱلْمُجْرِمُونَ (٤٣) يَطُوفُونَ بَيْنَهَا وَبَيْنَ حَمِيمٍ ءَانٍ (٤٤) فَبِأَيِّ ءَالَآءِ رَبِّكُمَا تُكَذِّبَانِ (٤٥) وَلِمَنْ خَافَ مَقَامَ

رَبِّهِ جَنَّتَانِ (٤٦) فَبِأَيِّ ءَالَاءِ رَبِّكُمَا تُكَذِّبَانِ (٤٧) ذَوَاتَآ أَفْنَانٍ (٤٨) فَبِأَيِّ ءَالَاءِ رَبِّكُمَا تُكَذِّبَانِ (٤٩) فِيهِمَا عَيْنَانِ تَجْرِيَانِ (٥٠) فَبِأَيِّ ءَالَاءِ رَبِّكُمَا تُكَذِّبَانِ (٥١) فِيهِمَا مِن كُلِّ فَكِهَةٍ زَوْجَانِ (٥٢) فَبِأَيِّ ءَالَاءِ رَبِّكُمَا تُكَذِّبَانِ (٥٣) مُتَّكِئِينَ عَلَىٰ فُرُشٍ بَطَآئِنُهَا مِنْ إِسْتَبْرَقٍ وَجَنَى ٱلْجَنَّتَيْنِ دَانٍ (٥٤) فَبِأَيِّ ءَالَاءِ رَبِّكُمَا تُكَذِّبَانِ (٥٥) فِيهِنَّ قَاصِرَاتُ ٱلطَّرْفِ لَمْ يَطْمِثْهُنَّ إِنسٌ قَبْلَهُمْ وَلَا جَآنٌّ (٥٦) فَبِأَيِّ ءَالَاءِ رَبِّكُمَا تُكَذِّبَانِ (٥٧) كَأَنَّهُنَّ ٱلْيَاقُوتُ وَٱلْمَرْجَانُ (٥٨) فَبِأَيِّ ءَالَاءِ رَبِّكُمَا تُكَذِّبَانِ (٥٩) هَلْ جَزَآءُ ٱلْإِحْسَٰنِ إِلَّا ٱلْإِحْسَٰنُ (٦٠) فَبِأَيِّ ءَالَاءِ رَبِّكُمَا تُكَذِّبَانِ (٦١) وَمِن دُونِهِمَا جَنَّتَانِ (٦٢) فَبِأَيِّ ءَالَاءِ رَبِّكُمَا تُكَذِّبَانِ (٦٣) مُدْهَآمَّتَانِ (٦٤) فَبِأَيِّ ءَالَاءِ رَبِّكُمَا تُكَذِّبَانِ (٦٥) فِيهِمَا عَيْنَانِ نَضَّاخَتَانِ (٦٦) فَبِأَيِّ ءَالَاءِ رَبِّكُمَا تُكَذِّبَانِ (٦٧) فِيهِمَا فَكِهَةٌ وَنَخْلٌ وَرُمَّانٌ (٦٨) فَبِأَيِّ ءَالَاءِ رَبِّكُمَا تُكَذِّبَانِ (٦٩) فِيهِنَّ خَيْرَاتٌ حِسَانٌ (٧٠) فَبِأَيِّ ءَالَاءِ رَبِّكُمَا تُكَذِّبَانِ (٧١) حُورٌ مَّقْصُورَاتٌ فِى ٱلْخِيَامِ (٧٢) فَبِأَيِّ ءَالَاءِ رَبِّكُمَا تُكَذِّبَانِ (٧٣) لَمْ يَطْمِثْهُنَّ إِنسٌ قَبْلَهُمْ وَلَا جَآنٌّ (٧٤) فَبِأَيِّ ءَالَاءِ رَبِّكُمَا تُكَذِّبَانِ (٧٥) مُتَّكِئِينَ عَلَىٰ رَفْرَفٍ خُضْرٍ وَعَبْقَرِيٍّ حِسَانٍ (٧٦) فَبِأَيِّ ءَالَاءِ رَبِّكُمَا تُكَذِّبَانِ (٧٧) تَبَٰرَكَ ٱسْمُ رَبِّكَ ذِى ٱلْجَلَٰلِ وَٱلْإِكْرَامِ (٧٨)

The Most Gracious (Allâh)! (1) He has taught (you mankind) the Qur'ân (by His Mercy). (2) He created man. (3) He taught him eloquent speech. (4) The sun and the moon run on their fixed courses (exactly) calculated with measured out stages for each (for reckoning). (5) And the herbs (or stars) and the trees both prostrate themselves. (to Allah). (6) And the heaven He has raised it high, and He has set up the Balance. (7) In order that you may not transgress (due) balance. (8) And observe the weight with equity and do not make the balance deficient. (9) And the earth He has put down (laid) for the creatures. (10) Therein are fruits, date-palms producing sheathed fruit-stalks (enclosing dates). (11) And also corn, with (its) leaves and stalk for fodder, and sweet-scented plants. (12) **Then which of the Blessings of your Lord will you both (jinn and men) deny?** (13) He created man (Adam) from sounding clay like the clay of pottery. (14) And the jinn He created from a smokeless flame of fire. (15) **Then which of the Blessings of your Lord will you both (jinn and men) deny?** (16) (He is) the Lord of the two easts (places of sunrise during early summer and early winter) and the Lord of the two wests (places of sunset during early summer and early winter). (17) **Then which of the Blessings of your Lord will you both (jinn and men) deny?** (18) He has let loose the two seas (the salt and the fresh water) meeting together. (19) Between them is a barrier which none of them can transgress. (20) **Then which of the Blessings of your Lord will you both (jinn and men) deny?** (21) Out of them both come out pearl and coral. (22) **Then which of the Blessings of your Lord will you both (jinn and men) deny?** (23) And His are the ships going and coming in the seas, like mountains. (24) **Then which of the Blessings of your Lord will you both (jinn and men) deny?** (25) Whatsoever is on it (the earth) will perish. (26) And the Face of your Lord full of Majesty and Honour will remain forever. (27) **Then which of the Blessings of your Lord will**

you both (jinn and men) deny?
(28) Whosoever is in the heavens and on earth begs of Him (its needs from Him). Every day He is (engaged) in some affair (such as giving honour or disgrace to some, life or death to some, etc.)! (29) **Then which of the Blessings of your Lord will you both (jinn and men) deny?** *(30) We shall attend to you, O you two classes (jinn and men)! (31)* **Then which of the Blessings of your Lord will you both (jinn and men) deny?** *(32) O assembly of jinn and men! If you have power to pass beyond the zones of the heavens and the earth, then pass beyond (them)! But you will never be able to pass them, except with authority (from Allâh)! (33)* **Then which of the Blessings of your Lord will you both (jinn and men) deny?** *(34) There will be sent against you both, smokeless flames of fire and (molten) brass, and you will not be able to defend yourselves. (35)* **Then which of the Blessings of your Lord will you both**

(jinn and men) deny? *(36) Then when the heaven is rent asunder, and it becomes rosy or red like red-oil, or red hide (37)* **Then which of the Blessings of your Lord will you both (jinn and men) deny?** *(38) So on that Day no question will be asked of man or jinni as to his sin, [because they have already been known from their faces either white (dwellers of Paradise - true believers of Islamic Monotheism) or black (dwellers of Hell - polytheists; disbelievers, criminals)]. (39)* **Then which of the Blessings of your Lord will you both (jinn and men) deny?** *(40) The Mujrimûn (polytheists, criminals, sinners) will be known by their marks (black faces), and they will be seized by their forelocks and their feet. (41)* **Then which of the Blessings of your Lord will you both (jinn and men) deny?** *(42) This is Hell which the Mujrimûn (polytheists, criminals, sinners) denied. (43) They will go between it (Hell) and the fierce boiling water! (44)* **Then which of the Blessings of your**

*Lord will you both (jinn and men) deny?
(45) But for him who fears the standing
before his Lord, there will be two Gardens
(i.e. in Paradise). (46)* **Then which of the
Blessings of your Lord will you both
(jinn and men) deny?** *(47) With spreading
branches. (48)* **Then which of the
Blessings of your Lord will you both
(jinn and men) deny?** *(49) In them (both)
will be two springs flowing (free). (50)* **Then
which of the Blessings of your Lord will
you both (jinn and men) deny?** *(51) In
them (both) will be every kind of fruit in
pairs. (52)* **Then which of the Blessings of
your Lord will you both (jinn and men)
deny?** *(53) Reclining upon the couches
lined with silk brocade, and the fruits of the
two Gardens will be near at hand. (54)* **Then
which of the Blessings of your Lord will
you both (jinn and men) deny?**
*(55) Wherein both will be Qasirat-ut-Tarf
[chaste fmales (wives) restraining their
glances, desiring none except their*

husbands], *with whom no man or jinni has had Tamth before them.* (56) **Then which of the Blessings of your Lord will you both (jinn and men) deny?** (57) *(In beauty) they are like rubies and coral.* (58) **Then which of the Blessings of your Lord will you both (jinn and men) deny?** (59) **Is there any reward for good other than good?** (60) **Then which of the Blessings of your Lord will you both (jinn and men) deny?** (61) *And besides these two, there are two other Gardens (i.e. in Paradise).* (62) **Then which of the Blessings of your Lord will you both (jinn and men) deny?** (63) *Dark green (in colour).* (64) **Then which of the Blessings of your Lord will you both (jinn and men) deny?** (65) *In them (both) will be two springs gushing forth.* (66) **Then which of the Blessings of your Lord will you both (jinn and men) deny?** (67) *In them (both) will be fruits, and date- palms and pomegranates.* (68) **Then which of the Blessings of your Lord will you both** (jinn and men) deny? (69) Therein (Gardens) will be Khairâtun-Hisân [fair (wives) good and beautiful]. (70) **Then which of the Blessings of your Lord will you both (jinn and men) deny?** (71) Hûr (beautiful, fair females) guarded in pavilions; (72) **Then which of the Blessings of your Lord will you both (jinn and men) deny?** (73) With Whom no man or jinni has had Tamth before them. (74) **Then which of the Blessings of your Lord will you both (jinn and men) deny?** (75) Reclining on green cushions and rich beautiful mattresses. (76) **Then which of the Blessings of your Lord will you both (jinn and men) deny?** (77) Blessed is the Name of your Lord (Allâh), the Owner of Majesty and Honour. (78)

Quran 56:8-9

فَأَصْحَٰبُ ٱلْمَيْمَنَةِ مَآ أَصْحَٰبُ ٱلْمَيْمَنَةِ (٨) وَأَصْحَٰبُ ٱلْمَشْئَمَةِ مَآ أَصْحَٰبُ ٱلْمَشْئَمَةِ (٩)

So those on the Right Hand (i.e. those who will be given their Records in their right hands) — how (fortunate) will be those on the Right Hand? (As a respect for them, because they will enter Paradise). (8) And those on the Left Hand (i.e. those who will be given their Record in their left hands) — how (unfortunate) will be those on the Left Hand? (As a disgrace for them, because they will enter Hell). (9)

Quran 56:57-74

نَحْنُ خَلَقْنَـٰكُمْ فَلَوْلَا تُصَدِّقُونَ (٥٧) أَفَرَءَيْتُم مَّا تُمْنُونَ (٥٨) ءَأَنتُمْ تَخْلُقُونَهُ ۤ أَمْ نَحْنُ ٱلْخَـٰلِقُونَ (٥٩) نَحْنُ قَدَّرْنَا بَيْنَكُمُ ٱلْمَوْتَ وَمَا نَحْنُ بِمَسْبُوقِينَ (٦٠) عَلَىٰٓ أَن نُّبَدِّلَ أَمْثَـٰلَكُمْ وَنُنشِئَكُمْ فِى مَا لَا تَعْلَمُونَ (٦١) وَلَقَدْ عَلِمْتُمُ ٱلنَّشْأَةَ ٱلْأُولَىٰ فَلَوْلَا تَذَكَّرُونَ (٦٢) أَفَرَءَيْتُم مَّا تَحْرُثُونَ (٦٣) ءَأَنتُمْ تَزْرَعُونَهُ ۤ أَمْ نَحْنُ ٱلزَّٰرِعُونَ (٦٤) لَوْ نَشَآءُ لَجَعَلْنَـٰهُ حُطَـٰمًا فَظَلْتُمْ تَفَكَّهُونَ (٦٥) إِنَّا لَمُغْرَمُونَ (٦٦) بَلْ نَحْنُ مَحْرُومُونَ (٦٧) أَفَرَءَيْتُمُ ٱلْمَآءَ ٱلَّذِى تَشْرَبُونَ (٦٨) ءَأَنتُمْ أَنزَلْتُمُوهُ مِنَ ٱلْمُزْنِ أَمْ نَحْنُ ٱلْمُنزِلُونَ (٦٩) لَوْ نَشَآءُ جَعَلْنَـٰهُ أُجَاجًا فَلَوْلَا تَشْكُرُونَ (٧٠) أَفَرَءَيْتُمُ ٱلنَّارَ ٱلَّتِى تُورُونَ (٧١) ءَأَنتُمْ أَنشَأْتُمْ شَجَرَتَهَآ أَمْ نَحْنُ ٱلْمُنشِئُونَ

(٧٢) نَحْنُ جَعَلْنَـٰهَا تَذْكِرَةً وَمَتَـٰعًا لِّلْمُقْوِينَ (٧٣) فَسَبِّحْ بِٱسْمِ رَبِّكَ ٱلْعَظِيمِ (٧٤)

We created you, then why do you believe not? (57) Then tell Me (about) the (human) semen that you emit? (58) Is it you who create it (i.e. make this semen into a perfect human being), or are We the Creator? (59) We have decreed death to you all, and We are not outstripped, (60) To transfigure you and create you in (forms) that you know not. (61) *And indeed, you have already known the first form of creation (i.e. the creation of Adam), why then do you not remember (or take heed)? (62) Then tell Me about seed that you sow in the ground? (63) Is it you that make it grow, or are We the Grower?* (64) Were it Our Will, We could crumble it to dry pieces, and you would be regretful (or left in wonderment). (65) (Saying): "We are indeed Mughramûn (i.e. ruined or have lost the money without any profit, or are punished

by the loss of all that we spend for
cultivation)! (66) "Nay, but we are
deprived!" (67) **Then tell Me about the
water that you drink? (68) Is it you who
cause it from the rainclouds to come
down, or are We the Causer of it to
come down? (69) If We willed, We verily
could make it salt (and undrinkable),
why then do you not give thanks (to
Allâh)? (70) Then tell Me about the fire
which you kindle? (71) Is it you who
made the tree thereof to grow, or are We
the Grower?** (72) We have made it a
Reminder (of the Hell-fire, in the Hereafter);
and an article of use for the travellers (and
all the others, in this world). (73) Then
glorify with praises the Name of your Lord,
the Most Great. (74)

Quran 56:75-95

۞ فَلَا أُقْسِمُ بِمَوَٰقِعِ ٱلنُّجُومِ (٧٥) وَإِنَّهُ ۥ لَقَسَمٌ لَّوْ تَعْلَمُونَ
عَظِيمٌ (٧٦) إِنَّهُ ۥ لَقُرْءَانٌ كَرِيمٌ (٧٧) فِى كِتَٰبٍ مَّكْنُونٍ
(٧٨) لَّا يَمَسُّهُ ۥٓ إِلَّا ٱلْمُطَهَّرُونَ (٧٩) تَنزِيلٌ مِّن رَّبِّ
ٱلْعَٰلَمِينَ (٨٠) أَفَبِهَٰذَا ٱلْحَدِيثِ أَنتُم مُّدْهِنُونَ

(٨١) وَتَجْعَلُونَ رِزْقَكُمْ أَنَّكُمْ تُكَذِّبُونَ (٨٢) فَلَوْلَآ إِذَا
بَلَغَتِ ٱلْحُلْقُومَ (٨٣) وَأَنتُمْ حِينَئِذٍ تَنظُرُونَ (٨٤) وَنَحْنُ
أَقْرَبُ إِلَيْهِ مِنكُمْ وَلَٰكِن لَّا تُبْصِرُونَ (٨٥) فَلَوْلَآ إِن كُنتُمْ
غَيْرَ مَدِينِينَ (٨٦) تَرْجِعُونَهَآ إِن كُنتُمْ صَـٰدِقِينَ (٨٧) فَأَمَّآ
إِن كَانَ مِنَ ٱلْمُقَرَّبِينَ (٨٨) فَرَوْحٌ وَرَيْحَانٌ وَجَنَّتُ نَعِيمٍ
(٨٩) وَأَمَّآ إِن كَانَ مِنْ أَصْحَـٰبِ ٱلْيَمِينِ (٩٠) فَسَلَـٰمٌ لَّكَ مِنْ
أَصْحَـٰبِ ٱلْيَمِينِ (٩١) وَأَمَّآ إِن كَانَ مِنَ ٱلْمُكَذِّبِينَ ٱلضَّآلِّينَ
(٩٢) فَنُزُلٌ مِّنْ حَمِيمٍ (٩٣) وَتَصْلِيَةُ جَحِيمٍ (٩٤) إِنَّ هَـٰذَا
لَهُوَ حَقُّ ٱلْيَقِينِ (٩٥)

So I swear by the setting of the stars.
(75) And verily, that is indeed a great oath,
if you but know. (76) That (this) is indeed
an honourable recitation (the Noble
Qur'ân). (77) In a Book well-guarded (with
Allâh in the heaven i.e. Al-Lauh Al-
Mahfûz). (78) Which (that Book with Allâh)
none can touch but the purified (i.e. the
angels). (79) A Revelation (this Qur'ân)
from the Lord of the 'Alamîn (mankind, jinn
and all that exists). (80) **Is it such a talk
(this Qur'an) that you (disbelievers)
deny?** (81) And instead (of thanking Allâh)
for the provision He gives you, you deny

(Him by disbelief)! (82) **Then why do you not (intervene) when (the soul of a dying person) reaches the throat?** *(83) And you at the moment are looking on. (84) But We (i.e. Our angels who take the soul) are nearer to him than you, but you see not, (85)* **Then why do you not, if you are exempt from the reckoning and recompense (punishment) — (86) Bring back the soul (to its body), if you are truthful?** *(87) Then, if he (the dying person) be of the Muqarrabûn (those brought near to Allâh), (88) (There is for him) rest and provision, and a Garden of Delights (Paradise). (89) And if he (the dying person) be of those on the Right Hand, (90) Then there is safety and peace (from the Punishment of Allâh) for those on the Right Hand. (91) But if he (the dying person) be of the denying (of the Resurrection), the erring (away from the Right Path of Islâmic Monotheism), (92) Then for him is entertainment with boiling water. (93) And*

*burning in Hell-fire. (94) Verily, this! This
is an absolute Truth with certainty. (95)*

Quran 57:10-11

وَمَا لَكُمْ أَلَّا تُنفِقُوا۟ فِى سَبِيلِ ٱللَّهِ وَلِلَّهِ مِيرَٰثُ ٱلسَّمَـٰوَٰتِ
وَٱلْأَرْضِ لَا يَسْتَوِى مِنكُم مَّنْ أَنفَقَ مِن قَبْلِ ٱلْفَتْحِ وَقَـٰتَلَ
أُو۟لَـٰٓئِكَ أَعْظَمُ دَرَجَةً مِّنَ ٱلَّذِينَ أَنفَقُوا۟ مِنۢ بَعْدُ وَقَـٰتَلُوا۟ وَكُلًّا
وَعَدَ ٱللَّهُ ٱلْحُسْنَىٰ وَٱللَّهُ بِمَا تَعْمَلُونَ خَبِيرٌ (١٠) مَّن ذَا ٱلَّذِى
يُقْرِضُ ٱللَّهَ قَرْضًا حَسَنًا فَيُضَـٰعِفَهُۥ لَهُۥ وَلَهُۥٓ أَجْرٌ كَرِيمٌ
(١١)

*And what is the matter with you that
you spend not in the Cause of Allâh?
And to Allâh belongs the heritage of the
heavens and the earth. Not equal among you
are those who spent and fought before the
conquering (of Makkah with those among
you who did so later). Such are higher in
degree than those who spent and fought
afterwards. But to all, Allâh has promised
the best (reward). And Allâh is All-Aware of
what you do. (10)* **Who is he that will
lend Allâh a goodly loan, then (Allâh)
will increase it manifold to his credit**

(in repaying), and he will have (besides)
a good reward (i.e. Paradise)? (11)

Quran 57:16

﴿ أَلَمۡ يَأۡنِ لِلَّذِينَ ءَامَنُوٓاْ أَن تَخۡشَعَ قُلُوبُهُمۡ لِذِكۡرِ ٱللَّهِ وَمَا
نَزَلَ مِنَ ٱلۡحَقِّ وَلَا يَكُونُواْ كَٱلَّذِينَ أُوتُواْ ٱلۡكِتَـٰبَ مِن قَبۡلُ
فَطَالَ عَلَيۡهِمُ ٱلۡأَمَدُ فَقَسَتۡ قُلُوبُهُمۡۖ وَكَثِيرٌ مِّنۡهُمۡ فَـٰسِقُونَ ﴿١٦﴾

Has not the time come for the hearts of
those who believe to be affected by
Allâh's Reminder (this Qur'ân), and
that which has been revealed of the
truth, lest they become as those who
received the Scripture [the Taurât
(Torah) and the Injeel] before (i.e. Jews
and Christians), and the term was
prolonged for them and so their hearts
were hardened? And many of them were
Fâsiqûn (the rebellious, the disobedient to
Allâh). (16)

Quran 58:7-8

أَلَمۡ تَرَ أَنَّ ٱللَّهَ يَعۡلَمُ مَا فِى ٱلسَّمَـٰوَٰتِ وَمَا فِى ٱلۡأَرۡضِۖ مَا
يَكُونُ مِن نَّجۡوَىٰ ثَلَـٰثَةٍ إِلَّا هُوَ رَابِعُهُمۡ وَلَا خَمۡسَةٍ إِلَّا هُوَ

سَادِسُهُمْ وَلَآ أَدْنَىٰ مِن ذَٰلِكَ وَلَآ أَكْثَرَ إِلَّا هُوَ مَعَهُمْ أَيْنَ مَا
كَانُوا۟ ثُمَّ يُنَبِّئُهُم بِمَا عَمِلُوا۟ يَوْمَ ٱلْقِيَٰمَةِ إِنَّ ٱللَّهَ بِكُلِّ شَىْءٍ عَلِيمٌ
(٧) أَلَمْ تَرَ إِلَى ٱلَّذِينَ نُهُوا۟ عَنِ ٱلنَّجْوَىٰ ثُمَّ يَعُودُونَ لِمَا نُهُوا۟
عَنْهُ وَيَتَنَٰجَوْنَ بِٱلْإِثْمِ وَٱلْعُدْوَٰنِ وَمَعْصِيَتِ ٱلرَّسُولِ وَإِذَا
جَآءُوكَ حَيَّوْكَ بِمَا لَمْ يُحَيِّكَ بِهِ ٱللَّهُ وَيَقُولُونَ فِىٓ أَنفُسِهِمْ لَوْلَا
يُعَذِّبُنَا ٱللَّهُ بِمَا نَقُولُ حَسْبُهُمْ جَهَنَّمُ يَصْلَوْنَهَا فَبِئْسَ ٱلْمَصِيرُ
(٨)

Have you not seen that Allâh knows whatsoever is in the heavens and whatsoever is on the earth? *There is no Najwa (secret counsel) of three, but He is their fourth (with His Knowledge, while He Himself is over the Throne, over the seventh heaven), nor of five but He is their sixth (with His Knowledge), not of less than that or more, but He is with them (with His Knowledge) wheresoever they may be; And afterwards on the Day of Resurrection, He will inform them of what they did. Verily, Allâh is the All-Knower of everything.* (7) *Have you not seen those who were forbidden to hold secret counsels, and afterwards returned to that which they had been forbidden, and conspired together for sin and wrong doing and disobedience to the Messenger (Muhammad)? And when they come to you, they greet you with a greeting wherewith Allâh greets you not, and say within themselves: "Why should Allâh punish us not for what we say?" Hell will be sufficient for them, they will burn therein, and worst indeed is that destination! (8)*

Quran 58:12-15

يَـٰٓأَيُّهَا ٱلَّذِينَ ءَامَنُوٓا۟ إِذَا نَـٰجَيْتُمُ ٱلرَّسُولَ فَقَدِّمُوا۟ بَيْنَ يَدَىْ نَجْوَىٰكُمْ صَدَقَةً ذَٰلِكَ خَيْرٌ لَّكُمْ وَأَطْهَرُ فَإِن لَّمْ تَجِدُوا۟ فَإِنَّ ٱللَّهَ غَفُورٌ رَّحِيمٌ (١٢) ءَأَشْفَقْتُمْ أَن تُقَدِّمُوا۟ بَيْنَ يَدَىْ نَجْوَىٰكُمْ صَدَقَـٰتٍ فَإِذْ لَمْ تَفْعَلُوا۟ وَتَابَ ٱللَّهُ عَلَيْكُمْ فَأَقِيمُوا۟ ٱلصَّلَوٰةَ وَءَاتُوا۟ ٱلزَّكَوٰةَ وَأَطِيعُوا۟ ٱللَّهَ وَرَسُولَهُ ۚ وَٱللَّهُ خَبِيرٌۢ بِمَا تَعْمَلُونَ (١٣) ۞ أَلَمْ تَرَ إِلَى ٱلَّذِينَ تَوَلَّوْا۟ قَوْمًا غَضِبَ ٱللَّهُ عَلَيْهِم مَّا هُم مِّنكُمْ وَلَا مِنْهُمْ وَيَحْلِفُونَ عَلَى ٱلْكَذِبِ وَهُمْ يَعْلَمُونَ (١٤) أَعَدَّ ٱللَّهُ لَهُمْ عَذَابًا شَدِيدًا إِنَّهُمْ سَآءَ مَا كَانُوا۟ يَعْمَلُونَ (١٥)

O you who believe! When you (want to) consult the Messenger (Muhammad) in private, spend something in charity before your private consultation. That will be better and purer for you. But if you find not (the means for it), then verily, Allâh is Oft-Forgiving, Most Merciful. (12) **Are you afraid of spending in charity before your private consultation (with him)?** *If then you do it not, and Allâh has forgiven you, then (at least) perform Salât (Iqâmat¬as¬Salât) and give Zakât and obey Allâh (i.e. do all that Allâh and His Messenger order you to do). And Allâh is All-Aware of what you do.* (13) **Have you (O Muhammad) not seen those (hypocrites) who take as friends a people upon whom is the Wrath of Allâh (i.e. Jews)?** *They are neither of you (Muslims) nor of them (Jews), and they swear to a lie while they know.* (14) *Allâh has prepared for them a severe torment. Evil indeed is that which they used to do.* (15)

Quran 59:11-12

۞ أَلَمْ تَرَ إِلَى ٱلَّذِينَ نَافَقُواْ يَقُولُونَ لِإِخْوَٰنِهِمُ ٱلَّذِينَ كَفَرُواْ مِنْ أَهْلِ ٱلْكِتَـٰبِ لَئِنْ أُخْرِجْتُمْ لَنَخْرُجَنَّ مَعَكُمْ وَلَا نُطِيعُ فِيكُمْ أَحَدًا أَبَدًا وَإِن قُوتِلْتُمْ لَنَنصُرَنَّكُمْ وَٱللَّهُ يَشْهَدُ إِنَّهُمْ لَكَـٰذِبُونَ (١١) لَئِنْ أُخْرِجُواْ لَا يَخْرُجُونَ مَعَهُمْ وَلَئِن قُوتِلُواْ لَا يَنصُرُونَهُمْ وَلَئِن نَّصَرُوهُمْ لَيُوَلُّنَّ ٱلْأَدْبَـٰرَ ثُمَّ لَا يُنصَرُونَ (١٢)

Have you (O Muhammad) not observed the hypocrites who say to their friends among the people of the Scripture who disbelieve: "(By Allâh) If you are expelled, we (too) indeed will go out with you, and we shall never obey any one against you, and if you are attacked (in fight), we shall indeed help you."? But Allâh is Witness, that they verily, are liars. (11) Surely, if they (the Jews) are expelled, never will they (hypocrites) go out with them, and if they are attacked, they will never help them. And (even) if they do help them, they (hypocrites) will turn their backs, and they will not be victorious. (12)

Quran 61:2-3

يَـٰٓأَيُّهَا ٱلَّذِينَ ءَامَنُوا۟ لِمَ تَقُولُونَ مَا لَا تَفْعَلُونَ (٢) كَبُرَ مَقْتًا
عِندَ ٱللَّهِ أَن تَقُولُوا۟ مَا لَا تَفْعَلُونَ (٣)

O you who believe! **Why do you say that**
which you do not do? *(2) Most hateful it*
is with Allâh that you say that which you do
not do. (3)

Quran 61:7-11

وَمَنْ أَظْلَمُ مِمَّنِ ٱفْتَرَىٰ عَلَى ٱللَّهِ ٱلْكَذِبَ وَهُوَ يُدْعَىٰٓ إِلَى
ٱلْإِسْلَـٰمِۚ وَٱللَّهُ لَا يَهْدِى ٱلْقَوْمَ ٱلظَّـٰلِمِينَ (٧) يُرِيدُونَ لِيُطْفِـُٔوا۟
نُورَ ٱللَّهِ بِأَفْوَٰهِهِمْ وَٱللَّهُ مُتِمُّ نُورِهِۦ وَلَوْ كَرِهَ ٱلْكَـٰفِرُونَ
(٨) هُوَ ٱلَّذِىٓ أَرْسَلَ رَسُولَهُۥ بِٱلْهُدَىٰ وَدِينِ ٱلْحَقِّ لِيُظْهِرَهُۥ
عَلَى ٱلدِّينِ كُلِّهِۦ وَلَوْ كَرِهَ ٱلْمُشْرِكُونَ (٩) يَـٰٓأَيُّهَا ٱلَّذِينَ
ءَامَنُوا۟ هَلْ أَدُلُّكُمْ عَلَىٰ تِجَـٰرَةٍ تُنجِيكُم مِّنْ عَذَابٍ أَلِيمٍ
(١٠) تُؤْمِنُونَ بِٱللَّهِ وَرَسُولِهِۦ وَتُجَـٰهِدُونَ فِى سَبِيلِ ٱللَّهِ
بِأَمْوَٰلِكُمْ وَأَنفُسِكُمْۚ ذَٰلِكُمْ خَيْرٌ لَّكُمْ إِن كُنتُمْ تَعْلَمُونَ (١١)

And who does more wrong than the one
who invents a lie against Allâh, while
he is being invited to Islâm? *And Allâh*
guides not the people who are Zâlimûn
(polytheists, wrong-doers and disbelievers)
folk. (7) They intend to put out the Light of
Allâh (i.e. the Religion of Islâm, this

Qur'ân, and the Prophet Muhammad) with
their mouths. But Allâh will bring His Light
to perfection even though the disbelievers
hate (it). (8) He it is Who has sent His
Messenger (Muhammad) with guidance and
the religion of truth (Islâmic Monotheism)
to make it victorious over all (other)
religions even though the Mushrikûn
(polytheists, pagans, idolaters, and
disbelievers in the Oneness of Allâh and in
His Messenger Muhammed) hate (it). (9) O
You who believe! **Shall I guide you to a
trade that will save you from a painful
torment?** (10) That you believe in Allâh
and His Messenger (Muhammad), and that
you strive hard and fight in the Cause of
Allâh with your wealth and your lives, that
will be better for you, if you but know! (11)

Quran 63:1-4

إِذَا جَآءَكَ ٱلْمُنَـٰفِقُونَ قَالُواْ نَشْهَدُ إِنَّكَ لَرَسُولُ ٱللَّهِ وَٱللَّهُ يَعْلَمُ
إِنَّكَ لَرَسُولُهُ ۚ وَٱللَّهُ يَشْهَدُ إِنَّ ٱلْمُنَـٰفِقِينَ لَكَـٰذِبُونَ (١) ٱتَّخَذُوٓاْ
أَيْمَـٰنَهُمْ جُنَّةً فَصَدُّواْ عَن سَبِيلِ ٱللَّهِ ۚ إِنَّهُمْ سَآءَ مَا كَانُواْ يَعْمَلُونَ
(٢) ذَٰلِكَ بِأَنَّهُمْ ءَامَنُواْ ثُمَّ كَفَرُواْ فَطُبِعَ عَلَىٰ قُلُوبِهِمْ فَهُمْ لَا

يَفْقَهُونَ (٣) ۞ وَإِذَا رَأَيْتَهُمْ تُعْجِبُكَ أَجْسَامُهُمْ وَإِن يَقُولُواْ تَسْمَعْ لِقَوْلِهِمْ كَأَنَّهُمْ خُشُبٌ مُّسَنَّدَةٌ يَحْسَبُونَ كُلَّ صَيْحَةٍ عَلَيْهِمْ هُمُ ٱلْعَدُوُّ فَٱحْذَرْهُمْ قَٰتَلَهُمُ ٱللَّهُ أَنَّىٰ يُؤْفَكُونَ (٤)

When the hypocrites come to you (O Muhammad), they say: "We bear witness that you are indeed the Messenger of Allâh." Allâh knows that you are indeed His Messenger and Allâh bears witness that the hypocrites are liars indeed. (1) They have made their oaths a screen (for their hypocrisy). Thus they hinder (men) from the Path of Allâh. Verily, evil is what they used to do. (2) That is because they believed, then disbelieved, therefore their hearts are sealed, so they understand not. (3) And when you look at them, their bodies please you; and when they speak, you listen to their words. They are as blocks of wood propped up. They think that every cry is against them. They are the enemies, so beware of them. May Allâh curse them! **How are they denying (or deviating from) the Right Path?** (4)

Quran 64:5-6

أَلَمْ يَأْتِكُمْ نَبَؤُاْ ٱلَّذِينَ كَفَرُواْ مِن قَبْلُ فَذَاقُواْ وَبَالَ أَمْرِهِمْ وَلَهُمْ عَذَابٌ أَلِيمٌ (٥) ذَٰلِكَ بِأَنَّهُۥ كَانَت تَّأْتِيهِمْ رُسُلُهُم بِٱلْبَيِّنَٰتِ فَقَالُوٓاْ أَبَشَرٌ يَهْدُونَنَا فَكَفَرُواْ وَتَوَلَّواْ وَّٱسْتَغْنَى ٱللَّهُ وَٱللَّهُ غَنِيٌّ حَمِيدٌ (٦)

Has not the news reached you of those who disbelieved aforetime? And so they tasted the evil result of their disbelief, and theirs will be a painful torment. (5) That was because there came to them their Messengers with clear proofs (signs), but they said: "Shall mere men guide us?" So they disbelieved and turned away (from the truth), But Allâh was not in need (of them). And Allâh is Rich (Free of all needs), Worthy of all praise. (6)

Quran 66:1

يَٰٓأَيُّهَا ٱلنَّبِيُّ لِمَ تُحَرِّمُ مَآ أَحَلَّ ٱللَّهُ لَكَ تَبْتَغِى مَرْضَاتَ أَزْوَٰجِكَ وَٱللَّهُ غَفُورٌ رَّحِيمٌ (١)

O Prophet! **Why do you forbid (for yourself) that which Allâh has allowed to you, seeking to please your wives?**

And Allâh is Oft-Forgiving, Most Merciful.
(1)

Quran 67:3-4

ٱلَّذِى خَلَقَ سَبْعَ سَمَٰوَٰتٍ طِبَاقًا ۖ مَّا تَرَىٰ فِى خَلْقِ ٱلرَّحْمَٰنِ مِن تَفَٰوُتٍ ۖ فَٱرْجِعِ ٱلْبَصَرَ هَلْ تَرَىٰ مِن فُطُورٍ (٣) ثُمَّ ٱرْجِعِ ٱلْبَصَرَ كَرَّتَيْنِ يَنقَلِبْ إِلَيْكَ ٱلْبَصَرُ خَاسِئًا وَهُوَ حَسِيرٌ (٤)

*Who has created the seven heavens one above another, you can see no fault in the creation of the Most Gracious. Then look again: "**Can you see any rifts?**" (3) Then look again and yet again, your sight will return to you in a state of humiliation and worn out (4)*

Quran 67:13-23

وَأَسِرُّوا۟ قَوْلَكُمْ أَوِ ٱجْهَرُوا۟ بِهِۦ ۖ إِنَّهُۥ عَلِيمٌۢ بِذَاتِ ٱلصُّدُورِ (١٣) أَلَا يَعْلَمُ مَنْ خَلَقَ وَهُوَ ٱللَّطِيفُ ٱلْخَبِيرُ (١٤) هُوَ ٱلَّذِى جَعَلَ لَكُمُ ٱلْأَرْضَ ذَلُولًا فَٱمْشُوا۟ فِى مَنَاكِبِهَا وَكُلُوا۟ مِن رِّزْقِهِۦ ۖ وَإِلَيْهِ ٱلنُّشُورُ (١٥) ءَأَمِنتُم مَّن فِى ٱلسَّمَآءِ أَن يَخْسِفَ بِكُمُ ٱلْأَرْضَ فَإِذَا هِىَ تَمُورُ (١٦) أَمْ أَمِنتُم مَّن فِى ٱلسَّمَآءِ أَن يُرْسِلَ عَلَيْكُمْ حَاصِبًا ۖ فَسَتَعْلَمُونَ كَيْفَ نَذِيرِ (١٧) وَلَقَدْ كَذَّبَ ٱلَّذِينَ مِن قَبْلِهِمْ فَكَيْفَ كَانَ نَكِيرِ (١٨) أَوَلَمْ يَرَوْا۟ إِلَى ٱلطَّيْرِ فَوْقَهُمْ صَٰٓفَّٰتٍ وَيَقْبِضْنَ ۚ مَا

يُمۡسِكُهُنَّ إِلَّا ٱلرَّحۡمَـٰنُ‌ۚ إِنَّهُۥ بِكُلِّ شَىۡءٍۭ بَصِيرٌ (١٩) أَمَّنۡ هَـٰذَا ٱلَّذِى هُوَ جُندٌ لَّكُمۡ يَنصُرُكُم مِّن دُونِ ٱلرَّحۡمَـٰنِ‌ۚ إِنِ ٱلۡكَـٰفِرُونَ إِلَّا فِى غُرُورٍ (٢٠) أَمَّنۡ هَـٰذَا ٱلَّذِى يَرۡزُقُكُمۡ إِنۡ أَمۡسَكَ رِزۡقَهُۥ‌ۚ بَل لَّجُّواۡ فِى عُتُوٍّ وَنُفُورٍ (٢١) أَفَمَن يَمۡشِى مُكِبًّا عَلَىٰ وَجۡهِهِۦۤ أَهۡدَىٰٓ أَمَّن يَمۡشِى سَوِيًّا عَلَىٰ صِرَٰطٍ مُّسۡتَقِيمٍ (٢٢) قُلۡ هُوَ ٱلَّذِىٓ أَنشَأَكُمۡ وَجَعَلَ لَكُمُ ٱلسَّمۡعَ وَٱلۡأَبۡصَـٰرَ وَٱلۡأَفۡـِٔدَةَ‌ۖ قَلِيلاً مَّا تَشۡكُرُونَ (٢٣)

And whether you keep your talk secret or disclose it, verily, He is the All-Knower of what is in the breasts (of men). (13) **Should not He Who has created know?** And He is the Most Kind and Courteous (to His slaves) All-Aware (of everything). (14) He it is, Who has made the earth subservient to you (i.e. easy for you to walk, to live and to do agriculture on it), so walk in the path thereof and eat of His provision, and to Him will be the Resurrection. (15) **Do you feel secure that He, Who is over the heaven (Allâh), will not cause the earth to sink with you, and then it should quake?** (16) **Or do you feel secure that He, Who is over the heaven (Allâh), will not send** *against you a violent whirlwind? Then you shall know how (terrible) has been My Warning. (17)* **And indeed those before them belied (the Messengers of Allâh), then how terrible was My denial (punishment)? (18) Do they not see the birds above them, spreading out their wings and folding them in?** *None upholds them except the Most Gracious (Allâh). Verily, He is the All-Seer of everything. (19)* **Who is he besides the Most Gracious that can be an army to you to help you?** *The disbelievers are in nothing but delusion (20)* **Who is he that can provide for you if He should withhold His provision?** *Nay, but they continue to be in pride, and (they) flee (from the truth). (21)* **Is he who walks (without seeing) on his face, more rightly guided, or he who (sees and) walks upright on a Straight Way (i.e. Islâmic Monotheism)? (22)** *Say it is He Who has created you, and endowed you with hearing* *(ears), seeing (eyes), and hearts. Little thanks you give. (23)*

Quran 67:28-30

قُلْ أَرَءَيْتُمْ إِنْ أَهْلَكَنِيَ ٱللَّهُ وَمَن مَّعِىَ أَوْ رَحِمَنَا فَمَن يُجِيرُ ٱلْكَٰفِرِينَ مِنْ عَذَابٍ أَلِيمٍ (٢٨) قُلْ هُوَ ٱلرَّحْمَـٰنُ ءَامَنَّا بِهِۦ وَعَلَيْهِ تَوَكَّلْنَا فَسَتَعْلَمُونَ مَنْ هُوَ فِى ضَلَٰلٍ مُّبِينٍ (٢٩) قُلْ أَرَءَيْتُمْ إِنْ أَصْبَحَ مَآؤُكُمْ غَوْرًا فَمَن يَأْتِيكُم بِمَآءٍ مَّعِينٍ (٣٠)

Say (O Muhammad): "Tell me! **If Allâh destroys me, and those with me, or He bestows His Mercy on us — who can save the disbelievers from a painful torment?"** *(28) Say: "He is the Most Gracious (Allâh), in Him we believe, and in Him we put our trust. So you will come to know who is it that is in manifest error."* *(29) Say (O Muhammad): "Tell me!* **If (all) your water were to sink away, who then can supply you with flowing (spring) water?"** *(30)*

Quran 68:35-41

أَفَنَجْعَلُ ٱلْمُسْلِمِينَ كَٱلْمُجْرِمِينَ (٣٥) مَا لَكُمْ كَيْفَ تَحْكُمُونَ (٣٦) أَمْ لَكُمْ كِتَٰبٌ فِيهِ تَدْرُسُونَ (٣٧) إِنَّ لَكُمْ فِيهِ لَمَا تَخَيَّرُونَ (٣٨) أَمْ لَكُمْ أَيْمَٰنٌ عَلَيْنَا بَٰلِغَةٌ إِلَىٰ يَوْمِ ٱلْقِيَٰمَةِ إِنَّ لَكُمْ لَمَا تَحْكُمُونَ (٣٩) سَلْهُمْ أَيُّهُم بِذَٰلِكَ زَعِيمٌ (٤٠) أَمْ لَهُمْ شُرَكَآءُ فَلْيَأْتُواْ بِشُرَكَآئِهِمْ إِن كَانُواْ صَٰدِقِينَ (٤١)

Shall We then treat the Muslims (believers of Islamic Monotheism, doers of righteous deeds) like the Mujrimûn (criminals, polytheists and disbelievers)? (35) What is the matter with you? How judge you? (36) Or have you a Book where in you learn, (37) That you shall therein have all that you choose? (38) Or have you oaths from Us, reaching to the Day of Resurrection that yours will be what you judge? (39) Ask them, which of them will stand surety for that? (40) Or have they "partners"? Then let them bring their "partners" if they are truthful! (41)

Quran 68:46-47

أَمْ تَسْـَٔلُهُمْ أَجْرًا فَهُم مِّن مَّغْرَمٍ مُّثْقَلُونَ (٤٦) أَمْ عِندَهُمُ
ٱلْغَيْبُ فَهُمْ يَكْتُبُونَ (٤٧)

Or is it that you (O Muhammad) ask them a wage, so that they are heavily burdened with debt? (46) Or that the Ghaib (unseen) is in their hands, so that they can write it down? (47)

Quran 69:1-3

ٱلْحَاقَّةُ (١) مَا ٱلْحَاقَّةُ (٢) وَمَآ أَدْرَىٰكَ مَا ٱلْحَاقَّةُ (٣)

The Inevitable (i.e. the Day of Resurrection)! (1) **What is the Inevitable? (2) And what will make you know what the Inevitable is? (3)**

Quran 69:5-8

فَأَمَّا ثَمُودُ فَأُهْلِكُواْ بِٱلطَّاغِيَةِ (٥) وَأَمَّا عَادٌ فَأُهْلِكُواْ بِرِيحٍ
صَرْصَرٍ عَاتِيَةٍ (٦) سَخَّرَهَا عَلَيْهِمْ سَبْعَ لَيَالٍ وَثَمَٰنِيَةَ أَيَّامٍ
حُسُومًا فَتَرَى ٱلْقَوْمَ فِيهَا صَرْعَىٰ كَأَنَّهُمْ أَعْجَازُ نَخْلٍ خَاوِيَةٍ
(٧) فَهَلْ تَرَىٰ لَهُم مِّنْ بَاقِيَةٍ (٨)

As for Thamûd, they were destroyed by the awful cry! (5) And as for 'Ad, they were destroyed by a furious violent wind!

*(6) Which Allâh imposed on them for seven nights and eight days in succession, so that you could see men lying overthrown (destroyed), as if they were hollow trunks of date-palms! (7) **Do you see any remnants of them? (8)***

Quran 70:36-39

فَمَالِ ٱلَّذِينَ كَفَرُواْ قِبَلَكَ مُهْطِعِينَ (٣٦) عَنِ ٱلْيَمِينِ وَعَنِ ٱلشِّمَالِ عِزِينَ (٣٧) أَيَطْمَعُ كُلُّ ٱمْرِئٍ مِّنْهُمْ أَن يُدْخَلَ جَنَّةَ نَعِيمٍ (٣٨) كَلَّا ۖ إِنَّا خَلَقْنَـٰهُم مِّمَّا يَعْلَمُونَ (٣٩)

So what is the matter with those who disbelieve that they hasten to listen from you (O Muhammad), in order to belie you and to mock at you, and at Allâh's Book (this Qur'ân) (36) (Sitting) in groups on the right and on the left (of you, O Muhammad)? (37) Does every man of them hope to enter the Paradise of Delight? (38) No, that is not like that! Verily, We have created them out of that which they know! (39)

Quran 73:17-18

فَكَيْفَ تَتَّقُونَ إِن كَفَرْتُمْ يَوْمًا يَجْعَلُ ٱلْوِلْدَانَ شِيبًا (١٧) ٱلسَّمَآءُ مُنفَطِرٌ بِهِ كَانَ وَعْدُهُ مَفْعُولاً (١٨)

Then how can you avoid the punishment, if you disbelieve, on a Day (i.e. the Day of Resurrection) that will make the children grey-headed?
(17) Whereon the heaven will be cleft asunder? His Promise is certainly to be accomplished (18)

Quran 74:27-31

وَمَآ أَدْرَىٰكَ مَا سَقَرُ (٢٧) لَا تُبْقِى وَلَا تَذَرُ (٢٨) لَوَّاحَةٌ لِّلْبَشَرِ (٢٩) عَلَيْهَا تِسْعَةَ عَشَرَ (٣٠) وَمَا جَعَلْنَآ أَصْحَٰبَ ٱلنَّارِ إِلَّا مَلَٰٓئِكَةً وَمَا جَعَلْنَا عِدَّتَهُمْ إِلَّا فِتْنَةً لِّلَّذِينَ كَفَرُواْ لِيَسْتَيْقِنَ ٱلَّذِينَ أُوتُواْ ٱلْكِتَٰبَ وَيَزْدَادَ ٱلَّذِينَ ءَامَنُوٓاْ إِيمَٰنًا وَلَا يَرْتَابَ ٱلَّذِينَ أُوتُواْ ٱلْكِتَٰبَ وَٱلْمُؤْمِنُونَ وَلِيَقُولَ ٱلَّذِينَ فِى قُلُوبِهِم مَّرَضٌ وَٱلْكَٰفِرُونَ مَاذَآ أَرَادَ ٱللَّهُ بِهَٰذَا مَثَلاً كَذَٰلِكَ يُضِلُّ ٱللَّهُ مَن يَشَآءُ وَيَهْدِى مَن يَشَآءُ وَمَا يَعْلَمُ جُنُودَ رَبِّكَ إِلَّا هُوَ وَمَا هِىَ إِلَّا ذِكْرَىٰ لِلْبَشَرِ (٣١)

And what will make you know (exactly) what Hell-fire is? (27) It spares not (any sinner), nor does it leave (anything unburnt)! (28) Burning and blackening the

skins! (29) Over it are nineteen (angels as
guardians and keepers of Hell). (30) And
We have set none but angels as guardians of
the Fire, and We have fixed number (19)
only as a trial for the disbelievers, in order
that the people of the Scripture (Jews and
Christians) may arrive at a certainty [that
this Qur'ân is the truth as it agrees with
their Books regarding their number (19)
which is written in the Taurât (Torah) and
the Injeel] and that the believers may
increase in Faith (as this Qur'ân is the
truth) and that no doubt may be left for the
people of the Scripture and the believers, and
that those in whose hearts is a disease (of
hypocrisy) and the disbelievers may say:
"What Allâh intends by this (curious)
example ?" Thus Allâh leads astray whom
He wills and guides whom He wills. And
none can know the hosts of your Lord but
He. And this (Hell) is nothing else than a
(warning) reminder to mankind. (31)

Quran 74:49-56

فَمَا لَهُمْ عَنِ ٱلتَّذْكِرَةِ مُعْرِضِينَ (٤٩) كَأَنَّهُمْ حُمُرٌ مُّسْتَنفِرَةٌ
(٥٠) فَرَّتْ مِن قَسْوَرَةٍ (٥١) بَلْ يُرِيدُ كُلُّ ٱمْرِئٍ مِّنْهُمْ أَن
يُؤْتَىٰ صُحُفًا مُّنَشَّرَةً (٥٢) كَلَّا بَل لَّا يَخَافُونَ ٱلْأَخِرَةَ
(٥٣) كَلَّا إِنَّهُ تَذْكِرَةٌ (٥٤) فَمَن شَاءَ ذَكَرَهُ
(٥٥) وَمَا يَذْكُرُونَ إِلَّا أَن يَشَاءَ ٱللَّهُ هُوَ أَهْلُ ٱلتَّقْوَىٰ وَأَهْلُ
ٱلْمَغْفِرَةِ (٥٦)

Then what is wrong with them (i.e. the
polythesists the disbelievers) that they
turn away from (receiving) admonition?
(49) As if they were (frightened) wild
donkeys. (50) Fleeing from a hunter, or a
lion, or a beast of prey. (51) Nay, everyone
of them desires that he should be given pages
spread out (coming from Allâh with a
writing that Islâm is the right religion, and
Muhammad has come with the truth from
Allâh the Lord of the heavens and earth).
(52) Nay! But they fear not the Hereafter
(from Allâh's punishment). (53) Nay,
verily, this (Qur'ân) is an admonition.
(54) So whosoever will (let him read it), and
receive admonition (from it)! (55) And they
will not receive admonition unless Allâh

wills; He (Allâh) is the One, deserving that mankind should be afraid of, and should be dutiful to Him, and should not take any Ilâh (God) along with Him, and He is the One Who forgives (sins). (56)

Quran 75:1-5

لَآ أُقۡسِمُ بِيَوۡمِ ٱلۡقِيَـٰمَةِ (١) وَلَآ أُقۡسِمُ بِٱلنَّفۡسِ ٱللَّوَّامَةِ (٢) أَيَحۡسَبُ ٱلۡإِنسَـٰنُ أَلَّن نَّجۡمَعَ عِظَامَهُ ۚ (٣) بَلَىٰ قَـٰدِرِينَ عَلَىٰٓ أَن نُّسَوِّيَ بَنَانَهُ ۚ (٤) بَلۡ يُرِيدُ ٱلۡإِنسَـٰنُ لِيَفۡجُرَ أَمَامَهُ ۚ (٥)

I swear by the Day of Resurrection; (1) And I swear by the self-reproaching person (a believer). (2) **Does man (a disbeliever) think that We shall not assemble his bones?** (3) Yes, We are Able to put together in perfect order the tips of his fingers. (4) Nay! (Man denies Resurrection and Reckoning. So he) desires to continue committing sins. (5)

Quran 75:34-40

أَوْلَىٰ لَكَ فَأَوْلَىٰ (٣٤) ثُمَّ أَوْلَىٰ لَكَ فَأَوْلَىٰ (٣٥) أَيَحْسَبُ الْإِنسَـٰنُ أَن يُتْرَكَ سُدًى (٣٦) أَلَمْ يَكُ نُطْفَةً مِّن مَّنِيٍّ يُمْنَىٰ (٣٧) ثُمَّ كَانَ عَلَقَةً فَخَلَقَ فَسَوَّىٰ (٣٨) فَجَعَلَ مِنْهُ الزَّوْجَيْنِ الذَّكَرَ وَالْأُنثَىٰ (٣٩) أَلَيْسَ ذَٰلِكَ بِقَـٰدِرٍ عَلَىٰ أَن يُحْيِـَۧ الْمَوْتَىٰ (٤٠)

Woe to you [O man (disbeliever)]! And then (again) woe to you! (34) Again, woe to you [O man (disbeliever)]! And then (again) woe to you! (35) **Does man think that he will be left neglected [without being punished or rewarded for the obligatory duties enjoined by his Lord (Allâh) on him]?** (36) Then he became an 'Alaqa (a clot); then (Allâh) shaped and fashioned (him) in due proportion. (38) **Is not He (Allâh Who does that), Able to give life to the dead?** (40)

Quran 76:1-3

هَلْ أَتَىٰ عَلَى الْإِنسَـٰنِ حِينٌ مِّنَ الدَّهْرِ لَمْ يَكُن شَيْـًٔا مَّذْكُورًا (١) إِنَّا خَلَقْنَا الْإِنسَـٰنَ مِن نُّطْفَةٍ أَمْشَاجٍ نَّبْتَلِيهِ فَجَعَلْنَـٰهُ سَمِيعًا بَصِيرًا (٢) إِنَّا هَدَيْنَـٰهُ السَّبِيلَ إِمَّا شَاكِرًا وَإِمَّا كَفُورًا (٣)

Has there not been over man a period of time, when he was nothing to be mentioned? (1) Verily, We have created man from Nutfah drops of mixed semen (discharge of man and woman), in order to try him, so We made him hearer, seer. (2) Verily, We showed him the way, whether he be grateful or ungrateful. (3)

Quran 77:7-28

إِنَّمَا تُوعَدُونَ لَوَاقِعٌ (٧) فَإِذَا ٱلنُّجُومُ طُمِسَتْ (٨) وَإِذَا ٱلسَّمَاءُ فُرِجَتْ (٩) وَإِذَا ٱلْجِبَالُ نُسِفَتْ (١٠) وَإِذَا ٱلرُّسُلُ أُقِّتَتْ (١١) لِأَيِّ يَوْمٍ أُجِّلَتْ (١٢) لِيَوْمِ ٱلْفَصْلِ (١٣) وَمَا أَدْرَىٰكَ مَا يَوْمُ ٱلْفَصْلِ (١٤) وَيْلٌ يَوْمَئِذٍ لِّلْمُكَذِّبِينَ (١٥) أَلَمْ نُهْلِكِ ٱلْأَوَّلِينَ (١٦) ثُمَّ نُتْبِعُهُمُ ٱلْآخِرِينَ (١٧) كَذَٰلِكَ نَفْعَلُ بِٱلْمُجْرِمِينَ (١٨) وَيْلٌ يَوْمَئِذٍ لِّلْمُكَذِّبِينَ (١٩) أَلَمْ نَخْلُقكُّم مِّن مَّاءٍ مَّهِينٍ (٢٠) فَجَعَلْنَـٰهُ فِى قَرَارٍ مَّكِينٍ (٢١) إِلَىٰ قَدَرٍ مَّعْلُومٍ (٢٢) فَقَدَرْنَا فَنِعْمَ ٱلْقَـٰدِرُونَ (٢٣) وَيْلٌ يَوْمَئِذٍ لِّلْمُكَذِّبِينَ (٢٤) أَلَمْ نَجْعَلِ ٱلْأَرْضَ كِفَاتًا (٢٥) أَحْيَاءً وَأَمْوَاتًا (٢٦) وَجَعَلْنَا فِيهَا رَوَاسِىَ شَـٰمِخَـٰتٍ وَأَسْقَيْنَـٰكُم مَّاءً فُرَاتًا (٢٧) وَيْلٌ يَوْمَئِذٍ لِّلْمُكَذِّبِينَ (٢٨)

Surely, what you are promised must come to pass. (7) Then when the stars lose their

lights; (8) And when the heaven is cleft
asunder; (9) And when the mountains are
blown away; (10) And when the Messengers
are gathered to their time appointed;
(11) **For what Day are these signs
postponed?** (12) For the Day of sorting out
(the men of Paradise from the men destined
for Hell). (13) **And what will explain to
you what is the Day of sorting out?**
(14) Woe that Day to the deniers (of the Day
of Resurrection)! (15) **Did We not destroy
the ancients?** (16) So shall We make later
generations to follow them. (17) Thus do We
deal with the Mujrimûn (polytheists,
disbelievers, sinners, criminals)! (18) Woe
that Day to the deniers (of the Day of
Resurrection)! (19) **Did We not create you
from a despised water (semen)?**
(20) Then We placed it in a place of safety
(womb), (21) For a known period
(determined by gestation)? (22) So We did
measure, and We are the Best to measure
(the things). (23) Woe that Day to the

deniers (of the Day of Resurrection)!
(24) *Have We not made the earth a
receptacle? (25) For the living and the
dead? (26) And have placed therein firm,
and tall mountains; and have given you
to drink sweet water? (27)* Woe that Day
to the deniers (of the Day of Resurrection)!
(28)

Quran 77:50

فَبِأَيِّ حَدِيثٍ بَعْدَهُ ۥ يُؤْمِنُونَ (٥٠)

*Then in what statement after this (the
Qur'ân) will they believe? (50)*

Quran 78:1-7

عَمَّ يَتَسَاءَلُونَ (١) عَنِ ٱلنَّبَإِ ٱلْعَظِيمِ (٢) ٱلَّذِى هُمْ فِيهِ
مُخْتَلِفُونَ (٣) كَلَّا سَيَعْلَمُونَ (٤) ثُمَّ كَلَّا سَيَعْلَمُونَ (٥) أَلَمْ
نَجْعَلِ ٱلْأَرْضَ مِهَٰدًا (٦) وَٱلْجِبَالَ أَوْتَادًا (٧)

*What are they asking (one another
about)? (1) About the great news, (i.e.
Islâmic Monotheism, the Qur'ân, which
Prophet Muhammad brought and the Day of
Resurrection), (2) About which they are in*

disagreement. (3) Nay, they will come to know! (4) Nay, again, they will come to know! (5) **Have We not made the earth as a bed, (6) and the mountains as pegs? (7)**

Quran 79:15

هَلْ أَتَىٰكَ حَدِيثُ مُوسَىٰٓ (١٥)

Has there come to you the story of Mûsa (Moses)? (15)

Quran 79:27

ءَأَنتُمْ أَشَدُّ خَلْقًا أَمِ ٱلسَّمَآءُ بَنَىٰهَا (٢٧)

Are you more difficult to create, or is the heaven that He constructed? (27)

Quran 80:1-12

عَبَسَ وَتَوَلَّىٰٓ (١) أَن جَآءَهُ ٱلْأَعْمَىٰ (٢) وَمَا يُدْرِيكَ لَعَلَّهُۥ يَزَّكَّىٰٓ (٣) أَوْ يَذَّكَّرُ فَتَنفَعَهُ ٱلذِّكْرَىٰٓ (٤) أَمَّا مَنِ ٱسْتَغْنَىٰ (٥) فَأَنتَ لَهُۥ تَصَدَّىٰ (٦) وَمَا عَلَيْكَ أَلَّا يَزَّكَّىٰ (٧) وَأَمَّا مَن جَآءَكَ يَسْعَىٰ (٨) وَهُوَ يَخْشَىٰ (٩) فَأَنتَ عَنْهُ تَلَهَّىٰ (١٠) كَلَّآ إِنَّهَا تَذْكِرَةٌ (١١) فَمَن شَآءَ ذَكَرَهُۥ (١٢)

*(The Prophet) frowned and turned away,
(1) Because there came to him the blind man
(i.e. 'Abdullâh bin Umm-Maktûm, who
came to the Prophet while he was preaching
to one or some of the Quraish chiefs)
(2)* **And how can you know that he
might become pure (from sins)? (3) Or
that he might receive admonition, and
that the admonition might profit him?**
*(4) As for him who thinks himself self-
sufficient, (5) To him you attend; (6)* **What
does it matter to you if he will not
become pure?** *(from disbelief, you are only
a Messenger, your duty is to convey the
Message of Allâh) (7) But as to him who
came to you running (8) And is afraid (of
Allâh and His Punishment), (9) Of him you
are neglectful and divert your attention to
another, (10) Nay, (do not do like this),
indeed it (this Qur'ân) is an admonition,
(11) So whoever wills, let him pay attention
to it. (12)*

Quran 80:17-23

قُتِلَ ٱلْإِنسَٰنُ مَآ أَكْفَرَهُ (١٧) مِنْ أَيِّ شَىْءٍ خَلَقَهُ (١٨) مِن نُّطْفَةٍ خَلَقَهُ فَقَدَّرَهُ (١٩) ثُمَّ ٱلسَّبِيلَ يَسَّرَهُ (٢٠) ثُمَّ أَمَاتَهُ فَأَقْبَرَهُ (٢١) ثُمَّ إِذَا شَآءَ أَنشَرَهُ (٢٢) كَلَّا لَمَّا يَقْضِ مَآ أَمَرَهُ (٢٣)

Be cursed (the disbelieving) man! How ungrateful he is! (17) **From what thing did He create him?** (18) From Nutfah (male and female semen drops) He created him, and then set him in due proportion; (19) Then He makes the Path easy for him; (20) Then He causes him to die, and puts him in his grave; (21) Then, when it is His Will, He will resurrect him (again). (22) Nay, but (man) has not done what He commanded him. (23)

Quran 81:1-29

إِذَا ٱلشَّمْسُ كُوِّرَتْ (١) وَإِذَا ٱلنُّجُومُ ٱنكَدَرَتْ (٢) وَإِذَا ٱلْجِبَالُ سُيِّرَتْ (٣) وَإِذَا ٱلْعِشَارُ عُطِّلَتْ (٤) وَإِذَا ٱلْوُحُوشُ حُشِرَتْ (٥) وَإِذَا ٱلْبِحَارُ سُجِّرَتْ (٦) وَإِذَا ٱلنُّفُوسُ زُوِّجَتْ (٧) وَإِذَا ٱلْمَوْءُۥدَةُ سُئِلَتْ (٨) بِأَيِّ ذَنْبٍ قُتِلَتْ (٩) وَإِذَا ٱلصُّحُفُ نُشِرَتْ (١٠) وَإِذَا ٱلسَّمَآءُ كُشِطَتْ (١١) وَإِذَا ٱلْجَحِيمُ سُعِّرَتْ (١٢) وَإِذَا ٱلْجَنَّةُ أُزْلِفَتْ (١٣) عَلِمَتْ نَفْسٌ

مَّآ أَحْضَرَتْ (١٤) فَلَآ أُقْسِمُ بِالْخُنَّسِ (١٥) ٱلْجَوَارِ ٱلْكُنَّسِ (١٦) وَٱلَّيْلِ إِذَا عَسْعَسَ (١٧) وَٱلصُّبْحِ إِذَا تَنَفَّسَ (١٨) إِنَّهُ لَقَوْلُ رَسُولٍ كَرِيمٍ (١٩) ذِى قُوَّةٍ عِندَ ذِى ٱلْعَرْشِ مَكِينٍ (٢٠) مُّطَاعٍ ثَمَّ أَمِينٍ (٢١) وَمَا صَاحِبُكُم بِمَجْنُونٍ (٢٢) وَلَقَدْ رَءَاهُ بِٱلْأُفُقِ ٱلْمُبِينِ (٢٣) وَمَا هُوَ عَلَى ٱلْغَيْبِ بِضَنِينٍ (٢٤) وَمَا هُوَ بِقَوْلِ شَيْطَانٍ رَّجِيمٍ (٢٥) فَأَيْنَ تَذْهَبُونَ (٢٦) إِنْ هُوَ إِلَّا ذِكْرٌ لِّلْعَلَمِينَ (٢٧) لِمَن شَآءَ مِنكُمْ أَن يَسْتَقِيمَ (٢٨) وَمَا تَشَآءُونَ إِلَّآ أَن يَشَآءَ ٱللَّهُ رَبُّ ٱلْعَلَمِينَ (٢٩)

When the sun is wound round and lost its light (is lost and is overthrown). (1) And when the stars fall; (2) And when the mountains are made to pass away; (3) And when the pregnant she-camels are be neglected; (4) And when the wild beasts are gathered together; (5) And when the seas become as blazing Fire or overflow; (6) And when the souls are joined with their bodies (the good with the good and bad with the bad). (7) And when the female (infant) buried alive (as the pagan Arabs used to do) is questioned.(8) **For what sin was she killed?** (9) And when the (written) pages [of deeds (good and bad) of every person] are laid open; (10) And when the heaven is stripped off and taken away from its place; (11) And when Hell-fire is set ablaze. (12) And when Paradise is brought near, (13) (Then) every person will know what he has brought (of good and evil). (14) So verily, I swear by the planets that recede (i.e. disappear during the day and appear during the night). (15) And by the planets that move swiftly and hide themselves, (16) And by the night as it departs; (17) And by the dawn as it brightens; (18) Verily, this is the Word (this Qur'ân brought by) a most honourable messenger [Jibrail (Gabriel), from Allâh to the Prophet Muhammad] (19) Owner of power, (and high rank) with (Allâh) the Lord of the Throne, (20) Obeyed (by the angels in the heavens) and trustworthy. (21) And (O people) your companion (Muhammad) is not a madman; (22) And indeed he (Muhammad) saw him [Jibril (Gabriel)] in the clear horizon

*(towards the east) (23) And he
(Muhammad) withholds not a knowledge of
the unseen. (24) And it (the Qur'ân) is not
the word of the outcast Shaitân (Satan).
(25)* **Then where are you going?**
*(26) Verily, this (the Qur'ân) is no less than
a Reminder to (all) the 'Alamîn (mankind
and jinn). (27) To whomsoever among you
who wills to walk straight, (28) And you
cannot will, unless (it be) that Allâh wills,
the Lord of the 'Alamîn (mankind, jinn and
all that exists). (29)*

Quran 82:6

يَـٰٓأَيُّهَا ٱلْإِنسَـٰنُ مَا غَرَّكَ بِرَبِّكَ ٱلْكَرِيمِ (٦)

**O man! What has made you careless
about your Lord, the Most Generous?
(6)**

Quran 82:17-19

وَمَآ أَدْرَىٰكَ مَا يَوْمُ ٱلدِّينِ (١٧) ثُمَّ مَآ أَدْرَىٰكَ مَا يَوْمُ ٱلدِّينِ
(١٨) يَوْمَ لَا تَمْلِكُ نَفْسٌ لِّنَفْسٍ شَيْـًٔا ۖ وَٱلْأَمْرُ يَوْمَئِذٍ لِّلَّهِ
(١٩)

And what will make you know what the Day of Recompense is? (17) Again, what will make you know what the Day of Recompense is? (18) (It will be) the Day when no person shall have power (to do) anything for another, and the Decision, that Day, will be (wholly) with Allâh. (19)

Quran 83:4-6

أَلَا يَظُنُّ أُوْلَٰٓئِكَ أَنَّهُم مَّبْعُوثُونَ (٤) لِيَوْمٍ عَظِيمٍ (٥) يَوْمَ يَقُومُ ٱلنَّاسُ لِرَبِّ ٱلْعَٰلَمِينَ (٦)

Do they not think that they will be resurrected (for reckoning), (4) On a Great Day, (5) The Day when (all) mankind will stand before the Lord of the 'Alamîn (mankind, jinn and all that exists)? (6)

Quran 83:7-9

كَلَّآ إِنَّ كِتَٰبَ ٱلْفُجَّارِ لَفِى سِجِّينٍ (٧) وَمَآ أَدْرَىٰكَ مَا سِجِّينٌ (٨) كِتَٰبٌ مَّرْقُومٌ (٩)

Nay! Truly, the Record (writing of the deeds) of the Fujjâr (disbelievers, polytheists sinners, evil-doers and wicked) is (preserved) in Sijjîn. (7) **And what will make you know what Sijjîn is? (8)** A Register inscribed. (9)

Quran 83:18-21

كَلَّآ إِنَّ كِتَٰبَ ٱلْأَبْرَارِ لَفِى عِلِّيِّينَ (١٨) وَمَآ أَدْرَىٰكَ مَا عِلِّيُّونَ (١٩) كِتَٰبٌ مَّرْقُومٌ (٢٠) يَشْهَدُهُ ٱلْمُقَرَّبُونَ (٢١)

Nay! Verily, the Record (writing of the deeds) of Al-Abrâr (the pious and righteous), is (preserved) in 'Illiyyûn. (18) **And what will make you know what 'Illiyyûn is? (19)** A Register inscribed. (20) To which bear witness those nearest (to Allâh, i.e. the angels). (21)

Quran 83:29-36

إِنَّ ٱلَّذِينَ أَجْرَمُوا۟ كَانُوا۟ مِنَ ٱلَّذِينَ ءَامَنُوا۟ يَضْحَكُونَ (٢٩) وَإِذَا مَرُّوا۟ بِهِمْ يَتَغَامَزُونَ (٣٠) وَإِذَا ٱنقَلَبُوٓا۟ إِلَىٰٓ أَهْلِهِمُ ٱنقَلَبُوا۟ فَكِهِينَ (٣١) وَإِذَا رَأَوْهُمْ قَالُوٓا۟ إِنَّ هَٰٓؤُلَآءِ لَضَآلُّونَ (٣٢) وَمَآ أُرْسِلُوا۟ عَلَيْهِمْ حَٰفِظِينَ (٣٣) فَٱلْيَوْمَ

ٱلَّذِينَ ءَامَنُوا۟ مِنَ ٱلْكُفَّارِ يَضْحَكُونَ (٣٤) عَلَى ٱلْأَرَآئِكِ يَنظُرُونَ (٣٥) هَلْ ثُوِّبَ ٱلْكُفَّارُ مَا كَانُوا۟ يَفْعَلُونَ (٣٦)

Verily, (during the worldly life) those who committed crimes used to laugh at those who believed. (29) And whenever they passed by them, used to wink one to another (in mockery); (30) And when they returned to their own people, they would return jesting; (31) And when they saw them, they said: "Verily, these have indeed gone astray!" (32) But they (disbelievers, sinners) had not been sent as watchers over them (the believers). (33) But this Day (the Day of Resurrection) those who believe will laugh at the disbelievers (34) On (high) thrones, looking (at all things). (35) **Are not the disbelievers paid (fully) for what they used to do?** *(36)*

Quran 84:20

فَمَا لَهُمْ لَا يُؤْمِنُونَ (٢٠)

What is the matter with them, that they believe not? *(20)*

Quran 88:17-26

أَفَلَا يَنظُرُونَ إِلَى ٱلْإِبِلِ كَيْفَ خُلِقَتْ (١٧) وَإِلَى ٱلسَّمَآءِ
كَيْفَ رُفِعَتْ (١٨) وَإِلَى ٱلْجِبَالِ كَيْفَ نُصِبَتْ (١٩) وَإِلَى
ٱلْأَرْضِ كَيْفَ سُطِحَتْ (٢٠) فَذَكِّرْ إِنَّمَآ أَنتَ مُذَكِّرٌ
(٢١) لَّسْتَ عَلَيْهِم بِمُصَيْطِرٍ (٢٢) إِلَّا مَن تَوَلَّىٰ وَكَفَرَ
(٢٣) فَيُعَذِّبُهُ ٱللَّهُ ٱلْعَذَابَ ٱلْأَكْبَرَ (٢٤) إِنَّ إِلَيْنَآ إِيَابَهُمْ
(٢٥) ثُمَّ إِنَّ عَلَيْنَا حِسَابَهُم (٢٦)

Do they not look at the camels, how they are created? (17) And at the heaven, how it is raised? (18) And at the mountains, how they are rooted (and fixed firm)? (19) And at the earth, how it is outspread? (20) So remind them (O Muhammad) — you are only a one who reminds. (21) You are not a dictator over them — (22) Save the one who turns away and disbelieves. (23) Then Allâh will punish him with the greatest punishment. (24) Verily, to Us will be their return; (25) Then verily, for Us will be their reckoning. (26)

Quran 89:6-10

أَلَمْ تَرَ كَيْفَ فَعَلَ رَبُّكَ بِعَادٍ (٦) إِرَمَ ذَاتِ ٱلْعِمَادِ (٧) ٱلَّتِى لَمْ يُخْلَقْ مِثْلُهَا فِى ٱلْبِلَدِ (٨) وَثَمُودَ ٱلَّذِينَ جَابُواْ ٱلصَّخْرَ بِٱلْوَادِ (٩) وَفِرْعَوْنَ ذِى ٱلْأَوْتَادِ (١٠)

Saw you not how your Lord dealt with 'Ad (people) (6) Of Iram (Who were very tall) like (lofty) pillars, (7) The like of which were not created in the land? (8) And (with) Thamûd (people), who hewed out rocks in the valley (to make dwellings)? (9) And (with) Fir'aun (Pharaoh), who had the stakes (to torture men by binding them to stakes)? (10)

Quran 90:4-20

لَقَدْ خَلَقْنَا ٱلْإِنسَنَ فِى كَبَدٍ (٤) أَيَحْسَبُ أَن لَّن يَقْدِرَ عَلَيْهِ أَحَدٌ (٥) يَقُولُ أَهْلَكْتُ مَالاً لُّبَدًا (٦) أَيَحْسَبُ أَن لَّمْ يَرَهُ أَحَدٌ (٧) أَلَمْ نَجْعَل لَّهُ عَيْنَيْنِ (٨) وَلِسَانًا وَشَفَتَيْنِ (٩) وَهَدَيْنَهُ ٱلنَّجْدَيْنِ (١٠) فَلَا ٱقْتَحَمَ ٱلْعَقَبَةَ (١١) وَمَآ أَدْرَىٰكَ مَا ٱلْعَقَبَةُ (١٢) فَكُّ رَقَبَةٍ (١٣) أَوْ إِطْعَمٌ فِى يَوْمٍ ذِى مَسْغَبَةٍ (١٤) يَتِيمًا ذَا مَقْرَبَةٍ (١٥) أَوْ مِسْكِينًا ذَا مَتْرَبَةٍ (١٦) ثُمَّ كَانَ مِنَ ٱلَّذِينَ ءَامَنُواْ وَتَوَاصَوْاْ بِٱلصَّبْرِ وَتَوَاصَوْاْ بِٱلْمَرْحَمَةِ (١٧) أُوْلَئِكَ أَصْحَبُ ٱلْمَيْمَنَةِ (١٨) وَٱلَّذِينَ

كَفَرُواْ بِـَايَـٰتِنَا هُمْ أَصْحَـٰبُ ٱلْمَشْـَٔمَةِ (١٩) عَلَيْهِمْ نَارٌ
مُّؤْصَدَةٌ (٢٠)

Verily, We have created man in toil.
(4) **Does he think that none can**
overcome him? *(5) He says (boastfully): "I*
have wasted wealth in abundance!"
(6) **Does he think that none sees him?**
(7) **Have We not made for him a pair of**
eyes? *(8)* **And a tongue and a pair of**
lips? *(9)* **And shown him the two ways**
(good and evil)? *(10) But he has not*
attempted to pass on the path that is steep
(i.e. the path which will lead to goodness and
success). (11) **And what will make you**
know the path that is steep? *(12) (It is)*
Freeing a neck (slave) (13) Or giving food in
a day of hunger (famine), (14) To an orphan
near of kin. (15) Or to a Miskîn (poor)
cleaving to dust (out of misery). (16) Then
he became one of those who believed, (in the
Islamic Monothsim) and recommended one
another to perseverance and patience, and
(also) recommended one another to pity and

compassion. (17) They are those on the
Right Hand (i.e. the dwellers of Paradise),
(18) But those who disbelieved in Our Ayât
(proofs, evidences, verses, lessons, signs,
revelations, etc.), they are those on the Left
Hand (the dwellers of Hell) (19) The Fire
will be shut over them (i.e. they will be
enveloped by the Fire without any opening
or window or outlet.(20)

Quran 93:1-11

وَٱلضُّحَىٰ (١) وَٱلَّيْلِ إِذَا سَجَىٰ (٢) مَا وَدَّعَكَ رَبُّكَ وَمَا قَلَىٰ
(٣) وَلَلْأَخِرَةُ خَيْرٌ لَّكَ مِنَ ٱلْأُولَىٰ (٤) وَلَسَوْفَ يُعْطِيكَ
رَبُّكَ فَتَرْضَىٰ (٥) أَلَمْ يَجِدْكَ يَتِيمًا فَـَٔاوَىٰ (٦) وَوَجَدَكَ
ضَآلاًّ فَهَدَىٰ (٧) وَوَجَدَكَ عَآئِلاً فَأَغْنَىٰ (٨) فَأَمَّا ٱلْيَتِيمَ فَلَا
تَقْهَرْ (٩) وَأَمَّا ٱلسَّآئِلَ فَلَا تَنْهَرْ (١٠) وَأَمَّا بِنِعْمَةِ رَبِّكَ
فَحَدِّثْ (١١)

By the forenoon (after); (1) By the night
when it darkens (and stands still). (2) Your
Lord (O Muhammad) has neither forsaken
you nor hates you. (3) And indeed the
Hereafter is better for you than the present
(life of this world). (4) And verily, your Lord

will give you (all good) so that you shall be well-pleased. (5) **Did He not find you (O Muhammad) an orphan and gave you a refuge? (6) And He found you unaware (of the Qur'ân, its legal laws, and Prophethood) and guided you? (7) And He found you poor, and made you rich (self-sufficient with self-contentment)?** *(8) Therefore, treat not the orphan with oppression, (9) And repulse not the beggar; (10) And proclaim the Grace of your Lord (i.e. the Prophethood and all other Graces). (11)*

Quran 94:1-8

أَلَمْ نَشْرَحْ لَكَ صَدْرَكَ (١) وَوَضَعْنَا عَنكَ وِزْرَكَ (٢) ٱلَّذِىٓ أَنقَضَ ظَهْرَكَ (٣) وَرَفَعْنَا لَكَ ذِكْرَكَ (٤) فَإِنَّ مَعَ ٱلْعُسْرِ يُسْرًا (٥) إِنَّ مَعَ ٱلْعُسْرِ يُسْرًا (٦) فَإِذَا فَرَغْتَ فَٱنصَبْ (٧) وَإِلَىٰ رَبِّكَ فَٱرْغَب (٨)

Have We not opened your breast for you (O Muhammad)? (1) And removed from you your burden, (2) Which weighed down your back? (3) And have We not

raised high your fame? (4) *Verily, along with every hardship is relief,* (5) *Verily, along with hardship is relief* (6) *So when you have finished (your occupation), devote yourself for Allâh's worship.* (7) *And to your Lord (Alone) turn (all your) intentions and hopes.* (8)

Quran 95:7-8

فَمَا يُكَذِّبُكَ بَعْدُ بِٱلدِّينِ (٧) أَلَيْسَ ٱللَّهُ بِأَحْكَمِ ٱلْحَٰكِمِينَ (٨)

Then what (or who) causes you (O disbelievers) to deny the Recompense (i.e. Day of Resurrection)? (7) *Is not Allâh the Best of judges?* (8)

Quran 96:9-19

أَرَءَيْتَ ٱلَّذِى يَنْهَىٰ (٩) عَبْدًا إِذَا صَلَّىٰ (١٠) أَرَءَيْتَ إِن كَانَ عَلَى ٱلْهُدَىٰ (١١) أَوْ أَمَرَ بِٱلتَّقْوَىٰ (١٢) أَرَءَيْتَ إِن كَذَّبَ وَتَوَلَّىٰ (١٣) أَلَمْ يَعْلَم بِأَنَّ ٱللَّهَ يَرَىٰ (١٤) كَلَّا لَئِن لَّمْ يَنتَهِ لَنَسْفَعًا بِٱلنَّاصِيَةِ (١٥) نَاصِيَةٍ كَٰذِبَةٍ خَاطِئَةٍ (١٦) فَلْيَدْعُ نَادِيَهُ ۥ (١٧) سَنَدْعُ ٱلزَّبَانِيَةَ (١٨) كَلَّا لَا تُطِعْهُ وَٱسْجُدْ وَٱقْتَرِب 🕮 (١٩)

Have you seen him (i.e. Abû Jahl) who prevents, (9) A slave (Muhammad) when he prays? (10) Tell me, if he (Muhammad) is on the guidance (of Allâh) (11) or enjoins piety? (12) Tell me if he (Abû Jahl) denies (the truth, i.e. this Qur'ân), and turns away?
(13) **Knows he not that Allâh does see (what he does)?** *(14) Nay! If he (Abû Jahl) ceases not, We will catch him by the forelock — (15) A lying, sinful forelock! (16) Then, let him call upon his council (of helpers), (17) We will call the guards of Hell (to deal with him)! (18) Nay! (O Muhammad)! Do not obey him (Abû Jahl). Fall prostrate and draw near to Allâh! (19)*

Quran 97:1-5

إِنَّا أَنزَلْنَٰهُ فِى لَيْلَةِ ٱلْقَدْرِ (١) وَمَآ أَدْرَىٰكَ مَا لَيْلَةُ ٱلْقَدْرِ (٢) لَيْلَةُ ٱلْقَدْرِ خَيْرٌ مِّنْ أَلْفِ شَهْرٍ (٣) تَنَزَّلُ ٱلْمَلَٰئِكَةُ وَٱلرُّوحُ فِيهَا بِإِذْنِ رَبِّهِم مِّن كُلِّ أَمْرٍ (٤) سَلَٰمٌ هِىَ حَتَّىٰ مَطْلَعِ ٱلْفَجْرِ (٥)

Verily, We have sent it (this Qur'ân) down in the night of Al-Qadr (Decree)(1) **And what will make you know what the night of Al-Qadr (Decree) is?** *(2) The night of Al-Qadr (Decree) is better than a thousand months (i.e. worshipping Allâh in that night is better than worshipping Him a thousand months, i.e. 83 years and 4 months) (3) Therein descend the angels and the Rûh [Jibril (Gabriel)] by Allâh's Permission with all Decrees, (4) (All that night), there is Peace (and Goodness from Allâh to His believing slaves) until the appearance of dawn. (5)*

Quran 101:1-11

ٱلْقَارِعَةُ (١) مَا ٱلْقَارِعَةُ (٢) وَمَآ أَدْرَىٰكَ مَا ٱلْقَارِعَةُ (٣) يَوْمَ يَكُونُ ٱلنَّاسُ كَٱلْفَرَاشِ ٱلْمَبْثُوثِ (٤) وَتَكُونُ ٱلْجِبَالُ كَٱلْعِهْنِ ٱلْمَنفُوشِ (٥) فَأَمَّا مَن ثَقُلَتْ مَوَٰزِينُهُ (٦) فَهُوَ فِى عِيشَةٍ رَّاضِيَةٍ (٧) وَأَمَّا مَنْ خَفَّتْ مَوَٰزِينُهُ (٨) فَأُمُّهُ هَاوِيَةٌ (٩) وَمَآ أَدْرَىٰكَ مَا هِيَهْ (١٠) نَارٌ حَامِيَةٌ (١١)

Al-Qâri'ah (the striking Hour i.e. the Day of Resurrection), (1) **What is the striking (Hour)? (2) And what will make you know what the striking (Hour) is?** *(3) It is a Day whereon mankind will be like moths scattered about, (4) And the mountains will be like carded wool, (5) Then as for him whose balance (of good deeds) will be heavy, (6) He will live a pleasant life (in Paradise). (7) But as for him whose balance (of good deeds) will be light, (8) He will have his home in Hawiyah (pit, i.e. Hell) (9)* **And what will make you know what it is? (10)** *(It is) a fierce blazing Fire! (11)*

Quran 104:1-9

وَيْلٌ لِّكُلِّ هُمَزَةٍ لُّمَزَةٍ (١) ٱلَّذِى جَمَعَ مَالاً وَعَدَّدَهُ (٢) يَحْسَبُ أَنَّ مَالَهُ أَخْلَدَهُ (٣) كَلَّا لَيُنۢبَذَنَّ فِى ٱلْحُطَمَةِ (٤) وَمَآ أَدْرَىٰكَ مَا ٱلْحُطَمَةُ (٥) نَارُ ٱللَّهِ ٱلْمُوقَدَةُ (٦) ٱلَّتِى تَطَّلِعُ عَلَى ٱلْأَفْـِٔدَةِ (٧) إِنَّهَا عَلَيْهِم مُّؤْصَدَةٌ (٨) فِى عَمَدٍ مُّمَدَّدَةٍ (٩)

Woe to every slanderer and backbiter. (1) Who has gathered wealth and counted it,

(2) He thinks that his wealth will make him last forever! (3) Nay! Verily, he will be thrown into the crushing Fire (4) **And what will make you know what the crushing Fire is?** *(5) The fire of Allâh, kindled, (6) Which leaps up over the hearts, (7) Verily, it shall be closed upon them, (8) In pillars stretched forth (i.e. they will be punished in the Fire with pillars). (9)*

Quran 105:1-5

أَلَمْ تَرَ كَيْفَ فَعَلَ رَبُّكَ بِأَصْحَـٰبِ ٱلْفِيلِ (١) أَلَمْ يَجْعَلْ كَيْدَهُمْ فِى تَضْلِيلٍ (٢) وَأَرْسَلَ عَلَيْهِمْ طَيْرًا أَبَابِيلَ (٣) تَرْمِيهِم بِحِجَارَةٍ مِّن سِجِّيلٍ (٤) فَجَعَلَهُمْ كَعَصْفٍ مَّأْكُولٍ (٥)

Have you not seen how your Lord dealt with the Owners of the Elephant? [The elephant army which came from Yemen under the command of Abrahah Al-Ashram intending to destroy the Ka'bah at Makkah]. (1) Did He not make their plot go astray? (2) And He sent against them birds, in flocks, (3) Striking them with stones of Sijjîl (baked clay). (4) And He made them like (an empty field of) stalks (of which the corn has been eaten up by cattle). (5)

Quran 107:1-7

أَرَءَيۡتَ ٱلَّذِى يُكَذِّبُ بِٱلدِّينِ (١) فَذَٰلِكَ ٱلَّذِى يَدُعُّ ٱلۡيَتِيمَ (٢) وَلَا يَحُضُّ عَلَىٰ طَعَامِ ٱلۡمِسۡكِينِ (٣) فَوَيۡلٌ لِّلۡمُصَلِّينَ (٤) ٱلَّذِينَ هُمۡ عَن صَلَاتِهِمۡ سَاهُونَ (٥) ٱلَّذِينَ هُمۡ يُرَآءُونَ (٦) وَيَمۡنَعُونَ ٱلۡمَاعُونَ (٧)

Have you seen him who denies the Recompense? (1) That is he who repulses the orphan (harshly), (2) And urges not on the feeding of AlMiskîn (the poor),(3) So woe unto those performers of Salât (prayers) (hypocrites), (4) Those who delay their Salât (prayer from their stated fixed times), (5) Those who do good deeds only to be seen (of men), (6) And prevent Al-Mâ'ûn (small kindnesses like salt, sugar, water). (7)

.